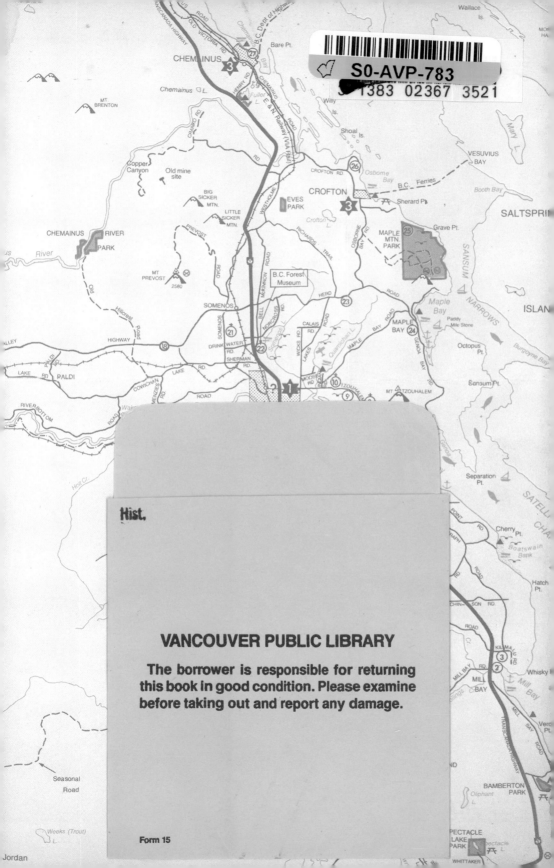

MEMORIES
EVER LOST

ERRATA: PAGE 60 – delete "Magnus" and insert "Christina" – see page 46.

Page: 112 – photo caption should read "William & Nora Kingston's home ......
245 – photo caption should read "William & Nora Kingston's home ......
255 – line 15 – "turstees" should read "trustees"
280 – below (Mrs. George H.Fleetwood) date should be 1882-1974
318 – caption beneath lower picture should read "Bay of Maples Tea Room"

MEMORIES
NEVER LOST

STORIES OF THE PIONEER WOMEN OF THE
COWICHAN VALLEY AND A BRIEF HISTORY
OF THE VALLEY 1850-1920

COMPILED BY THE PIONEER
RESEARCHERS

The Pioneer Researchers gratefully acknowledge
financial assistance received for this publication from
The New Horizons Program of The Department of National
Health and Welfare, Canada,
and
The British Columbia Heritage Trust of The
Government of British Columbia.

ISBN: 0-88925-724-8

Memories Never Lost
Compiled by the Pioneer Researchers

Printed and bound in Canada by D.W. Friesen & Sons, Ltd., Altona,
Manitoba.

"You will know that you have played your part;
Yours shall be the love that never dies,
You, with Heaven's peace within your heart,
You, with God and Glory in your eyes."

Robert Service

Preface

"Some of these pioneer women deserve more than inscribing their names upon a list of pioneer women. I knew them all many years; and their memories will linger with me until the end."

John N. Evans, pioneer and historian of
Cowichan's first decade.

History deals sparsely with the lives and life-style of pioneer women, and so in early 1984 a group of men and women undertook the task of providing some balance to the written history, at least so far as the Cowichan Valley was concerned. They formed the "Pioneer Researchers" group, their objective being to research the lives of pioneer women in the valley.

The time span they decided to cover was from the earliest white settlement in the valley to 1920, when conditions changed very rapidly. Ox-drawn stoneboats had given away to horsedrawn democrats and buggies, tallow candles to kerosene and gas lamps. Indian canoe or weekly steamer to Victoria were replaced by a passable road and daily train service. By 1920 electric light and telephone were beginning to reach into the rural areas, while farmers were acquiring cars. While it would be many years before the last farm family acquired these luxuries of the twentieth century, the rate of change accelerated to such a degree after 1920 (and the end of the Great War had its effect), that true pioneering became the exception rather than the rule.

The geographical area covered by this book extends from Maple Bay in the east to Cowichan Lake in the west, and from Cowichan Bay and Cowichan Station to the south to Westholme in the north.

The necessity for this work was underscored for the Researchers when they attempted to compile biographies of those female pioneers who left no descendents, or none who could be traced. Written documentation, even if fragmentary, existed for the lives of many of the male pioneers of the 1860's and 1870's, but there is no comparable record for the women.

An illuminating testimony to the changing definitions of "pioneer" can be found in two cairns in the little Pioneer Park at Cowichan Bay. The plaque on one reads: "To commemorate the landing of the first group of Pioneer settlers from HMS *Hecate* at Cowichan bay at 4 p.m. on the eighteenth day of August 1862. There were about 100 settlers in the group and His Excellency the Governor accompanied the expedition." (For many years it was thought that the list of these 1862 settlers had been lost. It was later discovered that the exact number was 78.)

The second cairn, erected by the late Magnus Colvin (a Native Son), is specifically a tribute to pioneer women. As a group the Native Sons argued that the second cairn was redundant, that the word "pioneers" included women. Colvin held that women should have their own memorial.

Years before this, in about 1930, John N. Evans, the historian mentioned above, in an undated paper prepared for the first Cowichan Historical Society (1928-1935) listed the names of the pioneer women of the 1860's. (see Appendix)

All those people with female Cowichan ancestors, who participated by furnishing their histories, became part of the Pioneer Researcher's project. Their accounts give the flavour of the period, in many ways more accurately than that provided by documentary evidence. The editors have not presumed to attempt to verify dates or other factual information.

While this book is about the women pioneers of the Cowichan Valley, it is necessary to put their stories in the context of their times. Therefore, the reader will find that the Valley's history has been divided into naturally occurring sections showing where development took place, the various periods being of unequal length. The first part of each section sketches the history of that period and is followed by the life stories of various women who settled in the Valley at that time. Readers familiar with Cowichan will see that some well-known family names are missing. The Researchers regret this, but have only been able to include those women who left descendants or relatives able to contribute their personal stories to the book. Each section includes essays on some of the more significant group activities of pioneer women.

Members of the
Pioneer Researchers Group

Elizabeth Blanche Norcross. Miss Norcross was author of "The Warm Land" and "Pioneers Every One," and co-author, with Doris Farmer Tonkin, of "Frontiers of Vancouver Island." Her grandfather was James Norcross, prominent in Cowichan affairs between 1886 and 1910. Unfortunately Miss Norcross passed away 8th May, 1986 and so did not see the completion of this book to which she was a major contributor.

Elaine Holm. Mrs. Holm is well known in the Cowichan Valley for her interviews on Channel 3 TV. Her work as a photographer and in real estate has given her a broad knowledge of the area and its historic homes.

Will Dobson. Mr. Dobson, a long-time resident of the area, was a reporter and later editor of the "Cowichan Leader" newspaper, and a minister of the Anglican Church. He is now retired.

Hank Wilkinson. Retired from the B.C. Telephone Company Mr Wilkinson has been a resident of Cowichan for many years. His great-uncle, Dr. Watson Dykes, was one of Cowichan's early medical doctors.

Doreen Wilkinson. Mrs. Wilkinson is granddaughter of David Evans, a pioneer who came to Cowichan in 1864 to farm, and has family connections to other early settlers. She is a former B.C. Telephone Company employee.

Geraldine M.R. Weld. Mrs. Weld's childhood was connected to the Cowichan Valley through her parents, grandparents, and attending Queen Margaret's School. She has been a newspaper columnist, a children's story writer and a frequent contributor of articles to the "Islander" section of the Victoria "Daily Colonist."

Jack Ashdown Green. A retired chartered accountant and hospital administrator, Mr. Green is grandson of Ashdown H. Green who was warden (reeve) of North Cowichan in 1874.

Shirley Green. Mrs. Green's lifetime hobby of photography has been put to good use in copying historic photographs for this book. She was born in the Kings Daughters' Hospital and is a retired hospital admitting officer.

Margery Sherman. Mrs. Sherman came to Duncan in 1924 to teach at Duncan Elementary School. She taught there until her marriage in 1935, and returned to teaching 1956-1964.

Priscilla Vipond. Mrs. Vipond recently moved from Nanaimo to Cowichan. She has a keen interest in Vancouver Island history and participated in the Nanaimo Historical Society book "Nanaimo Retrospective."

JoAnn Whittaker. Mrs. Whittaker has been a resident of the Cowichan Valley since 1964. She is a Registered Nurse and is currently completing her Master of Arts degree in history at the University of Victoria. Her thesis topic is "Nurses and Nursing in British Columbia."

Editor

Jan Gould. Mrs. Gould is noted as a journalist and is the author of "Women of British Columbia" and "The Boathouse Question." Her fiction was first published in the *Canadian Forum* and she has had stories aired on C.B.C. Radio. She has won numerous awards including the Rosalind Hulet Petch Memorial Prize for creative writing at the University of Victoria. She has been working on the biography of a Nootka Elder, and her time spent on B.C. Indian Reserves has generated many articles, as well as fiction. One story, "A West Coast Woman," is to be filmed.

Contents

SECTION III "Then came the Railway" Period 1887-1900

14

SECTION I
TRANSPLANT A WOMAN
The Period 1850-1866
by Elizabeth Blanche Norcross

Before the intrusion of white settlers, the Cowichan Valley was home to
the prosperous Cowichan Band, a part of the large family of Coast Salish
Indians. The women provided much of the food for their people. They
harvested the root of the blue camas (which was superseded by the potato
as an article of diet very soon after white contact). Also they gathered berries, dug clams, and for winter use they preserved the fish the men brought
home. They assisted frequently with the fishing itself.

Into this land of Cowichan where women played such a prominent part
in the economy, came lone white men who traded with the Indians, or
fished and hunted. We find written reports of their activities in the 1850s,
as in the correspondence of Samuel B. Harris with Governor James Douglas (to be found in the Provincial Archives), and in an account of the life of
Giovanni Baptiste Ordano printed in the Cowichan Leader, Duncan, on
July 1, 1916. Those two names we know and we can be fairly sure there
were others in view of the concern reported in the Victoria Colonist of the
late 1850s for the opening up to settlement of the Cowichan Valley.[5]

Civilization, as represented by Victoria, was infinitely farther from the
Cowichan Valley of the 1850s and 1860s than the present hour's drive over
a good highway. An active man in the Cobble Hill area might walk into the
city, stay overnight, pick up such supplies as he could carry on his back, and
walk home the next day. A settler living nearer Cowichan Bay, or still farther north in Somenos, might make his way on foot to the Bay, hire an
Indian canoe to take him across to Saanich, and then foot it into Victoria.
On today's roads, the first individual would undertake a trip of about 25
miles each way, for the Somenos man, an additional eight miles. Using
winding forest trails the distance would be greater. Such a trip "outside"
was virtually impossible for a women with young children.

What were the women missing? The Victoria of that date was undoubtedly a rough frontier town. Harry Gregson in his History of Victoria, published in 1970 writes: "A visitor to Victoria in 1862 would have found not a
city but a shacktown. There were only twenty-five hundred permanent
residents." And again: "There were only a few brick buildings in the whole
city. The visitor could have walked around the entire built-up area in twenty minutes ...."[21]

On the other hand, life in the little settlement at the south end of Vancouver Island was good for the well-to-do. It was a town of young people and

15

the tiny "Society" at the top enjoyed a very pleasant existence of riding parties, balls and shipboard dances given by officers of the Royal Navy. The ladies might, and did, complain about the difficulty of getting domestic help. The girls they brought out with them from England soon married which meant that their mistresses then had to depend on untrained Indian women.

N. de Bertrand Lugrin, author of The Pioneer Women of Vancouver Island, published in 1928, was in the fortunate position of being able to interview the immediate descendants of these early chatelaines. She draws an insightful comparision between a woman's life in Victoria and the lives of women who lived no farther away than Cowichan.

"For these charming chatelaines of young Victoria there was little or no hardship," she wrote. "Their wants were nearly always gratified. Beautiful things they had, those brides of long ago, splendid furniture .... lovely gowns and shawls .... finely tailored riding clothes.... There was as much difference between these fortunate young women and the others who went out and away to the Indian countries to make their homes as if they had lived on different planets."

There is something of an apples-and-oranges comparison here, as not all the women in Victoria lived in the lap of luxury, very few who belonged to the social and economic level left it to take up life in the "Indian countries."

There are at least two exceptions to this general rule whom we can identify. One was Mrs. Thomas (Mary) Skinner, whose biography is contained in this section; the other was Mrs. William Sheldon (M.L.) Reece, wife of the first resident clergyman in the district, a woman of whom we know very little.

H.M.S. Hecate.

In the course of the 1860s a handful of white women, probably no more than sixteen or eighteen, settled with their husbands in the Cowichan Valley. It was not until 1930 that anyone took the trouble to name them, and that was John Evans in a paper prepared for the first Cowichan Historical Society (1928-1935) -- the same John Evans mentioned at the head of our Introduction to this book.

On August 15, 1862, the Colonist newspaper of Victoria carried the official announcement which had been eagerly awaited. Her Majesty's ship Hecate, it said, would convey prospective Cowichan settlers. The expedition would start from Victoria harbour on August 18, at 7:00 a.m. and would also tow a sloop for carrying any provisions and implements the passengers might wish to take. Everyone planning to join the expedition was expected to meet at the Land Office, at which time they would sign a memorandum and the men would be assigned to one of three parties which would proceed, each with a guide, to Shawnigan, Quamichan or Somenos. The guides, one being the Surveyor General himself and another his assistant, were men qualified to locate the survey stakes for each settler.

There is no official mention of any women on the Hecate accompanying their husbands.

A number of these men had taken part in the California, New Zealand, Australia, Fraser River and Cariboo gold rushes. Disillusioned, they now were seeking land.

While the pioneer wife probably started her Cowichan life in a one-room cabin, in most instances that cabin was very soon replaced by a larger, but still log-constructed, home. One of those original log cabins, built in 1863 by the brothers Marshall at Cowichan Bay, survived and was occupied as late as 1955, but never was shared by a wife. They left the property to

David Evans' pre-emption — now the corner of First Street and Canada Avenue, Duncan built in 1864. It was also the "first" home for David's brothers John and James Evans.

Tom & Matt Marshall Cabin at Cowichan Bay, built about 1863.

bachelor nephews, John and Thomas Spear, who made only minimal improvements to the dwelling, mainly adding mill lumber sheathing to the exterior. They continued to cook in the fireplace, hang clothing from pegs on the walls and sleep in homemade bunks. These were men of some education and cultivated tastes like their uncles.

Regrettably, when the last Spear brother died the cabin was demolished. With its fieldstone fireplace and stick and clay chimney it had been the only survivor of the type of dwelling which had been the norm in Cowichan's earliest days of settlement.

Even in the 1860s there were exceptions to these very primitive dwellings. Mrs. Patrick Brennan, credited with being the first white woman in Cowichan, may possibly have had to make do with such a home when she first arrived. Her two-storey log house situated across the Bay from the wharf on what later became Khenipsen Road, was built as early as 1866. Considerably altered outwardly and inwardly, the essential core survives, a modern witness to the Biblical parable of the house built upon a rock. That house and its succession of occupants are described in an essay in Part Two of this section.

Another 1860s Cowichan home that did not follow the usual pattern was St. Peter's Rectory. The Colonist of March 28, 1867, reported: "Mr. Reece's (Episcopal) church has just been completed and the rector and family are domiciled in a very substantial house." A photograph of the Rectory depicts a dwelling that certainly appears commodious and must indeed have been, as it received a congregation of thirty-six persons one Sunday in May of 1866.

Fireplace built by Tom & Matt Marshall for their cabin.

For the young male colonists who constituted the great majority of the white population in Cowichan's early days, most of their capital lay in their youth and muscle. Very little monetary capital came into Cowichan in the first two decades of its history. Probably the years it took the men to improve their homesteads, combined with the shortage of white women on Vancouver Island, account for great disparity in the ages of the bride and groom with very young brides and older grooms in many 1870 marriages.

The description of early pioneer life which Evans has given us does not touch on what social life and recreation, if any, the settler enjoyed. There

Early rectory at St. Peter's, Quamichan.

were the roof-raising bees, there was hunting, and there were the business trips which took him to Victoria two or three times a year. If nothing else, those trips were a change from the monotony of life on the pre-emption.

The Cowichan Valley was very much a man's world. What, then, did the women do? A trip to Victoria as described here was not entirely a pleasure excursion and quite impossible for a woman with young children. If she did go, who would mind the children? If the husband was the one to be absent, there was no difficulty about his special responsibility for the stock. She would look after that. We do know of one woman, Jess Bell, who did assume the husband's role in going to Victoria but that was because he was elderly and unfit.

The economic contribution the pioneer wife made to the family was considerable. She not only performed the ordinary housewifely duties (under extraordinary difficulties); but she was there, as we have noted, to take care of the stock if her husband should be away from home. Like her Indian counterpart, she was a food producer, caring for the poultry and the vegetable garden and gathering and preserving berries. Again, like the Indian wife, she made a great deal of the family's clothing. She was also a casual labourer, taking part in the work on the land when extra hands were required.

It is only fair to observe that our pioneers owed a debt to the casual labour the Indian population supplied. Settlement of the land would have been much slower and more arduous if there had not been Indian hands to help with seasonal chores such as haying and lifting potatoes. Their women worked on the latter job and were a source of help in the home for those white women who could afford them. A day spent doing the wash was paid for at one dollar or less.

The decade of the 1860s in the Cowichan Valley was a period of time

Maple Bay, c.1900. Beaumont's hotel and wharf.

1871 photograph of Mission House and School, Cowichan, V.I. W.H. Lomas, Jane Lomas, W.A. Lomas and two Miss Alexanders with a group from Quamichan Indian Village.

distinct from what had gone before and what came after. Before 1860 there had been exploration and trading but no white settlement. During the decade there were isolated farms, mere clearings in the forest, connected one to another (occasionally) and to the wharfs at Cowichan Bay and Maple Bay by roughly slashed out trails. In terms of walking time these were an hour or more apart. There was no "white" community except in the broadest use of that term. By the close of the decade organized groups had begun to appear.

The early settlers recognized the uniqueness of that period and made lists of male settlers in the 1860s. It was only at a much later date that John Evans listed women pioneers of those same years.

A few brave young Sisters of St. Ann came to Cowichan in 1864 to work with the Indian girls and the few white Roman Catholic children of the district.

If any one individual were to be singled out as the hero (I use the term advisedly) among the trailbreakers of the early 1860s, it would have to be Jess (Mrs. Neill) Bell. A trained midwife, she served a wide area, travelling on foot as far from her Somenos home as to the Askews in Chemainus, some ten miles, and the Chisholms at Maple Bay, only a little less. By forest trail those distances would have been greater. Jess Bell's story is among the biographies in Part Two of this section.

The first steps towards the second stage in Cowichan's story were being taken before the decade of the sixties was out.

The Reverend Alex Garrett, Anglican, one of the itinerant clergy who visited the Valley, can be credited with the first of those steps towards giving scattered colonists the focal point they so badly needed. It was he who prompted them to put up a log building on the west shore of Somenos Lake on part of the property now occupied by the Forest Museum, which was designed to serve all community needs as schoolhouse, church and meeting house.

It was the appointment of 1866 of a resident clergyman to serve the white community in Cowichan which really marked the beginning of the second stage in the Valley's development, much more significant than the building of the Somenos Lake hall.

When the Reverend William Sheldon Reece came to Cowichan he had already served three years in Victoria. The occasional services conducted by visiting clergy in the log hall on Somenos Lake or in the John Bull Inn at Cowichan Bay, could not provide the sustained leadership the Valley needed. The cultural English background of the settlers made them ready to give the leadership role to their clergyman. Reece fulfilled that role admirably.

A church life was important for the women particularly. It not only gave them spiritual support needed in their hard lives but it provided regular opportunities for them to meet one another, opportunities that their widely scattered homes denied them. Doubtless Mrs. Reece was equally welcome with her husband but she seldom made her way into the record!

Cowichan now moved forward into the second chapter of its history.

PIONEER HOUSEKEEPING IN COWICHAN - 1860s
ESSAY ON THE COWICHAN DISTRICT
by John N. Evans
(presented March, 1933 to Early Historical Society)

With the advent of the white settlers the Cowichan district was nearly all heavy timber. There were a few small fern patches which we called prairies but the earlier settlers did not locate on any of them. Theirs was the tall timber, to hew out clearings to build homes. Their first shelter must have been tents or a brush shelter of pine boughs over poles to form a roof to keep out the rain. In any event their cooking must have been done out of doors by a log fire. No stoves were here for many years. The first settlers came in 1862 and there was only one cookstove, belonging to the Drinkwaters, in 1870.

Their cooking outfit would be very limited, consisting of a frying pan which was used for many different acts of cooking. There were flapjacks, breadmaking (with the use of yeast powder), frying venison and many other uses. It was the most indispensable of all items. The following would be about what an outfit would consist of:

Frying pan, iron pot to boil water, a tin teapot which was used also to make coffee, a Dutch oven to bake bread, tin dishes and tin cups, a tin wash dish, a tin wash bowl and a wooden wash tub.

Their first house would be of logs and mostly of the one-room variety, about twelve by sixteen feet. There would be a door in one corner, a half window on one side and a fireplace at the end away from the door, built of cobblestone and placed in puddled clay. Chimneys were built of split wood and clay and there might be a floor of some kind of split slabs or a whip-sawed lumber, or no floor at all, just Mother Earth. Buildings were chinked with wood between logs and further closed up by that friend of the settler, puddled clay filling in all small cracks. For furniture there would be wooden stools for chairs, a table of split wood or whip-sawed lumber, and blocks of wood were used as seats.

For food there was plenty of game with potatoes often used at every meal. Flour was brought in from Victoria by the barrel consisting of approximately four sacks. Sugar came the same way. A good supply of the staples of living were laid in. The little stores at wharfs only carried small stocks of provisions and the settler did not use the luxuries of life. Bedsteads were also home-made of wooden logs with straw mattresses and the old reliable Hudson Bay four point blanket for covering. One of the greatest drawbacks the women faced was the lack of stores where they could buy the necessary clothing to wear. The wharf stores did not stock any women's clothing and little for men, except for overalls, shirts, stockings and shoes.

Transportation was by oxen with sleds or a 'block wheel' cart. Wheels were made by sawing blocks out of logs in a width of six inches by four feet in diameter. Iron was used for tires with either a wooden axle or an iron axle with boxing. The only ones who had horses and a wagon were the Drinkwaters who had brought them out from Ohio.

Roads were tracks cut and levelled through the woods, wide enough to drive a team through. All supplies came by boat once a week and the mail

Sketch of kitchen of Miller home on Jubilee Street, Duncan.

to the post offices located at the several bays where boats called in. Neighbours were usually miles apart except in Somenos, so the women had to do any visiting by travelling many miles on foot.

At first the only school was in an old log Church at Somenos Lake, taught by William H. Lomas. After that came the old Maple Bay School taught by R.M. Cleminston. Children walked from Somenos, Chisholm and Alexander.

In the way of churches there were St. Peter's and the old Log Church on Somenos Lake. Father Rondeault at Cowichan built firstly a wood church and then the old stone church. The Methodist Church at Maple Bay was a long walk from the settler's homes and to the several other churches. Altogether they had a hard but happy life to live. So few of either men or women are left as most have gone to their rest. They blazed a trail that others may travel. Few will develop the noble traits of the pioneers for they will not be called upon to go through the same experiences which shaped our pioneers.

The Sisters of St. Ann in the Cowichan Valley
by J.W.A. Green

From 1859 to 1860 Father Peter Rondeault working with his native parishioners erected a log church at Comiaken Hill. The church was dedicated to St. Ann and continued in use until the Stone Church was opened in 1870.

Deciding that there was need for Christian education in Cowichan, in 1864 the Sisters of St. Ann in Victoria sent Mother Mary Providence and Sister Mary Bonsecours to select a site for a Mission School. Their journey took them first to Saanich, then by canoe to Cowichan Bay, and from there by canoe and overland to Tzouhalem. The site was chosen and log buildings started. In October of 1864, Sister Mary of the Sacred Heart and Sister Mary Conception came to Maple Bay on the S.S. Fideliter and thence to Tzouhalem to establish the school.

The Sisters came with little other than their personal possessions. Furniture, such as was essential, was to be made on the site. No beds or tables were required for the children as each would bring her own sleeping mat and blanket, squatting on the floor to eat. At the outset the children ate with their fingers but later learned the use of utensils.

With limited funding and difficult transportation the Sisters had to be self-reliant and to improvise to meet their needs. To reduce drafts and chill they themselves chinked the logs of the first buildings with moss and clay. They brought a cow to Tzouhalem and later added cows to provide milk and butter for the school, selling their surplus production. Three-foot logs were burnt to heat a stone oven so they could bake bread. After the logs had burnt, the ashes were scraped out, pans of dough inserted and the oven sealed. Bakeries in Victoria supplied flour sacks at little or no cost and these provided material for clothes. It was not until 1880 that a sewing

Sisters of St. Ann c.1921 at St. Ann's Boys School.

machine was donated, reducing the laborious hand stitching and giving good service for 25 years. The sisters operated a farm to provide vegetables. Flour, tea, sugar and some other groceries had to be brought from Victoria. Flour was expensive and for a time that amount of bread eaten was carefully controlled.

Before 1886, when the Esquimalt and Nanaimo Railway connected Victoria and Cowichan, supplies usually came by boat. They were unloaded at the Cowichan wharf and taken by canoe to the head of the bay close to Mount Cowichan, as Mount Tzouhalem then was called. The ships Maud and Cariboo Fly provided service to Cowichan Bay and others came in to Maple Bay. After landing, and a considerable walk, the Sisters would be met by an ox-team and cart. This was a help but not a comfort as the ox-carts of the times had no springs and the wheels were solid rounds of wood. The rounds would be sawn from a log and holes bored to fit the axle. This was practical and the wheels were easy to replace.

One Sister speaks of the problems of doing farm work and climbing fences while wearing long habits and protective aprons. Once, when the water supply failed, a newly arrived Sister had to climb part way up Mount Tzouhalem with two boys to clear leaves from the cistern. Not all work was done by the Sisters as some labourers were hired from nearby villages.

Though resources were limited the school was always able to provide plentiful wholesome food, clothing and bedding. The government did not assist with funding, and the Indians considered education to be the full responsibility of the newcomers, if desirable at all. The Diocesan Bishop had problems enough with funding the Diocese and so the Sisters of St. Ann had the full responsibility for providing the school. The Sisters did receive a lot of practical help and support from the Indians with whom relations were always good.

At the school instruction included religion, reading, writing, household duties and personal grooming. The initial enrolment was twenty-two girls aged fourteen to eighteen years. Some disliked the routine and discipline and by 1865 the enrolment had dropped to 12. From its opening in 1864 to the amalgamation with the Victoria Orphanage in 1875, the average number of students was some 20 girls.

By 1875 the Victoria Convent School and Orphanage had become very crowded and so with space available at Cowichan 24 girls, orphans aged three to 15, were sent there. This increased the Cowichan numbers to 45 girls. The Cowichan School had been established for Indians only but this change brought in whites, Mexicans, Kanakas and children of mixed origins. This phase of the school carried through until 1904 when the girls were moved to Nanaimo, and boys from the protectorate were brought to Cowichan.

A very high standard of cleanliness was maintained. The Sisters worked on their hands and knees to scrub the floors. The floors were then polished by having boys sit on pieces of old carpet and the sisters pulling them backwards and forwards.

Some of the school ceremonials were of interest. In 1878 Sister Mary Theodore describes the Christmas Eve midnight mass. Some 40 girls with flaming torches left the school about ten-thirty in the evening to follow a trail through the forest which joined the Quamichan-Comiaken trail. This was near the Rectory. Here they were met by a large group of Indians and all walked in procession by torch-light to St. Ann's Church (the Old Stone Church at that date).

Another ceremonial was the Cowichan Corpus Christi procession which, while attended by only a few whites, was very well supported by the Cowichan, Saanich and Songhees Indians. Chiefs carried the Cross, light, banner and the canopy, with the procession following the road from St. Ann's Church to the Convent. This observance commenced in 1889 when the roads were being developed. In later years children from the Kuper Island Indian School, with their brass band, joined in the procession, as did the Saanich Mission School with its band. A sports program followed the ceremony and there were races and lacrosse and baseball games with prizes for the victors.

To raise additional funds for the school the Sisters, in 1921, instituted piano lessons for outside students. One Sister drove a buggy to the Cowichan Merchants store in Duncan taking eggs, cream and butter, and returning with meat and other supplies.

By 1925 the role of the school again changed, and from being a protectorate it became a boys residential school. Some seventy boys were enrolled in grades I to VIII.

Day students no longer attended St. Ann's School after the opening of St. Catherine's School in 1940, a school which was government funded, the Sisters of St. Ann providing the instruction. The building which formerly housed St. Catherine's School is now the headquarters of the Cowichan Indian Band.

The Sisters of St. Ann closed the residential school in 1956 having provided dedicated service there for over ninety years.

Margaret Alexander (nee Bryce)
(Mrs. David Alexander)
1826-1895
by her great-granddaughter, Kathleen Derby

Miss Margaret Bryce was born in Forfar, Scotland and was married to David Alexander in 1845. Hearing from relatives in Australia of the wonderful gold discoveries they decided to try their luck there. They made their home in Adelaide where their daughter Jane was born in 1849. While her husband was digging for gold a fire broke out near their tent home, and she just managed to escape the flames with her baby whom she was bathing at the time. All she saved was her prayer book which was in the pocket of her apron. After this she decided not to follow her husband to the mining.

Later they went to Sydney where the other children were born. She lived in various tent cities that seemed to spring up overnight and later she would move on to the next and richer diggings. There was always dread of fire, and it was after David returned to find the whole town in ashes and

Margaret Alexander, nee Bryce, 1826-1895.

took some time before he discovered his family that he decided the country was too hazardous for his peace of mind.

They took passage on The Seaman's Bride for British Columbia in 1860. After a six-month journey, which was very trying for the mother but thoroughly enjoyed by the children who were made much of by the sailors, they arrived at Esquimalt. Here men were rushing off to the Cariboo to mine for gold. David found it was too rough a country for women and children so he decided to try farming instead.

He came to Cowichan in 1862 and pre-empted two hundred acres of land on each side of Somenos Creek where he built a small cabin of oak logs before he returned to Victoria for his family. They came to Cowichan Bay

Margaret Sutton, nee Alexander, 1852-?

with several other settlers for various parts of the district travelling in the H.M.S. Grappler, landing at the mouth of the Cowichan river. The gunboats Grappler and Forward were used at that time to convey settlers as far as Comox and also to patrol the coast and quell any trouble that might be caused by the Indians.

The Alexanders were met by Jean Compagnon one of the first settlers, who helped the father secure canoes and Indians to take their belongings up the river and creek to their new home, Oak Bank. Meanwhile, Father Rondeault guided Mrs. Alexander and her five children up the narrow

Indian trail, through the forest and tall bracken. The poor mother arrived very weary after her long walk, her youngest child being only two years old. There were no beds or furniture but the canoes had arrived with their bedding and they were soon asleep. Next morning they were delighted with their outlook of oak trees, flowers, berries and the creek with the yellow water-lilies.

Being used to camp life, Mrs. Alexander quickly adapted herself to the country and did not find cooking over an open fire using only a camp oven, very difficult. She soon became quite noted for her bannocks, scones and oat cakes.

The Indians terrified her at first. At one time little David was missing. The family feared he had been abducted. Father Rondeault spoke to the Indians who immediately became sympathetic and joined in the hunt. The child was found in a deep pit which the Indians used to trap deer. He had tumbled in and had become exhausted calling for help and had fallen asleep. After this the Indians became much more friendly. One old man paddled his canoe up the creek every week in quest of old nails or bits of iron. As he was clad only in an old blanket and shell earrings, Mrs. Alexander gave him a pair of old pants, asking him to wear them. He immediately put them on and seemed very pleased. However, on reaching the canoe he removed them and only wore them when visiting her.

The Indians were very acquisitive. They would sit in silence for hours on the floor, occasionally pointing to something and asking, "How much?", thinking everything was for sale.

It was years before Mrs. Alexander became accustomed to their weird wailing and monotonous cries over their sick and at their dances. She imagined them to be war cries and often felt they would all be scalped before morning.

Another terrifying experience was meeting a medicine man on the narrow trail. He walked with a peculiar, jerking movement, grunting every few yards and seemed to be entirely covered with downy feathers and paint. He was hung with strings of shells or dried deer hooves which rattled as he moved.

There was no school in the district until 1864 when a small Mission Chapel was built on the edge of Somenos Lake. Here a young Englishman, William H. Lomas, undertook to teach the settlers' children. He had to paddle a canoe over to get his pupils on the Quamichan side, among whom were the Alexanders.

The Reverend Garret came up to Cowichan on horseback once a month to hold services in the Chapel. Archdeacon Reece was the first resident clergyman, coming in 1866. Until the log church was built, services were held in the parsonage, the Somenos School Chapel and at the John Bull Inn at Cowichan Bay.

Mrs. Alexander was a very musical person and always regretted that her children were not getting a musical education. There was no piano in the settlement for Jane and Margaret to continue their lessons. They all inherited their mother's love of music and she taught them to sing many old Scottish ballads. As they grew older, each child played some instrument by ear, violin, flute, concertina or guitar. The family had concerts in the evenings when the day's work was done.

Though for hundreds of years the Indians had been killing all the deer, ducks, geese or fish they needed for their daily food and for their pot-latches, there still was any quantity of game to be had without the trouble of hunting for it. In the 1860s and 1870s large bowls of wild strawberries, raspberries and blackberries could be picked in a few minutes for jam, but all groceries came by boat from Victoria. At first the supplies were carried from the landing by the children but a yoke of oxen and sled were soon acquired.

In a few years Oak Bank became a prosperous farm, the log cabin was turned into a dairy and a six-room house built with a large storeroom up-stairs and a cellar beneath. The family killed their own animals and there were always hams, sides of bacon, corned beef and pork in barrels. Jam, jellies, wine, cheese, candles and soap were made on the farm, too. Nothing was wasted in those days. The lead from the lining of tea boxes was melted for bullets, old felt hats and cardboard made wads for cartridges, all fat was made into soap or candles, discarded garments were made into rugs for the floors or into quilts for the beds and feathers saved for pillows or mattresses.

The dairy was the pride of Margaret Alexander's life. She attended to the milk herself, making butter and sending it to Victoria twice a week. There were no deep-setters or separators; the milk was strained into shallow pans, twenty or thirty of these were skimmed every day. Water for washing the pans had to be carried from the well and heated over an open fire. The daughters helped their father and brothers with the milking, fed the calves and washed the milk pails, but their mother allowed no one in the dairy.

She was a quiet, home-loving woman, never missing a church service but never visiting people unless they needed help or were newcomers to the district. Her spare time was spent in knitting, making quilts or rugs. The Bible and later newspapers were her only reading matter. After her husband's death in 1892 she bought a house in Duncan and lived there with her two daughters until her death of pneumonia in 1895. The only Alexander grandson was killed in the war, but Margaret left fourteen other grandchildren.

Jenet (Jess) Bell
(Mrs. Neill Bell)
1818-1900
by her great granddaughter, Myfanwy Lumpp

I am indebted to the late John N. Evans, Miss E. Blanche Norcross and Mr. Elden W. Kier of Cowichan, and the Otago Early Settlers Museum, New Zealand, for much of this information.

My great-grandmother, Jess Jamieson Bell, was the second white woman to arrive in the Cowichan Valley, "the Warm Land", travelling via Australia and New Zealand from Scotland.

Born in Stirling, Scotland in 1818, her early past is lost. She was widowed with two small sons, Peter, born in 1841 and Alexander, born in 1843, and took up the honoured profession of registered midwife to support herself and the family.

It is not known how she travelled to Australia or where she married Neill Bell. There is a family legend that Peter, as a child, was used as a courier to convey gold past bushrangers in Australia where gold was discovered at Ballarat and Bendigo in Victoria in 1851.

Daughters Christina (Tina) and Jessie were born in Australia in 1851 and 1854. The Bells could not take up land there and this drove them to Otago in New Zealand where they arrived in 1855.

Jess and Neill Bell settled near Dunedin on the Otago Peninsula. Here Jess practised her profession as midwife, rowing a boat around the bays to the settlers' homes when needed and here, too, her sons Hugh, John and Angus were born, (1856, 1858 and 1861).

In 1861 gold was discovered in Otago, bringing many miners to Dunedin's Port Chalmers, from whom the Bells probably heard of land soon to be available in Cowichan.

When Jess and Neill decided to endure once again the discomfort of a long sea voyage, Peter and Alex decided to remain in New Zealand.

Jess made this voyage at the age of forty-four with an invalid husband and five children, the oldest being ten years and the youngest a baby in his arms. That she did so reflects the desperation of the poor of those days.

They made the journey to Cowichan on the ship Hecate, and the whole family was taken up the creek in canoes by the Indians to Somenos where their first log cabin home was built.

It was in this earth-floored cabin, with its pine bough beds, that the district's first church service was held.

All the Bell children attended the school William Lomas taught on Somenos Lake, and later they walked to school at Maple Bay where Tina's future husband, Robert M. Clemitson, was the first teacher.

In the early years Jess would travel by Indian canoe to Saanich and walk the trail to Victoria for supplies and to do the family business, the first white woman to walk that trail.

When her services were needed, she would act as district nurse and midwife, walking to the Askews at Chemainus and back, fully twenty-four miles, or to the Chisholms at Maple Bay. On her return she milked cows and churned butter. In that connection, she was one of the district's best butter makers. Butter was shaped in wooden tubs or moulds and stamped with a carved wooden intaglio.

In December of 1871 Jess applied to the Chief Commissioner of Land and Works, Victoria, to take up a Crown grant of sections five, six and seven, Range Five, Somenos in her own name. Thus, that land she had travelled so far to reach and which she had helped to clear was hers at last for the price of four shillings and two pence per acre.

Christina died in 1875 in Victoria, leaving a baby son, Robert. Hugh and Angus did not marry, John married Jean Blair and Jessie became the second wife of James Kier. Later, this couple moved to Detroit where they lived and died, leaving a daughter, Mrs. Applehof.

Jess was bedridden for a while before her death on February 10, 1900, and refused to allow other women to nurse her. To use the words of John N. Evans, "Son Angus nursed her with every care and love. I feel like lifting my hat to him in memory of his love and duty to a noble woman."

Neill died in 1885. In 1900 Jess was buried beside him in what is now the Mountain View Cemetery at Somenos with Angus nearby.

Elizabeth Blackmore
1819-1912
Compiled by the Researchers

In the year 1865 some disembodied spirit might have observed a middle-aged woman trudging the rough Indian trail from Victoria to Cowichan. Her progress was slow, as she was allowing the cow in her care to graze along the way. The rest of the party had gone ahead and made an early camp, and she was to catch up with them at the end of the day.

This Elizabeth Blackmore was said by some accounts to have been the first white woman to "foot it" to the Cowichan Valley. While the route taken was roundabout, via the Sooke Lakes and Shawnigan, it was the only possible one at that date. And while it called for considerable physical endurance, we also have to admire the courage of this Englishwoman who almost certainly had tales in her head of hostile Indians and wild beasts.

To tell Elizabeth's story, and to explain her presence in the Cowichan Valley at that early date, we must look at the history of her employer.

Dr. John Chapman Davie had come to Victoria in 1862 with three half-grown sons and this same Elizabeth Blackmore who even then, had been a member of his household for many years. She had been first engaged by the Davies as a nursemaid when one of the younger sons Horace was born. His oldest son and his only daughter had remained behind in England with their mother whose health was too poor to allow her to make the journey. The two youngest sons, also left behind, lost no time in joining father and brothers in the New World adventure. Horace apparently made himself so obnoxious at home and at school that he was allowed to follow his father while his little brother, Theodore, used the simple expedient of running away to join them.

Dr. Davie was a busy man in 1862, establishing one home in Victoria where he practised medicine and another in Cowichan. He took up land in the Somenos district and constructed, or caused to be constructed, a cabin. This wilderness cabin, which would be Elizabeth Blackmore's home for many years, was a standard colonist one room log cabin earth floor and a single fireplace which served both for cooking and heat. The property was far from being a gentleman's country estate, but Dr. Davie, who came up every few months on horseback for the hunting, seemed to regard Cowichan as his principal residence.

Dr. Davie was a conscientious father, seeing that his sons were established in the callings which best suited their talents and the needs of the

Elizabeth Blackmore, 1819-1912, — Housekeeper of Dr. J.C. Davie.

colony. He sent his namesake to San Francisco to study medicine, in due course. Alexander and Theodore continued their education in lawyers' offices and eventually became lawyers themselves and premiers of the province, Alexander 1887-1889 and Theodore 1892-1895. Horace and William were to be farmers, Horace because that was his natural bent, William because Horace would then always be near at hand to keep a sort of guardian's eye on him, he being not quite as bright as his brothers.

Now in 1865, the time had come to settle those two sons on the Somenos property. Elizabeth was assigned to make a home for these two and for any visiting Davies whenever they were disposed to take a country holiday which they often did.

We could wish someone had kept an account of Elizabeth's history-making trek from Victoria, and that more details of her life had come down to us. She was one of a kind in the Cowichan of the 1860s, and she lived long enough to be almost within living memory. It is tantalizing how few scraps of information we have about her.

One of the scraps is that she set to work at once to make the cabin more habitable by flagging the dirt floor with flat stones from the bed of the nearby stream. She carried these to the cabin, one by one, in her apron.

As the Davies got enough land cleared to build up a herd of cows, she did the milking and made Devonshire cream. Her great pride was her calves.

One of the Evans family contributed: "She was more than a mother to the Davie boys," and another, "She was a friend to all small fry of the district. She always had a goody for them when they visited." This last recollection was from Arthur Evans, young enough then to have been one of the neighbourhood small fry.

The oustanding feature of Elizabeth Blackmore's appearance that Arthur remembered was the she always wore her black hair in ringlets, even when her hair had turned grey.

If the female pioneers of the 1860s felt the hardship of isolation and loneliness, how much worse must it have been for Elizabeth with no family of her own but who had to be both head and servant in the home.

Change in the Cowichan Valley came slowly in the years between her "footing it" from Victoria and her death. Wheeled vehicles, even automobiles, had made their appearance but there was still a great deal of "footing it". No electric light, telephone or indoor plumbing were ever introduced to the cabin where she spent the second half of her life.

In old age, Elizabeth Blackmore liked to say that she had been born in the same years as Queen Victoria but she outlived that monarch and died in 1912.

Annie Bonsall (nee Botterill)
(Mrs. Henry Bonsall)
1859-1933
by her daughter, Marjorie McKay

In the early 1860s my mother, Annie Botterill, travelled from Ontario to Vancouver Island with her parents, Matthew and Mary Botterill. They came by the Panama route to Victoria and settled there for a short time while my grandfather worked for the Hudson's Bay Company. However, he had come west with a view to farming, and shortly after arrival he took up a pre-emption in the Maple Bay area.

Mrs. Henry Bonsall, nee Anna Botterill.

In the meantime, my father's mother and stepfather, a Mr. Bednall, had emigrated from England to Australia but by the mid-1860s they, too, had found their way to Cowichan. Henry Bonsall, my father, had remained in England but he now emigrated and joined the Bednalls at Maple Bay about 1866.

Annie Botterill and Henry Bonsall married and made their home at Maple Bay for a time. Henry worked during the week at the Chemainus mill and spent the weekends at home. The couple's three oldest children were born at Maple Bay.

It was about 1881 that Henry pre-empted land at Westholme and the family moved there. Annie's first home on this land was a one-room log cabin with a loft which served as sleeping quarters for the children. After they had moved into a larger home, Annie had a family of eight girls and seven boys. By the time the youngest was born, the oldest had moved away from home.

My mother was a very small woman and very active. She was a beautiful cook, sewed beautifully and was a keen and talented gardener. She visited neighbours on her bicycle.

I remember hearing how on one occasion that she had gone to church and seen Mrs. Lloyd, also a very small woman, at the organ. When she came home she reported that she had seen the smallest woman she had ever observed. Later, we heard that Mrs. Lloyd was making the same report of her!

Annie Bonsall had an Indian woman to help in the house, particularly with the washing which had to be done on a scrub board.

We children got our elementary education at the local one-room school. Even Duncan did not have a high school built until 1910.

Both our parents were very particular about our behaviour. My father did not allow any careless English and my mother saw to it that we attended Sunday School regularly.

Mrs. Patrick Brennan
compiled by the Researchers

One hesitates in writing history to ever use the words "first" or "unique," but for Mrs. Patrick Brennan we put forward her claim to being the first white woman in Cowichan. This is based on the statement of one E.X. Vautrait and an anonymous Indian. The year of her arrival was 1861.

She may have lived for a time in one of those typical one-room cabins, but it is more probable that she, with her husband and their two boys, lodged in Sam Harris' John Bull Inn. It appears that the two men were business associates, judging from Harris's correspondence with The Colonist.

Pat Brennan had not come to Cowichan to be a farmer-settler, but, like Harris, he wanted to get in on the ground floor of the business opportunities expected when settlement began. We know little about him beyond the fact that he ferried new settlers with their goods across the river. Even if it was true as some claimed that he over-charged, he must have had some other source of income. As likely as not, that source was trade with the Indians.

When the two-storey log house on the rocky point of land across the bay from the Government wharf was built in 1866, Mrs. Brennan could enjoy some luxuries denied other 1860s women pioneers. She had living space, and she could see all the "life" there was in the Valley of those days. On the weekly, or perhaps ever two weeks, steamer days, everyone who could possibly manage it met the boat. It was the best occasion the area afforded for socializing, and she was in a better position than most to take advantage of it. In between steamer days there was the view of the bay, where Indian canoes would be seen moving between villages or following migrating salmon to the rivers and the occasional naval vessels from Victoria.

More than this we do not know of Mrs. Patrick Brennan, not even her own Christian name. At some time towards the end of the 1860s, the family left the district. The solid log house still stands as evidence of their stay.

Mary Chisholm (nee Moore)
(Mrs. William Chisholm)
1840-1901
by her grandson Douglas MacAdams

My grandmother, Mary Chisholm was born in 1840 at Kilmartin, Coun-

*Mrs. William MacAdams, nee Annie Chisholm
and Mrs. Mary Jones, nee Chisholm, c.1890.*

ty of Dublin, Ireland. She was the third daughter of Dennis Moore and Mary Lacey.Her marriage to William Chisholm was celebrated on August 9, 1866, at St. Ann's, Cowichan. The source of this information is the parish records of St. Ann's. The "St. Ann's" in 1866 was Father Rondeault's log church on Comiaken Hill which preceded the Stone Church and the present St. Ann's Church.

William and Mary Chisholm lived at Maple Bay until their deaths in 1905 and 1901, respectively, and both are buried at St. Ann's.

Eight children were raised on the farm, four sons and four daughters. None of the sons married and so there are no descendants bearing the Chisholm name. However, three of the four girls married and raised families; my sister, brothers and cousins, all of whom knew the farm well from many summers spent there.

Annie Chisholm MacAdams.

Janet Flett (nee Flett)
(Mrs. John Flett)
1823-1909
and
Mary Elizabeth Flett (nee Evans)
(Mrs. John William Flett)
1873-1971
From an interview with Mabel Nixon, granddaughter & daughter

My grandmother, Janet Flett, came to Victoria in 1855. Originally she was from the Orkney Islands but she had lived in London for some years, keeping house for her widowed brother, a sea captain, and his two children. Life in London must have been comfortable as among the possessions that she brought to Canada were six lovely silk dresses.

Her husband-to-be, John Flett, had come out to Victoria from the Orkney Islands six years before, but he returned to the Islands to marry Janet, who was his cousin. They came out to his Victoria home, living there until 1870 when the Victoria property was exchanged with the Randall family for their Herd Road farm in Cowichan; and so the Fletts moved to Cowichan.

They made the trip by steamer from Victoria to Maple Bay, their belongings being brought from Maple Bay to the farm by ox-cart. On the way one of the cart wheels broke, but in those simple days the men just sawed a thin round off a log, pierced it with a hole to fit the axle, and carried on their way again.

The couple had four children, all boys. Three of them farmed, while one, James, was station agent for a time at Somenos. The fourth brother, Alfred, became Deputy Provincial Treasurer of British Columbia but died at the age of forty-one. My father, John William Flett, was the eldest of the sons. After Grandfather died in 1886, Grandmother would spend half the year with us and half with other members of the family. I remember her as a tall and heavy lady who walked with two sticks because of rheumatism in her knees. As she could not climb up into a buggy, heavy planks were kept handy and, aided by someone on either side, she could walk from the top of the steps to the buggy.

She did what she could around the house, washing dishes and things like that. She would read from her Bible with me sitting at her feet. Though she was a Presbyterian, the family helped build the Methodist Church since this was the only denomination available. Two of her boys became Presbyterians and two Methodists.

In 1893, John William Flett married Mary Elizabeth Evans, daughter of the John Evans who was a member of the Legislature. Mary Elizabeth had been born in Nortonville, California. Her mother was very afraid of Indians because the wagon train in which she had crossed the Plains had been attacked and a number of people killed by Indians. However, Mary Elizabeth had Indian children as her playmates and looked on them as friends.

She had come to Cowichan in 1877 and first attended school at the junction of Maple Bay and Tzouhalem Roads. Later, she attended the Koksilah School at the Fairbridge site and the Somenos School where Somenos and

Drinkwater Roads meet. She was also at the school (later to become the Scout Hall) at the corner of Indian and Maple Bay Roads. During the school week she stayed with the Keatings but went home for week-ends. There was no bridge across that part of the Cowichan River but for 25 cents an Indian would ferry her across the river in his canoe. Once she met a bear and was very afraid.

After marrying my father she had many farm chores and also raised chickens. She used to trade eggs to the Indian, Redcap of Maple Bay, receiving in exchange salmon that he had caught. She raised ducks, too. Some eggs would be preserved in waterglass for winter use, but these were only fit for cooking.

We never had electricity on the farm, it would have been too expensive. To keep food cool we would let it down into the well in a bucket. The well was at the bottom of the hill so water was carried up to the house in buckets. If visitors were coming, Mother would go to the well for fresh cold water in time for their arrival. For heating we had the stove and fireplace, and at night would put a large log on the fire to last through until morning. Just outdoor pit toilets were used.

We did not have time for amusements. In the evening there were cows to be milked, milk to be separated, and calves to be tended. With the hot stove and oil lamps, Mother was afraid of fire and could not leave me alone in the house so while she was milking I was tied to a pole in the barn! Afterwards, Dad would read a few verses from the Bible and we would go to bed.

Our cream was sent to the Creamery in big cans. Milk was used to fatten our pigs and calves. The Creamery would empty the cans and send them back unwashed. There was always some thick cream left in the cans and this would be sour from the heat of the day. It was too good to waste and Mother used it in cooking, particularly to make some buns that she called "ragged jacks" which were very popular. I still make them.

We grew our own cattle feed, hay, mangles, carrots and other vegetables. Neighbours would come to help with the plowing and harvest. We had a Chinese man who lived on the farm from March to November, staying in Duncan for the winter.

In earlier days, if you needed a dentist you travelled to Victoria. Drugs were sent up from a pharmacy in Victoria. One Sunday in 1907 I broke my wrist and we sent for Dr. Dykes in Duncan using the government phone at Aitken's. In Duncan the message was given to another doctor who came out but left in a huff without seeing me when he found that he was not the doctor who had been phoned. By the time that Dr. Dykes came out on the Wednesday, my wrist had started to knit out of line, so they put me to sleep on the kitchen table, broke the wrist and re-set it!

We used to have lots of visitors. Mother was always at home but I do not know how she managed to look after them all. She had the chickens to tend. Also she helped with the milking, cooked, baked bread, and did washing, ironing, sewing and darning. When I was small she made my dresses and there was housework and gardening, too. However, she was always cheerful.

When she got old she stayed with me. When she was in her nineties, and had a heart condition, I told her that she was not to chop wood any more.

After she came back from a stay in hospital with pneumonia she was miserable and wanted to at least chop kindling.

She died in December of 1971, a real pioneer of Cowichan.

The Fry Family in Cowichan
written in 1923 by Mary Elizabeth Mainguy (nee Fry), 1856-1923
submitted by her nephew Gerald Prevost

Henry Fry and Jane Carter, both born in Barnstaple, Devon, England, married March 15, 1850. They lived first in Lowler where two children were born, Henry on January 28, 1851, and Anna Jane, born in 1853. Then they went to Canada and had two more children, Mary Elizabeth born in 1856 and Edith, born in 1859.

They returned to England in 1862, but my father came back to British Columbia, leaving the family in Heavitree, a small village near Exeter, Devon. In August of 1864 my mother, with the four children, left Liverpool on the sailing ship General Wyndham and arrived in Esquimalt Harbour in January, 1865.

My father was then managing a farm in North Saanich near what is now known as Patricia Bay but was then known as Union Bay. At that time there was no road from Victoria up the Island except the trail over the Sooke Mountain. If a doctor was sent for in an emergency case, he would ride out to Saanich and cross from Union to Mill Bay in a "plunger" sailed by "The Bosun," who was a runaway sailor employed by my father. The Reverend Garrett, who went to give services once a month, often came that way.

We left Saanich in 1867, my father going to San Francisco and my mother and family remaining in Victoria. My father returned in 1869, and in October of 1870 we all moved to Chemainus to the farm now owned by Mr. Burkitt. By that time the little steamboat Sir James Douglas commanded by Captain Clarke was making weekly trips to Nanaimo, calling at Cowichan Bay and Chemainus. There was no wheeled vehicle in Chemainus and the settlers had all turned out with their ox sleighs to take us and our belongings to our new home.

We remained at Chemainus until 1876, then moved to Quamichan Lake and the home "Summerland" was kept there until May of 1889 when my mother died. Father then went to England for a short time. Of the four children only Mary Elizabeth is living.

Henry was a British Columbia land surveyor who did much work on Vancouver Island. He also was in charge of a section of the Canadian Pacific Railway when it was built. He died in 1912 and his widow is still living in Duncan.

Anna Jane was married at Chemainus in 1873 by Archeacon Reece.

Mary Elizabeth, who married the late Daniel Wishart Mainguy on January 30, 1884, is still living. They lived on Mainguy Island for seven years and then moved to a home on the highway near Westholme, now owned by Mr. A. Coles.

Edith married David Alexander of Oakbank Farm on September 29, 1880 and died in 1921.

Mrs. Archibald Kier, nee Mary Jane Towers, 1813-1901.

Mary Jane Kier (nee Towers)
(Mrs. Archibald R. Kier)
1813-1901
by her great-grandson, Elden Kier

It is believed that Mary Jane Towers was born in Liverpool, England, in 1813. Some time in the 1830s she met and married Archibald Renfrew Kier, a native of Scotland. About 1832, they emigrated to Canada West (Ontario), where they raised a family of six boys and four girls.

In 1862, Mary and Archibald Kier, with their older son James and youngest son William T., travelled west from an area near London, Ontario in a covered wagon by the old Lewis and Clark trail. From Portland, Oregon, they took a ship to Victoria.

Two of the older sons remained in Ontario. The second eldest daughter, Mary, and a young son, George, came to Vancouver Island via the Cape Horn route in the same year as their parents were crossing the continent overland. Two other children, Martha and Joseph, followed in 1865, by the Oregon trail. One daughter Jane was married while the family was moving west and remained in Oregon with her husband, James Elliott.

The Kiers senior took up two pre-emptions in Somenos, and their son James, one. After their arrival at Cowichan Bay on the H.M.S. Hecate, August 22, 1862, they took Indian canoes up Somenos Creek to Somenos Lake, and from there travelled on foot to select their land.

The original Kier cabin was of log construction, built on an outcropping of shale on the present west side of Somenos Road, just north of Drinkwater Road. It is believed that Mrs. Kier was among the first white women to live in this area.

As Archibald Kier was of an advanced age, it fell to Mary Jane to get supplies from Victoria. It was she, rather than her husband, who made the trip to Victoria several times a year, going on foot to Cowichan Bay from Somenos and then by canoe to Saanich, and then on foot to Victoria. According to pioneer settlers, Mrs. Kier also walked the old trail from Victoria to Cowichan with small children in her care after the government had let a contract for construction of a trail five feet wide from Victoria to Cowichan travelling around by the Sooke watershed and Shawnigan Lake.

It is a matter of speculation why she had ever walked that trail, but probably she had gone down to Victoria by the usual route to meet Martha and Joseph in 1865. She would have found that Martha had been badly frightened by Indians crossing the American plains and so she would have chosen the trail to get them to Somenos.

When Maple Bay became a regular port of call, about 1865, it was much easier to get supplies. After British Columbia joined Canada in 1871, the Kier home became the post office for the Somenos district, with Archibald as postmaster until his death in 1881. Mrs. Kier then took on the position until her own death in 1901. It was her young son Joseph's job to fetch the mail from the steamer at Maple Bay and bring it by horseback to the post office.

One of the social activities of pioneer times was to call for mail at the Kier residence and stay for a cup of tea and visit.

Along with Mrs. Jess (Neil) Bell, Mary Jane Kier acted as midwife for other women in the district. Most of the John Newell Evans family were brought into the world by Mrs. Kier.

It was also Mrs. Kier's place to help in the clearing of the land and to ensure a food supply. By 1881, she had a garden and some fruit trees with a fence around the garden to protect it from deer. According to her son, James, each time a child was born to a pioneer family, that family planted another row of potatoes.

It was Mary Jane and Archibald Kier who donated some of their farm for what is now known as Mountain View Cemetery at Somenos. It was they who helped build the Methodist Church on the Herd Road (the Maple Bay church) in 1869, and the Methodist Church at the corner of Drinkwater and Somenos Roads in 1874 which was situated on their farm.

Mary Jane Kier was a kindly soul who went out of her way to help anyone who required help.

When she died she was buried next to her husband at Mountain View Cemetery, Somenos.

Jane Lomas (nee Alexander)
(Mrs. William H. Lomas)
1849-1930
by her granddaughter, Kathleen Derby

Jane Lomas, nee Alexander, 1849-1930.

Jane Alexander, the eldest of five children, was born in Adelaide, Australia on August 28, 1849. She attended a private school in Sydney for a few years, later joining her parents at a mining camp where she learned to pan gold.

In 1862 the Alexanders decided to come to British Columbia. Jane's brothers and sisters went to the Mission Chapel School on Somenos Lake, but she was considered to be too old. The young schoolteacher, William Lomas, lent her books and helped her with lessons until Archeacon and Mrs. Reece arrived in 1866 when she continued her studies with them.

Jane and William Lomas were married in 1868. By this time he had been appointed Indian catechist. A mission house had been built and attached rooms were provided for the catechist. This was their first home.

The Lomas home was seldom free of Indians. They became accustomed to going to Mr. Lomas at the Mission and continued to take their difficulties about sickness, matrimonial affairs, gardening, needlework, trading, et cetera, to Mrs. Lomas. During her husband's absences she had many disputes to settle and much advice to give.

Later, Mr. Lomas was appointed Indian Agent. His territory extended from Comox to Victoria and included the Gulf Islands. At one time, when the four eldest children were almost recovered from whooping-cough, he engaged a large canoe with three Indians to man it and took the family with him, camping out each night in a different place. The two weeks were much enjoyed by the children though Mrs. Lomas was often concerned in the rough waters when even the Indians gave up hope of reaching shore safely.

Jane Lomas always took a keen interest in the Agricultural Society, exhibiting and taking many prizes. The first Cowichan Tennis and Polo clubs also had her warmest support, and several future tennis stars learned to play on the Lomas court.

The Lomas family consisted of: Mary, who married William M. Dwyer, Edward S., Alfred H., William A., who died young, H. Maud, who married Wilfred Prevost, Jennie E., who married Herbert Naden Clague, and David Henry Geoffrey. The name has died out in the district as the two grandsons left no children.

Mrs. Lomas was president of St. Peter's Guild for years but joined no other women's societies.

Christina Nelson (nee Englund)
(Mrs. John Nelson)
by her great-granddaughter, June White

John Nelson, a Swede, left his native land to go to sea at the age of sixteen. Eventually he arrived in the Cowichan Valley which must have been some years prior to the <u>Hecate</u> expedition of 1862, as he was there at the wharf to greet the intending settlers with farm produce.

Christina Nelson emigrated from Sweden to North America and went into service in New York. I do not know how she found her way out here to Vancouver Island, but she married John Nelson here. These two were my

Christina Nelson, nee Englund, 1840-1920.

great-grandparents. They had two children, Paulina (1876) and Alfred. Paulina is believed to be the first white child born at Cowichan Bay.

Some time in the late 1860s the Nelsons moved into the log house at Cowichan Bay which the Brennans had built and was the house which Mrs. Marriner, her three daughters and one son bought in 1894.

The late Nathan Dougan recorded that Christina was a wonderful gardener, particularly noted for her roses, geraniums and fuschias as well as all kinds of spring flowering bulbs.

Her granddaughters remembered visiting their grandmother, possibly in Victoria, and the dresses she made for them.

Mary L. Skinner
(Mrs. Thomas J. Skinner)
died 1896
Compiled by the Researchers

It was 1864 when Mr. and Mrs. Thomas J. Skinner with their children came to the Cowichan wilderness from pleasant, civilized Esquimalt.

The Skinners were one of the first white families to make Vancouver Island their home. They arrived in Fort Victoria on a January day in 1853 by the ship, Norman Morrison. Although Thomas had been appointed as bailiff to manage one of the Puget Sound Agricultural Company's farms (a subsidiary of the Hudson's Bay Company), and he and his family were expected, no provision had been made for their accommodation.

An empty hut close to the fort was found for them, hastily cleaned out by Indians using fir boughs for brooms. This was their first home in the new country. They tacked up blankets to divide the space into two parts, one for the family, the other for their servants. Eleven persons in all lodged there the first day but on the second day one of the maids returned to the ship and married its cook. She had disdained his courtship on the voyage out, but now any excuse that would get her back to England was good enough.

A month later, in that drafty hut with its leaking roof, Mrs. Skinner gave birth to a daughter, her sixth child.

The maid had solved her personal problem of accommodation in short order. For her employers, the solution took a little longer but in time - we do not know how much time - Thomas Skinner had a commodious home built at Esquimalt on the farm property adjoining Craigflower. He named it Oaklands.

Margaret Ormsby in British Columbia: a history, says he was the only one of the four bailiffs to make the farm in his care pay.

There is not much on record about Mary Skinner. A picture of her as a young woman shows a surprisingly modern-looking girl. Her lifted chin and direct gaze suggest someone who might easily have been a militant suffragette a little later in the century. Certainly she has the appearance of an "equal rights" woman.

The Skinner children grew into adolescence in a privileged society. They were part of the select group that enjoyed the balls, the riding parties, the concerts and the shipboard dances which characterized life for the tiny "aristocracy" of Victoria and Esquimalt in the late 1850s and 1860s.

And then, abruptly, this delightful, civilized life came to an end. Thomas Skinner fell out with his employers in the matter of his contract and moved his family to a truly pioneer life in Cowichan.

As early as 1859 he had taken up land on Quamichan Lake, this at a time when the Colonial Office dreamt of a landed gentry and was charging one pound sterling per acre. Perhaps he had thoughts at the time of claiming this as the farm his employers had promised him in his contract. At any rate, his feeling of injustice came to a head in 1864.

The Colonist newspaper of May 31, 1864 reported, "The gunboat Grappler carried to Cowichan yesterday Mr. James T. Skinner and family, who, after a residence of many years in the vicinity of Esquimalt, have been obliged to give up their old home and begin life anew in a remote settlement."

The decision was obviously made in haste, and whether or not Mrs. Skinner concurred, we do not know. The furniture she had brought with her from Oaklands had to remain at Maple Bay where it was covered with carpets until it could be transported piece by piece through the woods to the new home. For the transfer they had brought with them a democrat wagon but a tree fell on it and it was broken to pieces. It was no great loss as it was years before a trail was cut on which such a wagon could be used.

John Evans who did an invaluable work in collecting the histories of the earliest settlers, said the Skinners had a log cabin and two tents. The logs for the cabin were cut and it was erected in "work bees," but it was many months before lumber for flooring or lining could be obtained. Sawmills were small and few and the demand for lumber was great.

The isolation, the lack of any household conveniences and any social life must have been a very unhappy experience for the ladies of the family. Miss Mary Skinner, who was interviewed by N. de Bertrand Lugrin for Pioneer Women of Vancouver Island did not like to recall the hardships of that life. "Very lovingly," the author says, "Miss Skinner speaks of the fortitude and patience of her mother, who always contrived to have some little comforts for her children."

They were not young children any longer, of course, but events showed that Mrs. Skinner was a practical woman. She kept up her ties with Esquimalt. The first wedding in her family was that of daughter Annie who at sixteen became the bride of a naval officer. She had first met him when she was a little girl at Oaklands and so he claimed had fallen in love with her even then. He took her with him to England. That marriage was solemnized by a visiting Anglican priest in the small log house which was the Skinner's first Cowichan home.

The next girl to leave was Constance, the child who had been born in the miserable hut in Fort Victoria. Her wedding took place in the larger house that Thomas had built to succeed the pioneer-type log house. She married Alexander Edmond Batson Davie, the young Victoria lawyer who would later be premier of the province. Her sister, Ada, also married into politics, one Joseph Mason, Member of Parliament for Cariboo, and it was at Quesnel that their marriage took place. The Skinner girls were only Cowichan pioneers briefly, and it seems reluctantly.

As to their father, he took an active part in the Cowichan community. We see Mrs. Skinner only through the lives of others. In January of 1896 she died and was buried in St. Peter's churchyard beside her husband who had died in 1889.

Martha Smithe (nee Kier)
(Mrs. William Smithe)
1849-1923
By Elden Kier and Mrs. C. Alma Green, her granddaughter

Martha Kier was born 3 August 1849 in Ontario, the fourth daughter of

Mrs. William Smithe, nee Martha Kier, 1849-1923.

Mary Jane and Archibald Kier who settled in Somenos in 1862.

In 1865 Martha and her younger brother, Joseph, came overland in a covered wagon from Ontario to Portland and thence by ship to Victoria and finally to Cowichan. She was a light-haired girl, the Indians had tried to buy her and this left a lasting impression on her sixteen year-old mind. She used to tell of the massacre by Indians of the wagon train which followed theirs. This was in retaliation for a foolish action towards a dead Indian by a man travelling with her own train. Martha had not wanted to come overland but had wished to travel the safer Cape Horn sea route.

On July 3, 1873, Martha Kier married William Smithe who was then a Member of the Provincial Parliament which he continued to be until his death in 1887. In January of 1883 he became Premier.

The Smithes raised a family of one daughter and two sons, all born in Cowichan. One son, Ormond T., became mayor of Duncan. During the First World War he changed the spelling of his name to "Smythe" because of the confusion in the post office.

In her younger days Martha Smithe was closely associated with the life of the district and took a leading part in women's activities. When she died in Duncan on February 15, 1923, she was buried beside her husband in Mountain View Cemetery, at Somenos.

Martha's daughter, Eleanore, married Joe MacDonald. Her two sons, William (Limen) and Ormond Towers, lived for most of their lives in the Cowichan Valley.

SECTION II
ON THE LAND
The Period 1867-1886
by Elizabeth Blanche Norcross

The Reverend William Sheldon Reece had been sent to Cowichan by Bishop Hills with two major responsibilities. The first was to minister to the Indians over a wide area, from Chemainus in the north to Shawnigan Lake in the south -- about twelve miles to the north and twenty in the south by today's road -- and Salt Spring Island to the east. His second responsibility was to the white settlers in the same area. William Lomas had been appointed as catechist to the Indians.

The Reverend Mr. Reece already had been active in his new parish for a year and had either an uncompleted rectory in which to live or else a temporary dwelling.[1] We know that he had something to call a parsonage as his base where he could draw his parishioners together. Despite the lack of a church building, in 1866 he held an October Harvest Festival service in mid-week at the parsonage where 63 people attended.

There were women present at this first Harvest Home; a contemporary account informs us that there was "a goodly sprinkling of ladies at the party which followed the service."[2] This was probably the first social event to gather together all the white residents of the Cowichan Valley and it can be regarded as an important milestone in the building of a true community.

St. Peter's, a log church, was built on the present site the next year, and in addition to his services there, Mr. Reece rowed across Somenos Lake to conduct regular services in the log hall on its west shore.

For many years the Reece home served as the centre of the community. Mrs. Reece is a shadowy figure, but after the dance which followed the Harvest Home service of 1870 at which some 140 people were present, we are told that she served tea and cake.[3]

At the prompting of Mr. Reece, the Cowichan and Salt Spring Island Agricultural Society was formed with a purely male directorate.[4]

The second major contribution that Mr. Reece made to the secular life of the Valley was the founding of the Lending Library and Literary Institute. In initiating this he was following a practice common at the time of operating a reading room or institute in connection with the church.[5] While in other places these were designed primarily to provide a diversion for single men, in the highly literate Cowichan Valley a library would meet a need felt by most people, single or not.

To what extent did Mr. Reece's initiatives affect the lives of Cowichan women? We find that the annual Fall Fairs, inaugurated by the Agricultural

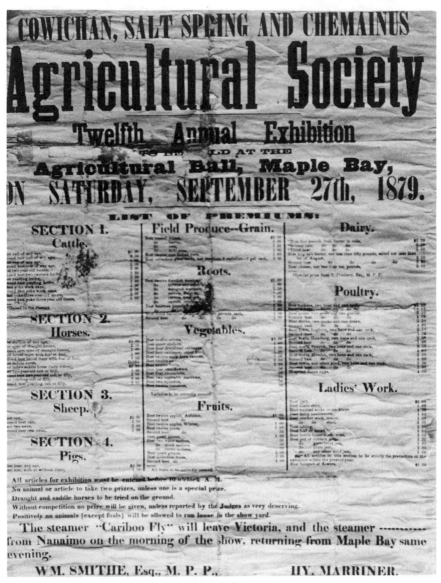

Poster of early Agricultural Exhibition.

Society, very early in their history made provision for women's work.

Indian women also benefited. For the history of their participation we start with a report in the Colonist of May 15, 1869. A general note about the work of the Church of England missions to the Cowichan Indians includes the following: "... and a gentlemen is about to teach them how to manufacture the wool produced in the vicinity into clothing, the mission being already provided with a carding machine."

As the gentleman in question (almost certainly this was the Indian cate-chist, William Henry Lomas) was married, it is a fairly safe guess that it was the lady of the house who would teach the manufacture of wool into clothing.

The teaching of the Fair Isle style of knitting adopted by the Cowichan Indians has been ascribed to various pioneer women of Scottish descent and also to the Sisters of St. Ann who definitely were not Scottish. Mrs. Jane Lomas, the catechist's wife, was a daughter of Margaret and David Alexander. While she herself had been born in Australia, her parents were Scots so she would have learned her knitting skills from her mother.

As to the Fall Fair connection, Mrs. Lomas was not only one of the keenest exhibitors herself, but one of her Indian pupils took a prize in needlework. Exhibits of Indian knitting came at a later date.

In 1869 the Agricultural Society built a hall at Maple Bay, that is to say, a mile or two inland, on the present Herd Road on 20 acres of land donated by the government.[6] By 1864, Maple Bay had become a port of call for the weekly steamer from Victoria and was taking precedence over Cowichan Bay as the preferred shipping point for the North Cowichan farmers. In time it would become a small-scale trading centre.

The inaugural meeting of the Lending Library was attended only by men. "March, 1871," the old minute book recorded, "at a meeting of the residents of Cowichan ..." and so on. At an early meeting following the inaugural one, a lone, brave woman, Miss E. Bell, invaded the male stronghold and enrolled as a member. In the ensuing years, women took no leadership position and all the offices were held by men. Presumably, Archdeacon Reece (as he became in 1868), had invited only men to form the Lending Library society, believing that its benefits would accrue to the women through their husbands, and probably they did. However, the choice of books and periodicals would not be theirs.[7]

The Methodists, like the Anglicans, had had itinerant ministers visiting the Valley in the earliest years of settlement. In this period of Cowichan's history, they built a church on what later became known as Herd Road. The church still is standing but has been converted to a house. In the spirit of the times, men of all denominations pitched in to help with the building. Supervising the work was the staunch Presbyterian, Archibald Kier. It was 1875 before the Methodists had a resident minister.[8]

St. Ann's, Tzouhalem, cared for the spiritual needs of the Roman Catho-lics of the district, white as well as Indian. In 1869-70, under Father Ron-deault's direction, they replaced their large log church on Comiaken Hill with the Stone Church which still stands, now converted to an Indian Arts and Crafts Centre.

In point of religious care, the small population of Cowichan was fairly well served.

Schools made their appearance in the Valley almost as soon as there were families. The first to open, was in the log hall on Somenos Lake, in 1864, with the schoolmaster rowing across the lake to fetch and return some of his pupils. Two other one-room schools were opened, one in the Maple Bay district, one south of the river, and thus, in a hit-or-miss fashion, the chil-dren were educated. For a time the same teacher was serving two schools,

Original log house of Dr. John Chapman Davie, built in 1863.

week and week about.[9]

Few of the children who attended these one-room schools and the later ones that were built as the population grew, could return home for the noon meal. Their sandwiches were wrapped in table napkins or scraps of cloth. Sometimes ordinary paper had to serve. Lard pails or syrup pails which came supplied with handles in those days, were provided as lunch containers. Boys might have workmen's lunch buckets. It was not until the 1920s that waxed paper was in general use.

Medical care was far down in the list of Cowichan's amenities. There was the trained midwife, Jess Bell, and other experienced women who helped as need arose. Dr. John Chapman Davie, the elder, rode up on horseback from Victoria every two or three months, primarily to see how his teen-aged sons were getting on with the farm. It was an opportunity for the settlers to consult him on medical problems. Otherwise, if they wished to see a doctor, and were well enough to make the trip, they went down to Victoria.

Dr. Davie died in 1869. His son and namesake, also a doctor, followed his father's custom of coming up from Victoria at intervals to visit the Valley. Family tradition has it that he made professional calls with a gun in the back of the buggy in order to get in a little shooting as he made his rounds. It was many years before there was a resident medical man in the Valley.

Another lack was a store that carried women's or children's wear. This must have been felt as a real privation as early (male) accounts of the period make special mention of it.[10] The women of these first years left no written record of their own.

A third lack, and this one constituting a daily hardship, was the absence of running water piped into the homes. Every bucket of water laboriously drawn from a well was a precious commodity to be used as thriftily as if it was actually in short supply.

After ten years of settlement, Cowichan Valley had only the most wretched of tracks through the forest to serve as roads. Jess Bell, mid-wife, still trudged on foot to her patients over the roughly slashed out trails. Somenos farmers still were forced to dedicate an eight-hour day by slow-paced ox team to take their produce to the steamer or to pick up supplies and mail. Women, for the most part, were still tied to home with young children and a never-ending round of chores.

Lack of roads was certainly a major social and economic deterrent to development of the Valley. Apart from the fact that white women were very much a minority on the whole of the west coast, men hesitated to ask women to share the hardships of wilderness living, hardships so much greater for them than for the men. We know that John Evans, who pre-empted Cowichan land in 1862, lived in California for a number of years thereafter, making summer visits to the Valley only at intervals, with his wife. Edward Marriner, another early pioneer, delayed for ten years before returning to England to find a bride. William Drinkwater obtained, so it is said, a "brideship" wife. Presumably she worked in Victoria for a few years after arrival for it was not until 1867 that Frances Knowles Douglas married William Drinkwater in St. Peter's Church, the first marriage celebrated there.

On the subject of the lack of roads and girls, John Evans injected a sly comment into a paper presented to the first Cowichan Historical Society. "Can any of you locate Lover's Lane?" he inquired. He answered his own question. This Lovers Lane he explained, started at Trunk Road, now known as Somenos, and was built by Joseph Drinkwater at his own expense. Before officially being designated "Drinkwater," when not described as Lover's Lane, it was known as the west end of Maple Bay Road. "We had several marriageable young ladies in Somenos," said Evans, "and a favourite walk was up Lover's Lane." Cowichan was progressing!

The Drinkwater brothers, William and Joseph, were the prop and stay of Cowichan in its early pioneer years. They were the exception among the settlers in that they had come with some modest capital which permitted them to equip their farm with all the agricultural machinery and tools then available. In consequence, their equipment was continually on loan, often to its owners' great inconvenience. The solution they applied was to buy a second complete set so that they had one for lending and one for their own use.

Now producing a surplus over their own needs, the settlers relied on the Victoria and Nanaimo markets, accessible only by steamer from either Maple Bay or Cowichan Bay. Wagon roads, rather than sled (stone boat) tracks were essential. It is true that government in Victoria sent a road construction crew into the Valley every summer. In the usual manner of visiting experts, the foreman would not listen to the locals who pointed out those patches of road that became impassable under winter conditions and were most in need of work.

Dissatisfied with the way road construction and maintenance were handled, the Cowichan settlers north of the river petitioned for municipal status.[11] (Not to be overlooked was the fact that road work meant wages for a cash short economy, or, just as satisfactory, remission of taxes.) The records we find in connection with the petition provide an insight into Cowichan's population at the time. It was required that the petition be signed by at least two-thirds of the male freeholders, householders, free miners (if any), pre-emptors and lease-holders for a term of not less than two years and that they were 21 years old and residents of Cowichan North and Chemainus. Seventy men met the requirements, and of that number fifty-five signed the petition.[12]

It was probably with a sigh of relief that Victoria turned the Valley's problems over to its residents, effective June 18, 1873.

South of the river the pioneer farmers were not affected by the new political entity. The Cowichan River, still not bridged, was a barrier to communication.

With incorporation of the District Municipality of North Cowichan, the Valley entered a new historic period. In practical terms, not a great deal changed.

The decade after incorporation was characterized by slow growth, stagnation, depression and loss of population. Victoria also suffered a depression at this time with loss of population, and Cowichan could scarcely be expected to fare better. This depression was widespread with the rise of urbanization.

A hard core of settlers who had cast their lot in the Cowichan Valley and stubbornly worked to open up the country did remain, but an almost equal number of transients came and went. Among the newcomers of the 1870s were some furnished with capital who bought partly developed properties and then built frame houses. There were others whose names appear once in the records and never reappear.

In the 1870s Cowichan enjoyed a sufficient level of prosperity that stoves were being set up in the settlers' homes, (the first on record to arrive in the district was in 1870). Women no longer had to cook and bake in the fireplace. No longer, also, were they forced to manufacture and work by tallow candles. Coal oil lamps became a commonplace and produced a new chore, that of the daily cleaning of their glass chimneys. The increasing prosperity resulted from developing of the farms and increased farm surpluses to sell in Victoria and Nanaimo.

In 1879 the telegraph line was put through from Victoria to Nanaimo. Of great interest here is the fact that the first operator and maintenance "man" for the section between Shawnigan Lake and the site of the present Ladysmith was reputedly a woman, Mary Glyde (Mrs. Ambrose) Skinner. Probably this is not strictly accurate. It seems that her husband held the post for a few months before his death. We do know that this Mrs. Skinner was the first woman to appear on North Cowichan's assessment roles.

The job on the telegraph line was undoubtedly important to the widow who had a small daughter to support but the line in itself was of minimal importance to the district as a whole; what the residents desperately needed was better access to markets through a road connection.

In incorporation year the Reverend David Holmes succeeded Archdeacon Reece. His initial enthusiasm and optimism led him to build two daughter churches to St. Peter's, those being St. Mary's, Somenos and All Saints, Westholme, as well as a new St. Peters. The two new churches were as important as St. Peter's was to women's lives.

In 1882 Mr. Holmes was lamenting, "... everything in Cowichan does not advance ... nothing to keep the population in the district."[13]

In this period William Sutton came from "Canada" (as British Columbians still referred to the central provinces) and set up a sawmill at Genoa Bay. With sawn lumber now becoming general for housebuilding, one would have expected the enterprise to be successful, but Sutton failed after several years of operation, as did his successors in the business.[14]

The little sawmill at Chemainus, founded in 1862, by three partners and bought in 1864 by T.G. Askew continued to operate through these years, continuing even when the owner was declared insolvent in 1880. When he died a few months later, the majority financial interest was in the hands of Mrs. Askew's stepfather, but for a few months the on-the-spot management was in her hands. She had been left virtually penniless, a young widow 30 years old with eight little children to support.[15]

William Penn Jaynes, a settler with capital, bought a property at Quamichan in 1878 with a newly built house on it. He conducted a store in a separate building. His trade was mainly with the Indians. The management of the post office which operated out of his home was registered in the name of Mrs. Jaynes.

The status of women was unaffected by incorporation. William's British Columbia Directory 1882-83 includes in the list of Cowichan residents a few women who apparently earned the right to an identity by becoming widows. We find Mrs. A. Kier, Somenos, postmistress; Mrs. Hall, Chemainus, farmer; Mrs. Askew, Chemainus, Mill owner (referred to as her husband's relic); Mrs. Ambrose Skinner, farmer; and, intriguingly, Mrs. Charley, Somenos, private hotel. The North Cowichan municipal elections cast a little light on this last as they show that in 1874 a James Charley had one hundred acres in Comiaken with a retail liquor licence, and that from 1882 to 1884 Mrs. James Charley was a householder in Somenos.[16]

The Directory also noted that in Cowichan the Indian Reserve had some of the best land which was not being developed. It might become available for purchase by whites within a few years as the Indians, "... and sorry is the writer to say it ...", are fast disappearing.[17]

Mr. Holme's discouraged report on Cowichan affairs in 1882, proved to be a case of the darkest hour before the dawn. Matters took a decided upswing; the long awaited for railway connection between Victoria and Nanaimo now became a certainty, though still in the future. The third stage in Cowichan's development, rapid increase in population and local capital, was at hand.

THE ANCIENT MARRINER
By Geraldine Weld

Johnny pointed a brown finger to where the sagging verandah roof leaned brokenly on posts soft with dryrot. "That old house is goin' to fall down pretty soon," he said flatly.

I looked at it with a twinge of misgiving. He had just put into plain words the thoughts that lurked in the eyes of our friends when they said politely, "It is a beautiful position." That was in 1962.

The builder had been Patrick Brennan. He had put in a bid for twenty or more acres of lands from the government before 1868. But due to the delay in defining the boundaries of the Indian reserve land, his grant did not come through until 1871. He built anyway, regardless of legality. A roving photographer, Fred Dally, took a picture of the semi-finished Stone Church on Comiaken Hill in 1869 and in the background this house stands out clearly.

Comiaken Hill showing old log Church and Stone Church under construction, c.1869-70. Photo by Fred Dally, itinerant photographer in 1860's and 1870's.

Pat Brennan was first mentioned in a Victoria newspaper in 1859 when he rescued a drowning Indian woman off Beacon Hill Park. Later accounts

59

Edward Marriner house from Khenipsen Rd.

of him were mainly for pulling a gun to settle an argument or putting his brand on other people's cattle. There is no mention of a Mrs. Brennan although the house has three bedrooms above its twenty-one by thirty-foot log frame.

The next owners in 1876 were Magnus and John Nelson. Here, their only child, Pauline Nelson, mother of Hilda McNichol, was born.

The property changed hands and pieces of land were sold in the following years. When Mrs. Augusta Marriner bought the house in 1894, it seems to have belonged, I think, to William Chalmers Duncan and William Lomas.

She moved with her family from their farm on the Cowichan flats to escape the winter damp of the land her husband had settled and where their children had been born. At this time she was still an active person, but knew that she was threatened with arthritis. The 200-acre farm, their livelihood stretched to the dykes on Cowichan Bay and included Marriner's Island.

The Marriner Family of Cowichan Bay.
Back row: Nettie, Arthur, Gertie.
Front row: Mary, Augusta (Mrs. Edward Marriner).

This, their new house, stood on a solid granite bluff in the sunshine, safely above the swollen river and the penetrating high tides from the bay. Underneath is a small walk-in area where the rock and log foundation shows. It is perfectly dry; we put suitcases there!

When my memories of the Marriners begin they had lived there for twenty-one years and it was known as the Marriner house. The three Misses Marriner, Mardie (Mary), Gertie and Nettie with their brother Arthur, continued to work the farm. Indian neighbours helped with crops and haying. Mardie told me long after that the Indians had always been very protective towards them.

They were small women in long, dark skirts. Mardie, the eldest, was the sturdiest and most outgoing. She played bridge and practised her golf swing in the field. But each day, in all weathers, they walked the long mile between their properties. They had no horse and buggy then, so they walked home again, carrying full baskets of produce.

On the farm they made butter, big, two-pound yellow rounds stamped on top with a fat cow standing under a tree. I can remember as a child taking bits from the edge of that butter, afraid of hurting the cow.

One year when the dykes protecting the flats from Cowichan Bay broke and water lay two feet deep over the farms, father took his boat down the riverlike roadside ditch to rescue the Marriners' pigs which were swimming in their sty.

During these years Mrs. Marriner had become a bedridden victim of the arthritis that she had feared. Her bedroom, lined with books, was off the sitting-room. The bay window overlooked lilac trees and the garden, but had no fireplace. I remember a fine-featured, parchment face, supported by pillows. She felt the cold bitterly. That was shortly before her death in 1916.

I was told a pathetic little story of the family's efforts to give her warmth and companionship that she craved. They had a wooden packing case that had held a piano. Into this they piled blankets, and I am sure a hot water bottle as well. Then they dragged this warm nest into the sitting room by the fire and carried her into it for the evening.

Around 1900 when Mrs. Marriner was still active they built an addition to the house so that they could take in boarders, mostly fly fishermen and wives whom Mardie would row on the trout-filled river, or down into the bay. Fly fishing for salmon was quite common then. She charged them fifteen cents an hour.

This new part, as it was always called, had a long hall with two bedrooms off each side. It was varnished V-joint with high sash windows. Two chimneys with a fireplace in each guest bedroom provided the heat. There must have been many (now valuable) chamber pots in those rooms.

As time went on they blocked off the upstairs bedrooms and moved into the new part. It was here later that we found Nettie's bed with a homemade straw mattress.

New neighbours from New Zealand, the Hutchinsons, bought the house across Khenipsen Road in 1911. They played tennis and encouraged Mardie's golf. It was they who put the diving board above the deep tidal pool below the house. I learnt to swim there, hanging from a rope around my middle and dog-paddling like mad! My father would command, "Swim properly or I will drop the rope." It seems typical of these pioneer women that they still found time and energy for fun. Their social life was largely through church socials, including everything from lantern slides to whist parties. They helped with the teas, births, deaths and the decorations for weddings. They made many devoted friends who often gave them rides to these affairs. Otherwise, they walked.

To eke out their very slim finances they did baby sitting jobs or cared for someone ill, and did sewing. Mardie travelled to Victoria several times by train.

Throughout the Marriners' lives there, visitors turned down a lane off Tzouhalem Road below the Stone Church. It went over Indian land to the bank of the Cowichan river, above the swimming hole that became known as Marriner's pool. From there a white picket gate led to a path to the house. It was not wide enough for a horse and buggy but always lined with flowers. Even when we took the place, clumps of bulbs pushed up through heavy grass to bloom. Their garden obviously was another thing that they found time to work in and enjoy.

The last time my husband and I saw Nettie was a year before her death in 1961 when she was a wisp of an eighty-year-old woman who insisted on making us tea. She had lived here alone with her dog since her sister Gertie's death in 1939.

While we waited, she joyfully showed us a looped electric wire that trailed between the kitchen and sitting room. Since the previous year, through the kindness of Miss Arabella Welsh, she did not have to carry an oil lamp anymore. Miss Welsh also had given Nettie an indoor toilet and a bath with a cold water tap. Until this gift there had been no improvements. In the kitchen, cold water still ran into the sink, and out into a bucket below. There had never been money to spend on frills.

In the sitting room nothing had changed, either. The tall antique chair where I had sat as a child with my feet far off the floor, was there. I remembered the rock cakes crunchy with butter and fruit. I could almost hear Mardie's voice, "Sit up now and do not swing your legs."

Behind the stove in the wide kitchen fireplace a heavy black chain with an iron hook hung from a metal bar that pierced through both sides of the brick chimney. For long after the Brennans occupied this house, a bubbling stewing kettle must have hung there. Trivets made from horseshoes would have stood below to keep things warm. In the rough board ceiling a shotgun blast had ripped a peppered hole into the room above.

I asked Nettie if she ever went to look at the old farm. "No," she laughed, stroking the grizzled muzzle of the Labrador beside her, "It is all right for me, but it's too far for Smoky."

She left the property to her kind neighbour, Arabella Welsh. We asked for a first refusal if she decided to sell. We knew that behind the tumbledown verandas was a farm house built of massive logs. The hand-hewn beams were hard as iron, though the original fir floors, worn paper thin in places, sloped away at all angles from the square central brick chimney.

Some owner had added the verandas and someone had prettied-up the sitting room. An ornate mantlepiece and wallpaper covered the old brick of the chimney. A V-joint wall and door closed the kitchen from the sitting room. We decided to strip it all off and get back to its original simplicity. Under the third layer of wallpaper we found sheets of newspaper from the Portland Intelligencer dated 1878. They were brown and brittle but still legible. There was also a whole seagulls' wing. We scraped the hewn beams of a hundred years of flaking whitewash, they were beautiful.

The stairway up is narrow and twisting and its steps steep and grooved with wear. When we unboarded the windows there, we found that the frames were cut at a slant through the logs, making a deep frame for the view across the estuary and Cowichan Bay to Saanich.

It was in the cupboard here that Mardie Marriner's diary (in four volumes) was found. It is now in private hands.

We had to take down the new addition as the base was full of dry rot, but the old bricks from the chimneys we built back into an entrance hall.

The other occupants of the house and property, rats, ants, and other squirmy things, had become arrogant with one little old lady there. They resented us bitterly.

The Ancient Marriner is now well into its second century and just as I had told Johnny that it would be, it still is standing strong.

Ella Estelle Auchinachie (nee Evans)
(Mrs. Peter Auchinachie)
1877-1949
by her daughter Doll Walker

Our mother, Ella Auchinachie, was born in a log cabin on First Street in Duncan, the child of John N. and Mary Jane Evans. Her parents had returned to Duncan to stay and settled the following spring on the Cowichan Lake Road property in a log cabin. Barns on the property still stand today.

Ella's brother, William, was born 14 months after her. The two children grew up very close and thus it was a great sorrow and loss to Ella when William died from injuries suffered while he was hunting for cows. Ella was in her early teens at the time.

Ella attended school at the old Somenos school on the corner of Drinkwater and Somenos Roads, opposite the cemetery.

My father, Peter Auchinachie, remembered seeing his future wife for the first time when she was about eight years old, while he was working on the construction of Drinkwater Road. He said she was a saucy little girl with dark, curly hair, always ready for a joke or fun.

Ella married Peter Auchinachie when she was eighteen years old on November 13th, 1895, taking up residence in Sahtlam on Riverbottom Road. This house burned down in the 1920s. It was not possible to dig a well but my mother did have running water. My father had hollowed logs which carried water to a tank on the roof from far up the hill near the old Jordan homestead.

Peter and Ella had a large family consisting of two boys and seven girls. They were: William, born in 1904, Stanley, born in 1905, Eva, born in 1896 (Mrs. John Clark), Maude, born in 1898 (Mrs. Jim Maitland), Elsie, born in 1901 (Mrs. Jim Green), Margaret, born in 1907 (Mrs. John Walker), Grace, born in 1910 (first Mrs. Washington, second Mrs. Burrows, and third Mrs. Colk), Katie, born in 1915 (Mrs. George Payne) and Helen, born in 1917 (Mrs. Dick Courney). The two oldest children were born at her mother's house and the next five of us were born at Sahtlam.

Men in those days had few ways of getting cash. Road construction in the summer months was their main occupation. Mother was often alone for weeks during the first summers. I remember her telling of carrying her second child, Maude in one arm and the milk pail in the other with Eva hanging onto her apron in the early fall evenings. She was glad to get back to the warmth and safety of the house.

The Indian Reserve was next to the property and she depended on the Indians for many things. They were true friends. I remember her telling of a Mrs. Douglas living farther on from the Reserve who was a good friend and neighbour and of the two of them picking wild strawberries by the bucket and preserving them.

One time when my father was away, a cougar came after the sheep. Mother shut my older sisters and brother in the house and ran to the Reserve for Indian Willie. He came and she went to the snake fence to show him where the cougar jumped the fence and there was the cougar eating a lamb! Indian Willie shot it. My sister, Maude, remembers the wolves around the house one night after Dad had killed lambs and how scary it was, as he had gone back to his work.

My two older sisters were enrolled in Sahtlam school at the age of two or three years to ensure enough pupils to warrant a teacher. It was a long way for two small girls to walk alone with nothing but a rough road through the bush for over three miles, sometimes seeing bears and also passing Jordan's cows accompanied by a nasty bull. My sisters remembered father showing them the pits the Indians made on deer trails to trap deer and his warnings to them to be careful to not fall in them.

Mother was a butter maker and sold her produce (eggs too), to the Cowichan Merchants. She had her own special paper for this printed with her name, Mrs. Peter Auchinachie. More than fifty pounds of butter a week was made in the spring and summer and sold for five cents more per pound than other butters. Her butter was once sent to the Pacific National Exhibition and won first prize.

With such a large family, mother did not have much time for social activities. She sewed and made all our clothes. On winter evenings some of the family would read aloud as the women and girls knitted and darned socks. There was a Bible reading twice a day and also prayers. The washing was done by an Indian woman for a dollar a day. We always called the women ladies and were never allowed to use the word "squaw."

The homestead on Riverbottom Road was sold in 1911 or 1912 and a house built on Auchinachie Road. Ella Auchinachie never left the Island. She died in 1949 at the age of 72.

Jean Wallace Bell (nee Blair)
(Mrs. John Bell)
1853-1941
by her niece Mary Peck

Jeanie Blair, the daughter of Mr. and Mrs. John Blair, was born at Rockford, Illinois. She came to Vancouver Island with her parents in 1884.

John Blair preceded his wife and daughters to Cowichan and established a home on Menzies Road. Mrs. Blair and the daughters remained in Victoria and followed him in 1886.

Jeanie Blair was a small and very active woman. It is probable that she had taught school in Illinois, and at one point in her career she taught at Wellington, perhaps in the interval before joining her parents on Menzies Road.

She was the second teacher at the Somenos School, the first being Stewart Wood. The first school register for the Somenos School runs from 1886 to 1889, having been started by Stewart Wood and this was continued by Miss Blair. It was she who arranged for the first Christmas tree and entertainment in a district school, the objective being to raise funds for an organ for the school, one of many community efforts in which she interested herself.

Jeanie boarded with the Drinkwaters. Farmers' hours were kept, so it was bedtime and lights out at eight o'clock in the evening.

In 1890 Sahtlam parents applied to the Department of Education for a school. The application was granted, provided an average attendance of seven could be guaranteed. A Mr. Currie donated the property on Cowichan Lake Road for the new school, which was built of logs, with volunteer labour.

Pending construction of the school, Miss Blair, now Mrs. John Bell, taught the Sahtlam children, commencing in September of 1890, in an empty house on Menzies Road owned by John Blair. Some of these children had been walking the seven and a half-mile round trip to the Somenos School.

In 1891 the log school was near enough completion that it could be used. The requisite number of pupils was obtained by admitting a three year-old!

The John Bells had no children of their own but adopted a daughter.

In 1906 they moved away from Cowichan, to Grand Forks and ultimately to the United States.

Paulina Best, nee Nelson 1876-1912.

Paulina Best (nee Nelson)
(Mrs. William Best)
1876-1912
by her granddaughter June White

My grandmother, Paulina Best, was the daughter of John and Christina Nelson. It is believed that she was the first white girl born at Cowichan Bay.

In 1901 Paulina married William Best. The couple lived at a number of locations on Vancouver Island including Victoria, Cobble Hill, Crofton, Alberni, Pachena Bay, Bamfield, and Uchucklesit (now called Kildonan) on the Alberni Canal.

Paulina Best died in childbirth at Uchucklesit in 1912. The new baby was cared for and raised to the age of ten by the Angus McKinnons, at which time her father brought her home to join the family.

After Paulina's death, the seven older children were placed temporarily in a Victoria orphanage. They used to visit their grandmother, Christina Nelson, who regularly made the girls two dresses each year. In the pockets of the dresses she always slipped in a little extra present, such as hair ribbons or flower seeds.

The Bests' eight children were--James K., Caroline Christina (who became Mrs. J. Robson), Hilda (Mrs. William McNichol), Alfred William, Herbert Edward (deceased), Thomas Keenan, Clarence Nelson, and Edith Pauline (Mrs. J. Yeowart).

Fanny Sophie Blythe (nee Edgson)
(Mrs. William E. Blythe)
1874-1965
by her daughter Nell Johnston

Fanny Edgson was born one mile from Maple Bay, on April 12, 1874 to Milton and Keturah (Kate) Edgson. She married William Ernest Blythe on April 19, 1899 and they left immediately for England on their honeymoon where they stayed with her father-in-law and sister-in-law until 1901. They came back to Duncan and lived there until their house was built on the Maple Bay Road. There Fanny lived until her death on March 19, 1965, her husband predeceasing her in 1924. Fanny would have been 91 years old on April 12.

They had two children that died at birth and two that lived, Walter Edgson Blythe and Ellen Kate Blythe (Johnston), known as Nell.

Fanny took an active interest in St. Peter's Church (Quamichan) and was a member of the Sewing Guild and the Women's Auxiliary. She was also a member of the Scattered Circle of King's Daughters, the organization which established the first hospital in Duncan. Her sister, Mrs. Fry, used to take groups to the hospital where they mended the linen and made new sheets; Mrs. Blythe was usually one of the party.

Elizabeth Castley (nee Evans)
(Mrs. Thomas S. Castley)
1880-1956
by her daughter Doris McEwan

Memories of our Mother, Elizabeth (Bessie) Castley, begin on Grandfather Castley's farm, "Rosgill," on Cowichan Lake Road. Heavy iron pots and kettles were used on a plain cast iron stove with a shelf in front of the fire box where you could keep dishes warm. The stove had no warming oven or hot water reservoir. Cold water was packed by the bucket from the well which was a fair distance from the house. All hot water had to be heated on the stove for house and dairy. Baths were taken in front of the stove in the kitchen with the wash tub serving as a bath tub.

I remember mother sitting with her blind brother-in-law who lived with us and reading to him. We lived with Grandfather and our uncle until we moved across the road to our own part of the farm in 1917.

Mother always looked after the milk, made butter for sale and had the cream ready for the Creamery. The eggs were cleaned and packed to be taken for sale as well. Besides helping to plant and tend a large vegetable garden, she always had time for her beloved flowers and her houseplants.

All our clothes were made by mother on her old Singer machine. Underwear, sheets, pillowcases, and tea towels, were all made from sugar and flour sacks after being bleached. We sometimes sent away to factories in Eastern Canada for bundles of sacks which were advertised in the Family Herald and Weekly Star. All the family looked forward to that paper as there was very little reading material around in those days and everyone read whatever came around.

All the family wash was done in the wash tub with a scrub board, with soap, usually made by mother from saved up grease to which lye was added. Light and white things were boiled on the stove in a copper boiler.

One year we had the Sahtlam school teacher as a boarder. It helped out finances although since teachers' wages were not very high at that time, room and board was low, too.

Mother had four girls who were all born on the old farm with the exception of the second daughter. When Dad and the oldest girl had whooping-cough, mother went to Duncan to a Mrs. Hanson a nurse who cared for patients in her home on First Street.

We were all christened at Sahtlam, either in the old log school or the Payne residence where the Anglican minister held services and we all attended. The old log school is where we all received our education, walking there in all weathers until they consolidated and we went by bus to Duncan Elementary School.

Mother had a busy day baking big pans of bread and buns on the wood stove. I will never forget the smell of fresh bread just out of the oven when we got home from school. Things that had to be attended to in a busy day were cleaning and filling the coal oil lamps and polishing the lamp chimneys. Care had to taken on cutting the wicks straight. No inside plumbing meant a chamber pot in every bedroom which had to be emptied and cleaned. Chicks hatching meant time preparing feed and looking after them. There was no prepared chick starter in those days.

Pig-killing day was another busy time for Mother as the meat had to be cut up and brine made. As there was no refrigeration the meat had to be cured. Bacon and hams were dry salted and stored in a wooden trough.

Summer was always a busy time of the year on a farm but there was visiting with family and friends on a Sunday. The twenty-fourth of May was celebrated by a big picnic with families of the Sahtlam district all going to the Riverbottom on the Cowichan river. It was nice grassy area where the younger folk played ball and the older ones sat in the shade catching up on the news. The children made the most of pools of water by the river for it was about the only time we were able to wade in nice sand and gravel pools. Everyone had a good appetite and made short work of the big baskets of food provided by the women.

July first was another day when horse and buggy made the trip with us all to the Cowichan Bay Regatta. We especially were interested in the "greasy pole" event and, of course, the Indian canoe races. That was one day in the year I remember having an ice-cream cone, a big treat. Another big day was the Fall Fair. Of great interest was the district exhibits and for us, the Sahtlam entry was special as Mother was chosen to make a crock of butter for it and received high marks. It was another day of meeting friends and sitting on benches on the Mound watching cattle and horses being judged in the ring which is where the city market and parking area is now. Another day for ice cream!

Winter was the time for parties and dances. Mother, being an Evans with many relatives and the Castley family too, there were gatherings for cards, singing and music. Our parents took us with them wherever they went and I well remember going to the old Sahtlam school on cold winter nights to dances. We children sat in the back of the "Democrat" on blankets and on the hay provided for the horse. The music was generally two violins and someone chording on the piano. Mother and Dad loved to dance and took part in all the quadrilles, Lancers and waltzes, minuettes, et cetera. If they were short of couples for a "square," the oldest children would participate and were pushed around through the different parts. The young children were bedded down on the benches under coats and blankets to sleep. Outside, the men had built a big fire and hung coal oil cans of water to boil for coffee and tea. The women provided plates of big sandwiches and cakes for refreshments after which the dance continued.

Mother was not a joiner of organizations, but she did belong to a branch of the Women's Institute that the late Mrs. Robson organized. They had many enjoyable meetings.

It was around 1922 when our parents decided to make a move. With four girls there were not very many opportunities for employment in the country, and not being blessed with any sons to carry on the farm, it seemed the best thing to do.

We bought our first car, a 1918 Ford in 1920, so transportation became easier. Our Dad, Mother and oldest sister drove it and it was quite a change from having to harness the horse, except that we still had to crank the car and it could be balky on cold days.

The eldest daughter, Amy, had a job as telephone operator in Duncan in 1922 and stayed with our aunt and uncle but she rode her bicycle home on her day off.

By this time Dad was working for the Municipality of North Cowichan on roads, so in 1923 we made the move to a small house on McDonald Street in Duncan. The farm was rented to a family who worked at the Hillcrest Mill a short distance away.

We were all delighted to have a house with electric lights. Although we could not afford to put in hot water right away, just cold water out of a tap was wonderful. Mother was especially thrilled with it all.

Not everything worked out well for her. The year after we moved, Dad was laid up with a tubercular hip joint and had to be put in a cast from his waist down, both legs to the ankles. He was bedridden for almost two years and Mother kept him at home where she nursed him faithfully and tenderly. All this time, with the breadwinner incapacitated and no other income except twenty dollars a month rent from the farm, it was up to the girls to find work. Amy, the eldest, already was at the telephone office, Doris, the second oldest, after working for Whittaker's candy shop, went there too. Kathleen, the third girl, went hairdressing for Mrs. Hitchcocks, and when she was through school, Ethel, the youngest went to the Sprott-Shaw Business College and later worked as a stenographer at Hillcrest Lumber company.

Dad was able to have the cast removed but he never again had free use of his legs; he became quite mobile using a cane. He and mother had many happy hours in the garden together and raised all the vegetables and planted fruit trees and berries. It was a great day when Dad got his first pension cheque, about forty dollars a month at that time. Not too long after that he died in 1940 after enjoying 38 years of happy wedded life.

Dad was buried at Mountain View Cemetery. I often would take mother there and walk through the original Methodist Church section. Later the Municipality of North Cowichan took over the cemetery and it was now open to all residents. She knew most that were laid to rest there and told me stories of them all. Too bad I did not have the foresight to write it all down at the time. Always a sympathetic person, she found time in later years to go to a neighbour who was bedridden with an incurable ailment and, being a born nurse, she would fix her up for the night and talk or read to her.

Not having any sons, she was as fond of her sons-in-law as they were of her. They were all avid hunters and fishermen. They always remembered to bring a share of venison or fish home to "Mom." As usual she helped cut the venison, pluck and clean the birds and clean the fish. She could out pluck us all when it came to preparing a bird.

Mother loved Christmas at home. She taught us girls to make paper chains to decorate tree and room out of red, green and white tissue paper. A homemade paste of flour and water was used. Lots of green boughs and holly decorated the house inside and there always was a Christmas tree which seemed to take up most of the room. It smelled so nice and I suppose due to the cold rooms, it lasted a long time. Turkey was not on our table at that time but we had a roast of beef, venison or roasted chicken. Potatoes, turnips, carrots, pickled beets with mince pie and Christmas cake. We always had a plum pudding with a piece of holly stuck on top with lovely sauce laced with a bit of rum.

In later years we acquired some real Christmas candles and holders for the Christmas tree. Great care was taken to put them on the tree away from the paper chains so as not to burn the place down. We lighted them and sat around enjoying the tree for a short time, then the candles were blown out and the parcels opened. It was especially a happy time for Mother when the grandchildren came on the scene. They all loved their "Granny." As we all lived not too far away, the children had many opportunities for being together to play at her place.

During the Second World War years, Mother was a great worker for the Red Cross and went as a volunteer to Queen Margaret's school where there was a depot for scrap material which the Girl Guides collected and which all had to be sorted. As she said, it was not the cleanest task, sometimes it was even like the sweepings from someone's house but still the material had to be sorted in case there was a bit of tinfoil there, also wanted for the war effort.

Mother saw a lot of changes from 1880 when she was born until she died in 1956. We finally were able to get hot water and inside plumbing which made things easier. We also acquired an electric washing machine. A big event was when Mother won an electric refrigerator as the door prize at the Cowichan Fall Fair. This was much better than the meat safe outside which used netting to ward off the insects. Another milestone in her life was getting the government pension. Although it was very small it seemed like a million to her and made her feel independent.

Looking back, I think of ways we made do, such as using a dried feather, chicken or duck wing to dust with and clean out cracks, et cetera. Also, Mother made our mops of rags cut in strips and nailed on the end of a broom handle. That was used only as a quick mop up, otherwise it was down on our hands and knees with cloth and bucket of water and scrub brush for a good job. Mother spent hours unravelling old socks and sweaters and re-knitting them into clothing for her family. Making rag rugs was another pastime, if you could call it that. Braiding strips of material and then sewing it into oval or round mats gave colour to an otherwise bare floor. Hinges for chicken coops and small sheds were made with leather cut from the upper parts of men's shoes, also a hole in a pot was made very serviceable by stuffing a thick piece of cloth through the hole. Under Mother's direction, my older sister and myself were shown how to clean cutlery with bathbrick, first shaving it off and then rubbing with a damp cork. It was wonderful when stainless steel knives were brought out.

No insulation in houses, or heat other than the kitchen stove or maybe a heater in the front room, made the bedrooms very cold. Mother always had the sad irons on the back of the stove or kept a brick in the oven and wrapped these in a piece of blanket or similar material to take to bed to warm us up. Waking up in the morning to a window covered with frost in pretty designs would have been lovely but we scratched our name on the frost and ran to the kitchen with our clothes to stand around the open oven door and dress while porridge was cooking. Bread, covered with a washed and bleached flour sack, which had been put to rise the night before in its big pan, was pushing its way up through the cover of blankets and coats which kept it warm all night. Many times in really cold weather, an old overcoat on top of our bed was extra warmth.

I wish I could end this on a happier note of our mother's life but it was not to be. After a life in doing so much for her family and others, in 1950, after a series of small strokes she was bedridden and not able to help herself or know us. In 1956 she died in a nursing home well cared for by dedicated nursing sisters at Colwood.

Bessie was laid to rest by her husband, Tom, in the Mountain View Cemetery in the shadow of old Mount Prevost in the valley where she had lived all her life.

Josephine Charter (nee Holmes)
(Mrs. Hugh Charter)
1883-1973
by her daughter Diana Setterfield

In 1883 Josephine Holmes, later know as "Zephie," was born in Duncan at the Anglican rectory on College Street, known as Holmesdale. Her father, the Reverend David Holmes had come to Cowichan ten years before.

As a girl, Zephie helped on the family farm and looked after a little girl, Gladys Speck Orton, who had lost her mother. Later, she wrote children's stories.

She married Hugh Charter in 1911 and lived in Duncan but in 1919 they moved to Crofton where she and her husband operated a farm until 1927. The couple had two children, Richard, born in 1914 and Diana (Setterfield), born in 1921.

Josephine Charter died in 1973.

26.9.1911 Wedding picture of Zephie Holmes & Hugh Charter.

Jennie Elizabeth Clague (nee Lomas)
(Mrs. Herbert Naden Clague)
1886-1962
by her daughter Mrs. Alathea James

Before her marriage, Jennie Lomas worked at the library in Duncan. It was not far from her home on Trunk Road where the Financial Building now stands. She lived with her mother, her older sister, Maud, and brother, Geoffrey.

After her marriage to Herbert Clague, a land surveyor, on March 5, 1912, she moved to her new home which her husband had had built for her on the corner of Coronation and Festubert Streets, then called Relingferg Road. The house still stands there today.

Her husband's work took him all over British Columbia, to Anyox, near Stewart, B.C., Kitimat and other remote areas in the northern half of the province. One very cold winter night when he was away from Duncan, the kitchen stove went out during the night. The water in the water jacket of the wood-burning stove froze. The following morning, Jennie lit the stove, unaware of the frozen pipes, and the whole stove exploded. She was stirring porridge at the time, and her small daughter, Helen, was playing with her dolls on the floor by the stove. Miraculously, neither of them was hit by the pieces of stove or the old fashioned sad irons which landed all around Helen. Parts of the stove were driven through the doors, ceiling and windows. Porridge was scattered all around and the family cat disappeared through a broken window. The sound of the explosion was heard for blocks. The other children (two) and their grandmother, Mrs. Lomas, were still upstairs in bed when the explosion occurred. The whole family spent the next week with their aunt, Mrs. Prevost, while the kitchen was being repaired and a new stove, without a water jacket, was bought. This house still stands in Duncan, more than 60 years later.

In 1921, Mr. Clague died and Jennie and her young family went to live in Victoria with an uncle of Mr. Clague's. When holidays such as Christmas, Easter or the summer arrived, the children and often their mother returned to Duncan to spend happy times there with their cousins.

Jeremina Colvin (nee Robertson)
(Mrs. Robert Colvin)
1858-1937
written by her daughter Edith M. Vaux
submitted by her granddaughter Geraldine E.G. Wilson

For Jeremina Robertson, 1886 was a very eventful year, first she married Robert Colvin on April 24, 1886, and then emigrated by boat from the Shetland Islands to the Cowichan Valley. As her husband had been out here previously in 1882, they felt a better life could be made in Cowichan near the railway, and fishing. Robert had built a log cabin on what now is called

Jeremina Colvin, nee Robertson, 1858-1937.

Riverside Road but then was referred to as near McPherson's Station, later Cowichan Station.

All supplies had to come from Victoria by steamer to Cowichan Bay and it was by the steamer Amelia that my mother came to Cowichan to make her home after her marriage. She told us, her children, of the trail which they had to walk from the nearest neighbours' log cabin to the place where she lived for the rest of her lifetime. My father and uncles had dug and levelled a good path through the forest which was about four feet wide. A log was felled over the Koksilah River and a side hewn flat for easy walking. Further up the trail a log had been cut over half way through and levelled off to let travellers know they were almost through the forest and into the clearing which became in later years the north field. In the clearing stood a very low log cabin which Mother thought must be the lambs' house, but it was to be her home until a house was built farther back in the forest.

Henrietta "Hattie" Colvin and one less predator.

There were few white people here then but Mother was never afraid of the Indians. She made friends and soon learned to converse in Chinook and was saying prayers for them and making friends for a lifetime. The first months were very lonely and the only communication for Mother and her nearest white neighbour who lived across the river was the bullhorn. These large animal horns (probably oxen) with a hole bored in the small end were their "telephones." At a certain hour during the day a blast from the horn meant everything was in order. Of course, the blast was returned by the opposite party.

Mother was an expert spinner and knitter. It has been stated in many articles and stories about the pioneers that Jeremina Colvin taught the Indians to knit which she did not. However, she did teach them the Fair Isle pattern which appears in a lot of their patterns today, or as part of a pattern. She also tried to teach them to card and spin a finer thread and was somewhat successful.

As my father was a Fisheries Inspector and was away a lot, my mother, with the eventual assistance of her children, ran the farm. There were six children, Mary Grace (Allman) 1887-1965, Jemina Henrietta 1889-1935, Robert Andrew 1891-1969, Magnus William 1893-1982, and Margaret and Edith, born in 1895. They were one of the earliest sets of twins born in the valley. Margaret died in 1911 and Edith (Vaux) in 1978. Jeremina died in 1937.

The Corfields...In Cowichan...1883-1920
by their granddaughter
Daphne Ralphs Borden - nee Corfield

The founders of this family in the Cowichan Valley were George Treffry Corfield and his wife, Christiana Ralphs from Cornwall. After their marriage in England in 1883 he preceded her to Cowichan and bought a farm beside the Koksilah River from Mr. Billy Richardson. They called the house The Maples and the land Eureka Farm. With him he brought a huge, locked packing case full of memories and treasures from his earlier days in the West Indies.

Christiana Ralphs proved to be a remarkable pioneer wife. In the big farmhouse she bore six of their seven sons between 1884-1895. One child (Reg) had been born in England. They named them: John Frederick, Herbert, Ernest Charles, Norman Tresseder, Walter Ralph, George Treffry and William Edgerton.

Four of her sons went Overseas during the First World War and Ernest Corfield notes, "Mother used to worry a lot about her sons Overseas."

During these years the Corfields expanded their land holdings. They bought the farm belonging to James Boal, Senior and took over another at the top of the Cowichan Bay hill from Ernest Leakey. They also managed the Marriner and Pimbury farms for a number of years. Adding these properties to their own land, they were farming almost the whole of the Cowichan Bay estuary.

Christiana Corfield must have been left on her own to cope with the household on that big farm, even to seeing that the boys did their chores. As well as this she raised seven sows to help the family finances.

Bridge over Koksilah River at Corfields.

She found time to enjoy social activities, playing cards and tennis as we see from the references to the Corfields in Mary Marriner's diary.

"4 July 1889 - Corfields had a picnic on the mountain. Played games Fox and Geese, Prisoner's Base and Up Jenkins.

17 July 1901 - Mrs. Corfield's Tennis tea, and again on 4 September.

15 September 1901 - Mrs. Corfield and Mr. Robert Service had tea with the Marriners.

27 January 1906 - Mary Marriner visited Corfields. After supper played 500 and Casino.

8 June 1907 - First day of tennis at courts given by Mr. Corfield to South Cowichan Tennis Club."

The Corfields ran a store and kept the Post Office; they both adjoined the farmhouse by the river. The address was Corfield, B.C. Ernest Leakey worked there as did Robert Service who came to their farm first as a "mud pup" handyman. He became a friend of the family and told harrowing stories to the boys at bedtime.

In the store they traded goods with the Indians in exchange for deer and strings of game birds. These were shipped from the Cowichan Bay wharf to Victoria. Sometimes the trades were eggs, a canoe or old fire-arms. The Marriners used to take out goods in trade for farm rental.

Ernest Corfield wrote: "In the early days Father employed six or eight white men on the farm and storekeeper and a Chinese cook. The farm-hands all slept in one large room over the store which was reached by a narrow stairway. The storekeeper had a separate room with a ladder down into the store and Post Office. The Chinese cook had a cabin near the house. The farm hands had their meals in the kitchen where they were served by the cook, the storekeeper had his meals with the family".

One Chinese cook couldn't have kept up with it all and Mrs. Corfield had no daughters to help her. Yet the Corfields and their sons were enthusiastic supporters of the tennis club years before it moved to its present location.

By this time their sons were grown up. In 1913 Ernest Corfield married Grace Muriel Montgomery, born in 1888 in Port Elizabeth, South Arica. They lived for a time near his parents' house on the Koksilah River, then established themselves at Cowichan Station where Muriel taught school. During the war years she helped on their farm as Ernest's brothers were away. Later, her mother, also a registered teacher, joined them and their three children. She came from England to their Cowichan Station home. The children were: Noel Leslie, Victor Norman, and Thelma Ralphs Corfield.

Muriel's father had been killed in South Africa by a shark when she was two weeks old. Muriel Corfield died in 1985 at the age of 97.

Two of the Corfield brothers married Holt-Wilson sisters, Joyce and Rachael. Both girls had been born in Suffolk, England in 1897 and 1899 respectively. After the death of their father, Rev. Holt-Wilson, in Toronto in 1913, they came out with their mother to live with her son on his Somenos farm.

In 1922 Rachael married George Treffry Corfield, Jr. They had two sons and two daughters and moved their family to Courtenay.

The elder sister, Joyce Holt-Wilson, married William Edgerton (Reg) Corfield in 1923. Their house still stands near his family's former farmhouse by the Koksilah River, Cowichan Bay. They had two children, Michael and Barbara, born in Duncan which was their home.

The following stories, personal memories of their family lives, are from the Corfield letters and their family tree. The collection now is with their granddaughter, Daphne Ralphs Borden at Courtenay. She is the daughter of Walter Ralphs Corfield, and was brought up in England as he stayed there after the First World War. Excerpts from Ernest Corfield Letters:

"I remember a trip we made to the farm (Ernest Leakey's farm) with a single horse and buggy with Mother driving and six or seven children packed in with me on the floor under the back seat. On the way home, coming down the long hill, the hold-back straps broke and the horse bolted and we all landed with the buggy upside-down on the beach. The horse, Polly, broke away and headed for home. Later, Father arrived in a terrible temper with a team of horses and carriage, one of the team being Polly."

In the next story Ernest Corfield feels that it may "seem strange," that his mother sent the mountainous piles of farm washing out to be done for her. He recorded:

"One thing that may seem strange to you is that for many years a very large crate of clothing was shipped to a Chinese laundry in Victoria once a week. For years we used to look forward to the Chinese New Year when the laundry box would come back filled with gifts of firecrackers, ginger, Leichi nuts, etc. Some for everyone of the family, with special bulbs for mother."

All these years the big packing case from the West Indies were kept in their father's bedroom. Though they had seen and touched the ancient revolvers and varied treasures that it held, like anything that is locked, the case intrigued his sons. When their home, "The Maples," burnt to the ground in 1920, it was one of the special things they tried to save. Unfortunately everything was lost.

Christiana Ralphs Corfield died at age sixty-five in 1916. Her husband, George Treffry, kept this love for the Cowichan Valley until his death in 1928.

Beatrice Day (nee Jaynes)
(Mrs. Athelstan Day)
1883-1983
excerpted from taped interview with Beatrice Day by Jim Griffin, Shawnigan Lake, in 1980

"My parents, William P. and Clara Jaynes, were married in 1869 and came out to Canada in 1870. They were in Barrie, Ontario for a few years. When they arrived in Canada, Sir John A. Macdonald, Prime Minister of Canada, said, "Why don't you go west, young man?"

They came out in 1878 and Sir John got my father a job managing a mill at Genoa Bay. My mother had three little children then. Eventually she had ten! About two years later my father was offered the opportunity to buy a little store which dealt mainly with the Indians. This was the first, or perhaps the second store in Duncan.

I was born in 1883, brought into the world by a midwife, since there was no resident doctor in those days. I was born in a log cabin on the corner of Maple Bay Road and christened, confirmed and married in St. Peter's Church.

I went to the little public school. I was more of a tomboy as instead of studying I played football with the boys and climbed trees with the boys.

I did a lot of riding, and played tennis as I grew older. I think I was about 14 when I stopped going to school.

After I left school I used to help my father and mother part-time in the store in Duncan and never got paid a bean for it!

We had lots of dances and fancy dress dances. I remember going to a fancy dress dance as a chicken. I had chickens and I sewed every feather onto my costume. I was quite old then. I went to the Indian potlatches until they were stopped by the Government.

Robert Service who was working at Corfields used to walk up to St. Peter's and sing in the choir when I did.

My oldest sister married Jim Whittome who started J.H. Whittome and Company. My other sister married another Englishman, Ernest Price. I too married an Englishman, Athelstan Day, in 1906.

My husband was an assayer in Dawson City and other places. I went to Dawson with him the year we were married and for several years thereafter, going as soon as the ice broke up on the river and staying until freeze-up.

That first year, I went by boat, the Princess Beatrice from Vancouver,

Day-Jaynes wedding group. 21 Feb./06. Athelstan Day. Miss Agate Sutton.
Miss Fawcett. Beatrice (Jaynes) Day. Photo by A. Lane.

then over the White Pass and Yukon Railway to Whitehorse and then down the river in a paddlewheel steamer.

Oh, I had a wonderful time in Dawson! I used to keep open house for the bank boys. I went up six times in all, and at the end it got rather expensive, having two children to take with me.

My hubby came back again and we bought the Buena Vista Hotel which overlooked Cowichan Bay. We were there for seven years from 1914 to 1920 when we sold it.

We had some wonderful people visit there, for instance, the Duke who was the Governor-General of Canada came, the Duke of Connaught.

After the Buena Vista we were looking for another hotel to buy. We went up to Parksville to see the Island Hall but there was nothing doing in Parksville in those days. Then we thought we would buy the old Commercial Hotel, but I went into the kitchen and the place was full of cockroaches. I said, "nothing doing." So we came home and tossed a coin; should Athelstan go back to assaying or should he buy a hotel? The coin said to go back to assaying and so he did. I stayed here with the children and he went to Stewart and all different places, assaying.

Beatrice Day, nee Jaynes, 1883-1983.

When he was nearly 65 he retired and after that he gardened and played a little golf. He died in 1953.

I had three children. There was Doreen Beatrice who was born in 1907. She died when she was 54, of cancer. Then George Athelstan was born in 1912. My children were so far apart! Then Dickie (Richard Chester) was born in 1920."

Mrs. Day was a very social person. When she was well into her eighties she was still giving her usual Boxing Day party. When she was 91 she cooked a full-course lunch for twelve people. For her ninetieth birthday an old friend presented her with flowers garnished with two bottles of champagne flanking one of rye. All items in the gift were very much appreciated!

Beatrice Day's husband and children all predeceased her. She was survived by five grandchildren and great-grandchildren. Towards the end of her life her sight and hearing failed, but she continued in her own home until the end.

Sarah Annie Duncan (nee Ingram)
(Mrs. William Chalmers Duncan)
1844-1937
by her granddaughter Shirley Garriock

My grandmother, Sarah Annie Ingram, was born in Donegal, Ireland, in 1844 and came to Victoria in 1872. She travelled by ship from Londonderry to New York, a thirteen-day voyage, then took the train, via Chicago, to San Francisco; after that she travelled by ship again to Victoria where she joined a married sister. Possibly she was husband hunting! If so, she was successful four years later when she married Cowichan pioneer William Chalmers Duncan.

Duncan's farm took in all the land which now makes up the City of Duncan, extending as far as the present highway. The original farmhouse stood on the little hill just east of the railway tracks where the funeral chapel now is. When the farm was subdivided and streets laid out, in 1886, Ingram Street was named for Sarah Annie.

Each summer, in her later years, Mrs. Duncan insisted on staying at her house at Maple Bay which was very rustic, with an outhouse and wood-burning stove. Sometimes she cut the wood and kindling for it herself. Hardy in every respect, she had a cold sponge bath every day. Water for household needs she obtained from a tap by the Maple Bay store, but she brought glass jars of drinking water from Duncan.

My cousin Doll and I, as girls in our early 'teens, spent summers with Gran, looking after her. One of our duties was to bring a bucket of salt water up to the house from the beach. She soaked her feet in this every night.

Sarah and William Duncan raised a family of four and there were three others who died young. The daughters were Isabella, who married Fred Holmes; Inez, who married W.B.B. McAdam who, for many years, was British Columbia's Agent-General in London, England; and Margaret, who married Reg Gooding. The son, Kenneth, became Duncan's first mayor.

Sarah Annie Duncan, nee Ingram (from Donegal), 1844-1937.

When Mr. Duncan died in 1919, Sarah Annie lived on for five or six years in their old home. The last years of her life were spent with her son Kenneth.

Mary Dwyer (nee Lomas)
(Mrs. William M. Dwyer)
1872-1951
by her daughter, Kathleen Derby

My mother, Mary Dwyer, was born on her mother's birthday, August 28, in the Anglican Mission House. It was situated across from the present Queen of Angels School on Tzouhalem Road. She was one of the first girls to be baptized at St. Peter's Church, Quamichan.

Mary Dwyer, nee Lomas, 1872-1951.

Her father, William Henry Lomas, came from Derbyshire, England, and her mother, of Scottish descent, from Australia.

Mary Lomas took part in all activities of the district, played the organ at St. Peter's for eleven years, acted in plays put on for local entertainment and played tennis. She also taught Indian classes, helping the children to learn reading and writing.

She must have been very popular. I found three letters from boyfriends asking her to marry them. There were none from her future husband; he had sense enough to ask her in person!

After her marriage to William M. Dwyer, February 7, 1903 at St. Peter's Church, they lived at Tyee, or Stratford's Crossing, a railway siding and road crossing north of Somenos, as her husband was running the aerial tramway that carried the copper from Mount Sicker Mine. They were there five years until the mine closed.

They then moved to Gibbins Road to a house which still stands at the end of Baker Road. Later, in 1912, half of his property was sold and a new house was built on part of the same property farther up Gibbins Road. The two Dwyer girls still at home had the house torn down after Mother died and built a modern home in which they still live.

As the mother of five girls, mother became interested in the Girl Guide movement, and as each daughter became old enough, she was enrolled in the Guides. Mrs. Dwyer was member of the Girl Guide Committee for many years. She received a "thanks badge" from the Company for her work. She was also a member of the Women's Institute and a strong supporter of St. John's Church where the family attended regularly.

Mary Dwyer's family consisted of daughters, Norah Nicolson, Eileen Dwyer, Kathleen Derby, Sheila Dwyer, Patricia James, and sons Philip and Michael.

Keturah Neale (Kate) Edgson (nee Hutchins)
(Mrs. Milton Edgson)
1850-1920
by her granddaughter Nell Johnston

My grandmother, Keturah (Kate) Edgson was born in England to Caroline and Mr. Hutchins. (I do not know his first name).

Mr. Hutchins died early. My great-grandmother came around the Horn as a chaperone on one of the bride ships. Her eleven year old daughter, Kate accompanied her.

Milton Edgson had come around Cape Horn in 1861, and met and married Kate Hutchins in 1866. They lived in Oregon first, where a son, John, was born to them there. Then they came to Maple Bay in 1867 or 1868 where her mother was living with her second husband, a Mr. Hales, on what is now Rice Road.

Milton and Kate Edgson took up three hundred acres or more of land a mile from Maple Bay and built a log house in which they lived until after 1904, when they built a larger house.

They operated a mixed farm of cows, horses, sheep, pigs and chickens. As there was no town of Duncan at that time, all their supplies came by ship to Maple Bay. They did have a few neighbours, among them the Peter Fletts and John Fletts who lived below them and across what now is known as Herd Road.

On New Year's Eve, my grandfather used to go out and fire his gun and then shout New Year's greetings to the Fletts who would return greetings in the same way.

The Edgson farm was called Rocklands, an appropriate name although

Keturah Edgson, nee Hutchins, 1850-1920.

eventually there were some good fields with wonderful black soil where my grandfather had an excellent vegetable garden.

Travelling on horse-back, my grandmother collected the stipend for the

Rector of St. Peter's Church for many years. The parish then extended down to Cowichan Bay and almost to Cobble Hill.

She acted as midwife in the district for some years, under the direction of a doctor in Victoria. One of her babies was the late Mrs. Wilfred Prevost (Maud Lomas), but there were many more and she never lost a baby. At least on one occasion she rode over the Malahat which was just a trail then, perhaps the journey was made to consult the doctor.

The Edgsons were good members of St. Peter's Church, and Kate belonged to the Sewing Guild which took orders for pyjamas, shirts, and other items to make money. Easter teas were also held and I think the women vied with each other to have the best table of food.

Here are some of the memories which my mother passed on to me: my grandfather had his baths in a tub outside with the water drawn fresh from the well.

The house was very isolated, and if the parents were away and only the children at home and they saw someone coming (there were many tramps in those days), they would hide. Most likely the tramps had seen them, and they would call out, "It is all right, little ones, could you give me something to eat?" What they gave out I do not know but the tramps went on their way without touching anything around the place.

As the family got older, there were many dances in the winter. As they had to go a long way, some used to ride horseback and the others go by wagon taking their ball gowns. They changed at their destination. They arrived home in the morning just in time to start their daily chores.

As there were no telephones in those days they had to be prepared at any time to feed a party. Sometimes quite a number of people would arrive unexpectedly. On one occasion (and it may have happened more than once), one of my uncles was sent up the mountain to shoot something for a meal. There was plenty of wild game and birds and one day my uncle came back with grouse, out of season. One of the guests was a Judge from Victoria who pronounced the "chicken" to be excellent!

Gaynor Elizabeth Elkington (nee Simpson)
(Mrs. William Howard Elkington)
1869-1928
Compiled by the Researchers

Mrs. Elkington was the daughter of Henry Simpson, a medical doctor in Lancashire, England. She was born in 1869. After completing her schooling, she emigrated to Canada with her sister, Ethel Leather and Ethel's husband, Frank Leather. They came out in 1883 by steamship, crossed Canada by Canadian Pacific Railway, and settled in Cowichan. They brought with them furniture, carriage and servants, purchasing land in Tzouhalem on which there was already a home and farm buildings.

William Howard Elkington was born in England in 1861. His father was a very successful silversmith in Birmingham who had developed the silver electroplating process; he headed the firm of Elkington and Company. The

Gaynor Elizabeth (Simpson) Elkington, 1869-1928.

Elkingtons were interested in Vancouver Island through Amy Lomas, a governess employed in their home whose brother, W.H. Lomas, was an Anglican catechist on Vancouver Island. The Elkingtons had sent him books, paintings and other aids to assist him in his instruction of the Indians. The letters received from Mr. Lomas describing hunting, fishing and Canadian life style, so appealed to William Elkington that he decided to spend a few years on Vancouver Island. The decision also got him away from having to study for the army, a future which really did not interest him. And so in 1883 he came to Cowichan, selecting that area because of its association with Mr. Lomas.

In Cowichan William Elkington bought four hundred acres of land from the Beaumont estate, the land extending from Quamichan Lake to near the summit of Mount Tzouhalem. He also bought a five-acre strip on the shores of Maple Bay as a recreation site. On the main holding there were already two barns, pig-stys, chicken houses and smoke house. At that time the cost of land was $2.50 per acre.

The Leathers lived at their Tzouhalem home for a number of years, Frank Leather's mother coming from England to join them. In 1889 William Elkington became engaged to Gaynor Simpson and they travelled to England where they were married on the thirtieth of January, 1890. Gaynor Elkington kept close contact with her family in England, returning there to visit every two years or so.

The couple had three children, sons, the eldest Lionel Frederick being born in 1890. He died in 1901. Eric W.H. was born in 1893. He commenced the study of medicine but with the First World War involving Britain and Canada, he left his studies to join the Royal Army Medical Corps. However, since doctors were desperately needed he returned to study at McGill University, obtaining his degree in medicine. He served with the Medical Corps in India and for several years practised in Guy's Hospital, London. He is well known in Victoria, having practised as an eye specialist there.

Gerald Erlan, the youngest son, graduated from the Royal Military College, Kingston, and following the first World War attended McGill University where he received his degree in electrical engineering. He was Chief Engineer and General Manager of the East Kootenay Power Company, Crow's Nest Pass Division for many years before returning to Quamichan Lake.

After William and Gaynor Elkington had been married for some ten years they lost their home through fire caused by an over-turned oil lamp. The fire destroyed the house and much of their furniture, including many wedding presents. A scorched piano is still retained by the family. The Leathers had suffered financial reverses and so were living in a cottage of the Elkingtons. After the fire, tents were set up around the cottage to accommodate the family while the present Elkington house was being built.

On the farm the Elkingtons employed Chinese labour. These included a cook and a gardener who lived near the house, and three labourers who lived in a shack adjacent to the barn. In general, with the Chinese help, life was comfortable and enjoyable. There were times of pressure, such as haying season, but there was plenty of time for recreation which was readily available and varied. Swimming, sailing and boating were popular in the summer, and the Elkington beach property was much used. There were boat trips to such places as Thetis Island and Butchart's Gardens. Picnics were enjoyed at Maple Bay, Mt. Tzouhalem and Cowichan Lake. Riding horses was both recreation and transportation. When the lakes froze there was skating and tobogganing. There were musical evenings, reading evenings and book teas at which books were exchanged. Each year Mrs. Elkington would hold one or two garden parties. Her husband had a regular evening when his friends came in for billiards.

Mrs. Elkington wrote poetry and was an active member of St. Peter's Church. Both she and Clive Phillipps-Wolley wrote coronation hymns which were sung at the church June 22, 1911 service to celebrate the coronation of King George V.

Tennis was played by both men and women, being the main participatory sport for women. Elaborate tennis teas were held in conjunction with the tennis to provide a social side. At the annual Cowichan Regatta there were events for women such as the ladies single and double sculls.

William Elkington and others appreciated the need of a school for the Quamichan area and so had a school built, bringing Mr. P.T. Skrimshire out from England as schoolmaster. This was a one-room school with Mr. Skrimshire the only teacher. Classes numbered from twenty-four to thirty boys, ranging in fairly widespread age categories. The school was very successful and a number of the students went on to become prominent citizens. Over the years many Cowichan families had sons attend the Quamichan Lake School.

Mr. Elkington was a trustee of the Cowichan County Club at the west end of Main Street, situated near the present Cowichan Lake and Boundary roads, which was formed in 1911. If introduced by members, ladies were permitted to visit the club, though of course restricted to those parts of the club and grounds designated for their reception!

Mrs. Elkington was very active in the King's Daughters organization which raised the funds to build the original hospital in Duncan. For a number of years she was on the Hospital Board representing the King's Daughters. She was a charter member of the Cowichan Women's Institute which was formed in September of 1912.

On November 28, 1928, Mrs. Elkington passed away after living nearly 40 years in Cowichan. William Elkington lived until May 31, 1946. Their Quamichan Lake land has been home to the Elkington family for over one hundred years, Mr. and Mrs. Gerald Erlan Elkington living there now.

Hattie Vian Evans (nee Sellier)
(Mrs. James Evans)
1859-1936
by Elden Kier

Hattie Vian Sellier, daughter of John and Margaret Sellier, emigrated west with them from Indiana in a covered wagon to California. They settled in the goldfields at a mining camp at Bath, Placer County, California. Hattie was then a young girl. There she met James Evans, whom she married on May 13, 1884.

In April of the next year, Hattie Evans came to Cowichan with her husband, James. Their first home was a log cabin situated on what is now First Street, near the site of the old St. Andrew's Presbyterian Church, now the Oddfellows Hall. Where St. John's Church (Anglican) now stands was the approximate corner of the James Evans and the Duncan farms. In that log cabin Hattie Evans raised a family of five sons and three daughters.

Where cars travel down Bell-McKinnon Road*, she and her family once creaked along behind oxen in homemade wagons, the wheels made of solid sections of trees. Where Jubilee Street now runs past St. John's Church to Hospital Hill she used to call the cows from the muskeg in the evenings.

90

Sometimes she found them stuck in the mud and had to get horses to pull them loose.

Hattie Vian (Evans) Kier, Hattie Evans (Sellier), 1859-1956, Dorothy (Kier) Fiander.

In 1907, Hattie and James built a new farmhouse not far from the old log cabin. Just prior to James's death in 1907 the couple had a house warming for their new home. The old farmhouse was still standing near the corner of Garden and James Streets until early 1986.

Part of the James Evans farm is now the site of the Cowichan Community Centre and sports fields. One street is named for her, Vian, and another major street, James, is named for her husband. James Street was the old gravel road that led from Duncan to the James Evans farmhouse.

Hattie Evans was active in the Ivy Rebekahs and was a past noble grand. She died in 1936 and is buried at Mountain View Cemetery.

*Canada Avenue was originally part of Bell-McKinnon Road

Margaret Nairn Evans (nee McLay)
(Mrs. David Evans)
1858-1934
by granddaughters Margaret Filion and Doreen Wilkinson

Margaret Nairn McLay was born on July 21, 1858, in Airdrie, Scotland, the eldest daughter of Robert and Elizabeth McLay.

When Mrs. McLay decided to join her husband in California in 1868, Margaret was ten years old and responsible for looking after her younger brother and two sisters during the rough sea voyage from Glasgow to New York when her mother was very seasick. While waiting for the train to California, Margaret remembered walking around the streets of New York,

Margaret Nairn Evans, Nee McLay, 1858-1934 and husband David Evans.

92

and her wonder at her first sight of the ripe tomatoes displayed on the fruit stands lining the sidewalks. She was so taken with those "pretty red apples" that she begged her mother to buy one. But what a disappointment when she first tasted it to find that it was sour and not sweet!

Their home in Somerville, California, on a hot, dry mountainside above the Sacramento Valley, was recalled by Margaret as a place of heat and dust, of rattlesnakes and tarantulas in the sand where they played. She was fifteen years of age when her family moved again, this time north to Vancouver Island by the sea. Once again she was a great help to her mother on the journey and on arrival at their destination which was a log cabin at Koksilah.

Margaret had attended school both in Scotland and California and she finished her schooling at Cowichan Bay. To get to school, she had to walk along the present Koksilah Road to Cowichan Station, along to the Fourways corner and down the Buena Vista Hill into Cowichan Bay. It seems a roundabout way but the only bridge across the Koksilah River was at Cowichan Station.

One of the tasks of the children of the family was to gather wild strawberries, elderberries and gooseberries to be made into jams and jellies. The McLay family always had pleasant associations with the neighbouring Indian families and Margaret became fluent in the Chinook dialect.

When she finished her schooling, Margaret was sent to Nanaimo to study the art of dressmaking with a Mrs. Stevenson. This was to stand her in good stead in later life. She did dressmaking and tailoring for her sisters and brothers. Later she made clothes of all kinds for her own children.

At the age of twenty, Margaret was married to David Evans, aged thirty-five, on April 17, 1878, by the Reverend David Holmes, in the McLay home at Koksilah. Her husband had arrived in Victoria from Wales in 1862 on his nineteenth birthday, and in 1864 had come to Cowichan, pre-empting 100 acres of land in what is now Duncan, where he built a log cabin. This farm he later turned over to his brother, James and he went to live in Tom Nichol's cabin at Tansor. It was in this cabin that David and Margaret started their married life. Their first child, Harry, was born there in 1879. This property was surrounded by wilderness, and prowling bears, cougars and wolves were a menace to the livestock. Margaret would be alone in the cabin at nightfall while her husband was down at the barn some two hundred yards away, and she would hear the cry of the wolves as they circled the barn. Even in daylight she would often see wolves from her cabin door.

Meanwhile, her husband had bought one hundred acres of land at Somenos from William Smithe, next to the William Drinkwater property. He decided on this particular piece of land because he wanted his wife to have a good neighbour like Mrs. Drinkwater close at hand.

While still living at the Tansor cabin, Margaret with the baby Harry in her arms, was returning home from a visit to Mrs. Drinkwater, and she was just going up the steep hill on Drinkwater Road when she heard the wolves starting to howl, as they were coming down from the mountain. She ran the rest of the way home, about a mile, and collapsed inside the cabin with exhaustion.

During the first years of her married life, whenever Margaret wanted to visit her parents at Koksilah, a distance of about five miles, she had to go on horseback, fording the Cowichan River on the way. One evening she was a bit late starting for home and she heard the wolves howling behind her. She was very frightened by the time she got safely indoors. After that she was always very careful to leave Koksilah well before dark.

Finally, in 1880, their new house, built of lumber, was ready and Margaret and David moved to their own farm, Willow Park at Somenos which was their home for the rest of their lives. Their second child, Elizabeth, was born there that same year, followed by the birth of Robert in 1882 and James in 1883.

As Margaret was very good at handling the cattle she took on the chore of milking the nine cows night and morning because her husband, besides clearing and improving his land, had undertaken the job of Superintendent of Roads for the Municipality of North Cowichan.

Water for the household was brought in a large barrel pulled by horse and stoneboat from a well some distance from the house.

Besides caring for her small children, cooking and sewing, Margaret made the butter and looked after the poultry and their vegetable garden. The butter and egg money went a long way in providing groceries. She made butter for sale and it would be packed in specially made boxes, taken to Maple Bay and shipped by steamer to Victoria. She not only churned her own butter, she also prepared for sale the butter churned by her bachelor neighbour, Joe Drinkwater. Until 1886 they had to spend the better part of a day once a week taking the team and wagon to Maple Bay to meet the boat, ship the butter and eggs and pick up their supplies from Victoria. Flour was bought by the barrel and sugar by the one hundred-pound sack.

Once the railroad came through in 1886, life was much easier as Somenos station was only a mile away. Then the butter and eggs could be shipped by express to Nanaimo. As soon as her eldest son, Harry, was fifteen, Margaret would send him to Nanaimo with the butter and he would spend the night with friends of his McLay grandparents from Scotland, then he would deliver the butter from a little wagon to regular customers.

Now Margaret could drive with the children down to her brother-in-law's place in Duncan, leave the horse there and walk to Koksilah over the railroad bridge. When the river was low in summer, they could ford the river with the team and wagon where the White Bridge now stands.

The family increased over the years by seven more children: John in 1885, Esther in 1886, Mary in 1887, William in 1889, George in 1892, Robina in 1897, and Margaret in 1899. There was no resident doctor in the district in the years before 1892, the nearest one being Dr. John Davie, in Victoria who would travel to Duncan by train on occasion. He was son of an earlier Davie from Victoria who treated some patients in Cowichan. There was a trained midwife, Mrs. Bell, who had come to Cowichan in 1862 and she helped to deliver all of Margaret Evans' children, except the three youngest.

As soon as the children were old enough, they had to help with the chores, such as fetching the cows home for milking. There were no fences yet and the cows wandered far and wide in the woods. The three eldest daughters were able to help their mother with cooking, housework, and the care of the younger children and the boys were able to take over the milking. But Margaret still supervised the baking, made the butter, knitted their stockings and did all the sewing, including suits for the boys and dresses and coats for the girls. Besides a large vegetable garden, she raised fruit of all kinds to be preserved for winter use and she was an expert at curing hams and shoulders of bacon.

She somehow found the time for handiwork. All the baby clothes were trimmed with tatted or crocheted edgings. She also had the skill, learned in California, of making flowers out of wool and wire, which were made into framed pictures. From this she became adept at making flowers out of locks of human hair. How she found the time and how she could see to do it at night by lamplight which was the only spare time available, is a mystery.

Margaret had another accomplishment, a good soprano singing voice. She would sing at her work. Her children remember her sitting at the old sewing machine by the window, working the treadle swiftly with her foot and singing away to her heart's content; a happy picture on their return from school. She was always in demand to sing solos at parties. Two of her most requested songs were, "I Dreamt that I Dwelt in Marble Halls," and "I'll Take You Home Again, Kathleen."

The older children first had to walk to school at Somenos Lake where the Forest Museum now stands. Later on a Somenos school was built at the southeast corner of Drinkwater and Somenos Roads, quite close to their farm and very handy for the children.

The first child to leave home was Elizabeth, who married Thomas Castley in 1903 at St. Mary's Church which adjoined the David Evans farm. Mrs. King, the wife of the Somenos schoolmaster, came to help Margaret and Elizabeth with the wedding preparations, making dresses for the two little sisters and helping to decorate the bride's table, pinning clusters of pale pink rosebuds on the tablecloth which was centered with the beautiful wedding cake made, of course, by Margaret.

Of the eleven children, all survived to old age except Mary who was married at the age of 22. She went to Calgary to live where she contracted pneumonia and died within a year. It was a terrible heartbreak for her mother. Mary and a younger sister had suffered rheumatic fever in the year previous to her marriage and this illness had left her with a weakened heart.

Margaret was noted for her hospitality and kindness to all. Passers-by were always sure of a warm welcome and a good meal. As the David Evans home had the largest living-room of any house in Somenos, the neighbours always gathered there for card parties and dances. People would come after the chores were done in the evening and stay until daylight in the summertime. There was always someone to play the violin and eventually they had a piano as well. The dancing would go on until the early hours of the morning.

There was always a great social gathering at Christmas at the schoolhouse. As it was not the custom in those days to have a decorated tree at home, one can imagine the excitement of the children arriving for the party in the evening to see the large Christmas tree laden with a present for each child. The gifts had been provided by the parents. The desks had been moved out of the way and ordinary chairs set in rows for the audience. After the program of recitations, songs and pageants put on by the pupils, the chairs were removed and the rest of the evening was spent in dancing waltzes, quadrilles, lancers and two-steps to the music of a violin, piano or organ. The mothers provided the refreshments and Margaret would be busy baking all day beforehand, her specialties being doughnuts and puff-pastry tarts. She was also famous for her shortbread.

Around 1906 when her parents became too ill to cope, Margaret and her husband took over the McLay farm at Koksilah and looked after the old couple. Margaret nursed her mother until she died in her old home, Willow Brook, in 1908 at the age of 77.

In 1910 when her husband was persuaded to go back to Wales for a visit after 48 years' absence, Margaret had the responsibility of running both farms. On David's return from Wales, the family decided to move back to Willow Park at Somenos, taking the grandfather with them. Old Mr. McLay was quite happy to be cared for by his daughter, Margaret until he died in 1915 at the age of 86.

Margaret was a small woman, barely five feet in height but of immense capabilities, adored by her children and remembered for her sweet nature by all who knew her.

In 1927, Margaret and David were both in failing health. Willow Park farm was taken over by their son, George, and later by their eldest son, Harry, whose descendants still own and occupy the remaining farm property on Somenos Road, between St. Mary's Churchyard and Mount Prevost School. Margaret and David moved to the home of their daughter, Robina, and her husband, Harold Truesdale who had bought two acres of land at the southwest corner of Willow Park. Thus they were able to live out their last years still on their own farmland.

By the time they celebrated their golden wedding, on April 17, 1928, (the first couple married in the Cowichan district to do so), Margaret was bed-ridden from a stroke. She was lovingly cared for by her daughters until her death in 1934 at the age of 75.

Mary Jane Evans (nee Davies)
(Mrs. John N. Evans)
1853-1937
Reminiscences by her daughter, Ruby O. Evans

Background comments and notes for this biography of Mary Jane Evans have been compiled from written accounts, including those of John N. Evans, supplied by members of the Evans family. The contribution from Ruby O. Evans is taken directly from a tape recorded interview with her in 1984, with minor editing. Miss Evans is looking forward to celebrating her ninety-fifth birthday in June 1986.

Mary Jane Evans, a tiny, slender young woman, had just turned twenty years old when she first arrived in Cowichan District in 1873 as the bride of

Back row, l. to r.: Margaret Lillian b.1883 married George Savage.
Ella Estelle b.1877, married Peter Auchinachie.
Mary Elizabeth (Mamie) b.1873, married John W. Flett.
Arthur Welsley b.1875, married Annie MacDonald and
after her death married Janet Grieve (cousin of 1st wife).

Front row, l. to r.: Ruby Olive b.1891.
John Newell Evans.
Newell Chester b.1886, married Gladys Gwilt.
Mary Jane Evans b.1853, nee Davies.
Elbert Warren b.1888.

John N. Evans. They had been married in Nortonville, California, on February 2nd of that year. John had purchased land with a cabin on it on an earlier visit to Somenos in 1871. This cabin is where they made their first home.

Mary Jane's father Joseph Davies, a miner from Wales, and her mother Mary (Evans) Davies had made their home in the rough goldfield settlements of California for the previous twelve years. For six of those twelve years, Mary Jane, eldest of the fourteen Davies children, whose mother was then an invalid, had taken care of the entire household.

So this wisp of a girl was no stranger to the trials and hardships of frontier life, a life which had begun for her in 1861 when she crossed two thousand miles of America by ox team and covered wagon. She was then eight years old.

In later years Mary Jane recounted stories to her children about that journey, the terrors, the adventures, and the happy times too, that she, her family and their relatives experienced as they travelled across the Plains and over mountains by wagon train. Some of the more traumatic episodes had a lasting effect on her young mind, especially that of her fear of Indians which she did not overcome for many years.

Highlights of these stories recalled by her youngest daughter Ruby, and by Ruby's own memories of her mother, give us a vivid picture of the endurance and courage shown by the women and children of those times.

....."my mother came to this District (Cowichan) in 1873 but she had crossed the Plains in a covered wagon with her parents when she was eight years old. They were an independent train of 48 ox drawn wagons, all in charge of a wagon master, starting from St. Joseph's, Missouri, in July 1861, bound for California."

The train had been organized by Mary Jane's maternal grandfather Thomas R. Evans (not related to John Evans). Thomas R. Evans drowned while inspecting a river bridge in preparation for the journey from Pennsylvania. The widowed grandmother (Jane Evans) and other members of the Evans and Davies families set out together as planned.

The wagon train was made up of different families who joined together as protection against hostile Indian tribes on the anticipated eleven-week trek, travelling twenty miles a day from station to station. At night the wagons were drawn into a circle, chained together with everyone inside except for four men on guard with firearms.

....."the Indians followed them for three weeks and came into their camp every night. The old chief would lay his blanket down then he'd take his pipe around to everyone, kids and all, then they would go and put something in his blanket - a little sugar, a little tea, anything like that. When they'd all done it he tied his blanket up, put it over his shoulder and walked out.

....they didn't have any trouble but they heard later that they (the Indians) had killed people on the wagon trains before and after theirs - one time because a white man had offended Indian customs...she told me about coming to a station and while looking for firewood they found (gruesome) remains from a recent Indian raid. But their train was never touched....

....my grandmother (Jane Evans) was a great believer in reading the stars and they had an astrologer with them who used to read the stars every night and tell them when to leave. My grandmother believed 'til she died that that is why they were saved..."

Despite the hardships of the Plains and later dangers of treacherous mountain trails, some of the travellers remembered the journey as a fairly happy time in their lives. They tell of singsongs around the campfire at night 'Juanita', 'Sweet Land of Liberty', 'Silver Threads Among the Gold', 'Oh Susanna', 'Alice Ben Bolt' and 'God Save the Queen' were remembered favourites.

"....they came from St. Jo's, Missouri to Salt Lake (City), Utah, and they all had to become Mormons in Salt Lake. So my mother was baptised as a Mormon, and all the others too except an uncle who hid.

....you see, Brigham Young (founder of Salt Lake Mormon settlement) wanted the women for wives! My mother said "this story isn't exaggerated", and she knew because she delivered newspapers that winter with the daughter of the man who published the first newspaper in Salt Lake City. His surname was Mortimer.

....at one of Brigham Young's own houses, either the Lion House or the Eagle House, there were eighty wives! The other house had 60 - and there were more out in the surrounding countryside. Oh, he was a brave man!

....the First Wife lived in either the Lion House or the Eagle House, I'm not sure which, but mother said she was all dolled-up in silks and satins, and a gold watch and chain and what-have-you. Mum said there were all kinds of kids creeping around on the floor, and at other houses and everywhere. All kinds of them.

....they wintered outside Salt Lake that winter of 1861-62 and left in the middle of the night in April 1862.

....when the family left in April they were running away. They had to leave secretly, travelling day and night for three days and two nights to get over the Nevada border."

They had been warned that Brigham Young's 'Avenging Angels' were on their trail. Safely in Nevada, three handsome, bearded men mounted on beautiful horses were pointed out to them as being the 'Angels'.

....an uncle of my mother who had crossed the mountains (Sierra Nevada) either seven or 17 times, came from California to Salt Lake to meet them and guide them through the mountains to California.

....they came to places of high cliffs where the women and children stayed in the wagons, the oxen taken out (of the shafts) and the wagons were dropped over the cliffs with ropes."

During weeks of hazardous travelling in rough terrain, fording many rivers (the River Platte was forded five times in one day), the women cooked on the campfires, no doubt there was game to be shot by the men. Mary Jane's mother put milk from the cow which was tied behind the wagon into a can which she hung under the wagon. The bouncing of the wagon churned it and turned it into butter.

...."when she first came to the District in 1873 Mother was scared of the Indians here but she didn't need to be. However, she was the farthest away white woman out in the woods, her nearest neighbour a mile and a half away and the four nearest neighbours were bachelors. No womenfolk.

....she had come out of a big family, grown up in mining towns and the isolation here made her ill. She was sick until my Dad took her back to California after a few months.

....my eldest sister Mary (Mamie) Elizabeth and my eldest brother Arthur Welsey were born in California."

In 1877 when Mary Jane's health was restored the John Evans family returned to Cowichan. At first they lived in a log cabin on John's brother's farm where Ella Estelle, the third child, was born that year. Soon after, the family moved back to the one-room cabin on their own farm in what is now the Tansor area.

...."when my mother came back in 1877 she was kept so busy. She looked after a niece, two orphaned boys - so Mother really raised eleven of us - and in the early years looked after Dad's three brothers too. (David, Harry and James)

....she did all the cooking at an open fireplace and baked her bread by the fire. She had what they called a 'Reflector'. It was tin, polished to keep it bright. The bread was set beneath it and you kept turning it around and the heat came down on the bread. She made bread that way from 1873 to 1882, nine years."

In time, homegrown wheat was sent to Crate's Mill to be ground into flour. The mill was on a creek coming out of Quamichan Lake just below the bridge near W.P. Jaynes home. After the flour had been kept in boxes a while, it got all caked and had to be broken with a hammer!

....."she made the men's work pants and all their shirts, by hand! How she did it God only knows.

....the log cabin was one room, 12 by 16 feet, with a ladder to go upstairs to the low attic, then a shed for a kitchen. It was a lean-to made out of whip-sawn lumber. When she got a stove it stayed out in the shed.

....The cabin (it fell in the Big Snow in 1916) was on a little hill. It just had one window in it and two doors, one to the front and one to the back, and a small window upstairs.

....I remember Mother got up at six o'clock in the morning, milked the cows, tended to the family and then 'did up' the house. Breakfast was porridge, sometimes bacon, and eggs galore in the spring when the hens were laying.

....the hens didn't lay in the winter. Extra eggs in the spring were 'put down' in a salt and lye mixture, the eggs were put in it and a lid on top. A dish of water beside it to wash the salt off the eggs when they were taken out. They couldn't be boiled but you could fry them or poach them and they tasted fine.

....to pickle beef you made a brine of salt with some saltpetre in it, boiled the brine then laid the meat in the barrels and poured the brine over it. They were whiskey barrels my Dad got somewhere, he didn't drink it.

....the toilet was outside and we were bathed (two and three in the same water) in a wash tub. Mum heated the water in a washboiler on the stove (earlier, on the fireplace). The water came from the creek just outside the house, the house that is there now.

....the old one-storey part of the big house was put up in 1882 - there was a beautiful fireplace. The bricks were made at the brickyard at the corner of Cowichan Lake and Menzies Roads. (The two-storey part was put up in 1908)

....the old part had a lean-to kitchen and one bedroom, two bedrooms off the dining room and the boys' room was over the storeroom where we had a heater. We had our baths in there.

....she did up a 100 pounds of butter a week and printed it all out by hand.

....my Mother made the first citron (type of melon) jam that was made in the district.

....she nursed the sick, laid out the dead, helped my uncle make the coffins - she helped to make her own child's coffin - and brought oodles of babies into the world without the help of a doctor.

....we kids all had our jobs to do. I had to get the firewood in, chop kindling, wipe the dishes and peel potatoes after I got in from school. I walked to the Brownsey house to school.

....I was the youngest of my Mother's eight children. Mary Elizabeth

(1873), Arthur Welsley (1875), Ella Estelle (1877), William Roderick (1879), Margaret Lillian (1883), Newell Chester (1886), Elbert Warren (1886), Ruby Olive (1891). (William and Elbert died young)

....Mum was just under five feet tall and weighed no more than ninety-eight pounds most of her life.

....how she done it, I don't know."

Mary Jane's story is shared in similar ways by hundreds of women who chose long and dangerous journeys with their menfolk to reach that 'Eldorado' - the goldfields of California and those in other parts of the world. Some of them also came to Cowichan and their descendents, with those of the Evans families, are an integral part of the Cowichan Valley today.

Mary Jane Evans lived out her life in her own home on the same land that, more than 60 years before, she had found too lonesome and too remote. Today it is a few minutes by car from the small city of Duncan.

Mary Jane died in 1937 and is buried at Mountain View Cemetery, Somenos. John Newell Evans was also buried there in 1944.

Annie Forrest (nee Rutledge)
(Mrs. E.H. Forrest)
1872-1951
by her daughter-in-law Joyce E. Forrest

Annie Rutledge, my husband's grandmother, was two or three years old when the family came to Cowichan about the year 1875. She was born near New Mexico.

The family came to this district because Annie's father was a doctor and wished to help the Indians. They travelled by wagon train across the United States and settled on Hillbank Road on their arrival.

In 1888 Annie Rutledge married E.H. Forrest, by whom she had four children. After his death, she married a second time, a Mr. Dougan.

The Forrest children were, Edward, Robert, Jessie and Marg. Edward had a son who was mayor of Lake Cowichan while Robert ran the farm at Hillbank. I married Robert's son.

Eleanor Brooke Fry (nee Edgson)
(Mrs. Henry Fry)
1875-1947
by her niece Nell Johnston

My Aunt Eleanor was born 24 November, 1875. She was the daughter of Milton and Kate Edgson of Maple Bay. In 1896 she married Henry Fry who later was killed by his horse running away and his vehicle overturning in consequence.

Eleanor Fry took an active part in work for the King's Daughters' Hospital, taking work parties up to the hospital to do mending and making new

Eleanor Brooke Fry, nee Edgson, 1875-1947.

sheets, etc. She was secretary of the Scattered Circle of the King's Daughters for about twenty years, until they disbanded.

Elizabeth Hall (nee Beardmore)
(Mrs. Lewis Hall)
Born 1826
compiled by the Researchers

In 1847 Elizabeth Beardmore married Lewis Hall in Wolverhampton, England. Two years later the couple sailed for Australia where they lived until 1856, when they returned to England. In 1862 they emigrated for a second time, on this occasion choosing Canada. After a three-month voyage by sailing ship across the Atlantic, they settled in Gloucester, Ontario.

It was in 1874 that the Halls moved to Vancouver Island. This trip was made via New York, crossing the isthmus of Panama by rail, then proceeding by ship once more to San Francisco. At San Francisco they took another vessel which carried them as far as Victoria. The next stage in their journey was made by a small coast boat to Chemainus, and finally from Chemainus they proceeded by ox team to what was once known as Hall crossing, about five miles south of Chemainus.

Mrs. Hall had twelve children, six boys and six girls. Two sons became medical doctors, Herbert practising in Calgary, George A.B. in Nanaimo. A third son, Lewis, became a dentist, practising in Victoria. One of the daughters, Harriett Elizabeth, married a Somenos pioneer, James Kier.

The Halls had to go to Chemainus for mail which came on a weekly steamer from Victoria. They could also pick up a paper, as the two Victoria newspapers put out a weekly condensed version of the news for up-island readers.

Supplies came on that steamer and were then brought out to the Hall farm by leisurely ox team or on the men's backs.

One of the descendants recalled some housekeeping details of the early years: "Light in the house was some coal oil lamps but mostly tallow dips made by melting the tallow, then filling the moulds with a wick hung in place. Cooking was done by the open fireplace with bread baked in camp ovens, butter made in the old plunger churn worked by hand and later revolving churns and butter presses, all operated by hand power."

Susan Herd (nee Salmond)
(Mrs. William Herd)
1863-1931
by her daughter Jeannette Marsh

My mother, Susan Salmond, emigrated from Perthshire, Scotland in 1887. She was engaged to William Herd who had left home three years before with his brother, Alex, and sister, Elizabeth. In 1884 these three had arrived in Victoria on their way to New Zealand. While their ship made a necessary stopover in Victoria the Herds took a look around, venturing as far as the Cowichan Valley. They liked what they saw and made up their minds not to proceed to New Zealand but to make their home in this new country.

William and Alex Herd settled first in Westholme about where the Quist farm is today and their neighbours were the Lloyds. Later they pre-empted three hundred and sixty acres of land on what is now Herd Road and built a log cabin. Soon after her arrival, Susan married William Herd and moved into the log house for their first home together. However, in 1890 or 1891, a more suitable house was built and in due course, their seven daughters were born in it.

My earliest recollection is of my mother's bedroom where the older children had gathered to see the new baby. I was two years old at the time, and in good spirits, my father tossed me up in the air. That was 1903 and the seventh girl had just joined our family.

Susan Herd, c.1886, Mrs. William Herd nee Salmond.

After his wife died in Scotland, my mother's father, Joseph Salmond, had emigrated bringing out my aunts Jeanne, Jessie and Maggie Salmond. Jeanne married Alex Herd and Jessie married W. Thompson, a blacksmith at Cowichan Station.

My sisters and I all went to Maple Bay School which was situated at the corner of Herd and Lakes Road. I think the old well from which we got water for the school is still in evidence at the corner there. Dad, who was a carpenter and bricklayer, built the Maple Bay School for twenty-five dollars, believe it or not! He and his brother, Alex, in partnership, cleared land and built a barn and eventually had twenty-four milking cows. My sisters and I were not boys but we worked like them, milking cows, cocking hay and planting spuds by the acre.

My mother was a wonderful cook and enjoyed feeding her family well. She was well known for her tasty pies. Over the years, so many of her friends have said "What a perfect hostess your mother was"! I always enjoyed hearing that.

We were ahead of the times in some ways. For instance, I think we were the first girls in the district to have "bobbed hair!" That would be about 1919.

Susan and William's Herd's children were, Winnifred Van Norman, Marion Pickard, Ivy Johnston, Jessibelle Johnston, Effie Thorpe, Jeannette Marsh and Hazel Hodding. Winnifred, Marion and myself settled in the Cowichan area. The others have all lived here from time to time.

Susan Abercrombie Holmes (nee Nagle)
(Mrs. David Holmes)
1840-1921
by her grandson Donald Roberts

"Rain! Rain! Rain!", lamented Susan Holmes in her diary. Of the several connecting links throughout her diary of life in Cowichan, one was certainly the part played by the rain. It kept her from hanging her clothes out or from working in the vegetable garden. The rain kept away visitors expected for dinner, for a card game, or for a musical evening. Above all it meant she had to stay home from church because the roads became muddy; an open buggy was an invitation to a wet-through costume and a bad cold.

Church was a second consistent element in her diary. Susan was a parson's wife but even after David became more of a farmer than a practicing clergyman, she and the children went off to Somenos, Quamichan or Duncan to attend services. If she was ill or the weather kept her home, she would hold a service for herself and for those remaining at home with her.

Susan was born on board ship in 1840 as her father, Captain Jeremiah Nagle and his wife, Catherine, sailed from Liverpool to Australia. The family settled in New Zealand but not for long; by 1850 her roving Irishman father was taking them to California. Here Jeremiah bought and sold land, was in the shipping business, and was one of the "Vigilantes" in wild San Francisco. In 1858 the family moved to Victoria. By now there were five girls and three boys, a close-knit family, very loyal to their father and mother. Jeremiah was a good father but not a very good provider. Perhaps this was a blessing because in their individual ways the children found ways of helping out.

Susan began school teaching at Yale in 1869. It was shortly before this that she began to keep a diary on a fairly regular basis. Now, one can follow

Back: Susan Holmes, Bella Holmes, Fred Holmes with Phyllis.
Front: Isabel Roberts, Rev. David Holmes, Beatrice Holmes.

her on her trip by steamer to New Westminster and then up the Fraser to Yale. She felt the break with her family rather acutely but her thoughts were also on her engagement to Algy Hall who was in the Colonial Service in British Honduras. There was little possibility of Algy being able to support a wife, it seemed, so the engagement was broken off. The Reverend David Holmes, the Anglican clergyman at Yale, became a suitor. At first Susan felt that she could never marry him but as she got to know him marriage seemed inevitable. They were married on June 14, 1871, at Victoria.

By 1873, David, Susan and their little boy, Harry, were at the Quamichan parsonage. For the next fifty years Susan was a part of the life of Cowichan. She raised six children, took part in community affairs, found ways of making a little money to help out, taught her children to sing and play the piano, watched over their health, fed stray bachelors and nearly every day wrote in her diary. In her later life she wrote many children's stories.

In her early years at the Quamichan parsonage Susan was often ill. Neighbours came to sit with her if David was away or they looked after Harry so that she could go to church. She tried to find a woman to work for her but she had little success in keeping anyone, probably because there was so much to do, with little pay. On the twentieth of August, 1897, she wrote: "Christine informed me this morning that she did not want to work anymore and wished to be paid." Susan asked her to stay until she could get someone else or at least to stay until the end of the month. "She was not satisfied to do this, so she took herself off. It is most annoying just now when I want someone. However, I will try to do the best I can."

106

Susan had to do most things on her own with David's help. She taught Sunday School, visited the sick, taking various home remedies along and tried to improve the parsonage by white-washing and papering. She kept up her diary and wrote endless letters to her parents and to her brothers and sisters.

Life had many pleasures. They had visitors, the names so familiar to those who remember early Cowichan, the Frys, the Alexanders, the Lomases, the Marriners, the Edgsons and the Skinners. Members of Susan's family came to visit from Victoria and San Francisco. David would drive to Maple Bay to pick them up. Susan's mother made the trip. Susan wrote,

"Fine morning. Busy all the morning and anxious to know whether or not Mama had come. David started for Maple Bay as the clock struck twelve, and got back, to our delight, Mama beside him at half past three-....Harry was glad to see Granma particularly when she gave him the story book of the Three Kittens and Mr. Fox."

The 24th of May was a time for pleasure. Unfortunately, as the day approached in May of 1876, Susan realized that the rain would spoil the outdoor picnic. She was busy making cakes. On the twenty-fourth she wrote:

"At length it was decided that it should be held in our barn and so Mr. Ashdown Green sent notes to the expected guests telling them of the change. About one o'clock all were assembled and partook of the repast, after which the small harmonium was brought from school and Mr. Green having his violin, we made music enough for the rest of them to join in the 'light fantastic,' about 5:00 p.m. they all adjourned to the parsonage and partook of cake and tea and then returned to their respective homes apparently well pleased with the day's amusement."

Christmas was always a very special occasion. On Christmas Eve in 1890, Susan made mince pies, stuffed the turkey which she had plucked the day before, made a Christmas cake and filled six stockings. By now she had three sons and three daughters. Harry was now eighteen and Phil, the youngest, was six. Christmas Day, 1890, began by being gloomy but turned out a lovely day, quite warm. David could not hold services at Chemainus because of bad roads so they held a service at home. Harry went to Quamichan service. They had a very good dinner. Afterwards David took a parcel of things to some neighbouring children. Susan recorded this: "Our young people played with some of their new games while Harry and I played some duets on the piano. I trust that everyone in the district has spent as pleasant a day."

As far as Susan was concerned, Sunday was given over to church-going as the principal element of the day. Cards, dancing, singing of frivolous songs and sports were to be avoided. When David moved from Quamichan to a large acreage to the north of Duncan and built the house called Holmesdale, there were three churches that they attended, often by walking; these were Somenos, Quamichan and St. John's at Duncan's Station as they then called it. Then when David was in charge at Chemainus and Westholme, there were trips to those churches by buggy or train. Susan put down the churches attended in her diary. On Sunday, February 1, 1891, she wrote with some satisfaction, "Fine frosty day, Harry and Fred went to

Quamichan in the morning and all the rest of us went to Somenos in the afternoon. I drove back with Mr. Leakey. The boys and Beatrice went in the evening to the service at the Station so the Holmes family have been well represented at church today."

When the boys grew up it was necessary, very necessary, that they find work. Susan travelled to Victoria with Harry to see her old friend from Yale days, Peter O'Reilly, retired Chief of Surveys of British Columbia (note: above information applies to 1890s) about "getting a billet for Harry on a survey." She was not one to waste time so she went to the dentist in Victoria the next day and had eight teeth out. She was given gas and did not feel the first four teeth but she did the others. "Had lunch at the Todds and went from there to the train."

Harry was employed and in following years the other two boys went out on these survey parties. Susan prepared their clothes and sent them off, admonishing them to write as soon as possible. They came back brown and strong-looking and she always was very pleased to welcome them home.

With a large family in a cold house and the children often tramping through rain and slush, there seemed always to be someone with a bad cold in winter and spring. Susan raised her six through some bad illnesses and only lost Phil, when he was in his twenties to pneumonia. A mustard plaster was her basic remedy. She had to nurse neighbours and once had to help at a serious and fatal operation on a neighbour. A little girl, Gladys Speck, left motherless by this operation, had to be taken home and looked after for years.

As the girls grew older, Susan accompanied them to dances. But first she had to make their dresses. On the 30th of November, 1898, she wrote, "Stitching away at Isabel's garment. I shall be glad when my young ladies can make their own dresses. I have had a good many years of this kind of work." The next night she went with them to the dance. "Isabel's dress was quite a success. She looked very nice and received plenty of attention; got home about two o'clock." On the 29th of December of that year there was a dance that they persuaded her to go to although she had said she would not. She and Beatrice drove and the others walked. "It was the best affair of the season and a great many were present. The girls wore their white silks and looked very nice, indeed there was quite a gathering of pretty girls, the Jaynes girls, Carrie Green, Edie Maitland, Annie Carmichael and others. I am afraid to say at what hour we got home. It must have been somewhere about four o'clock!"

There was little activity at the Holmes after a night like this one, but the Alexanders gave a party the next night. The boys went. "The girls were asked but I would not let them go. I think they might all have been satisfied with having been out all the night before."

In the summer they sometimes went camping at Maple Bay or Cowichan Bay. In August of 1903 Susan was busy preparing for a trip to Cowichan Bay. Harry took the girls a day ahead so that they could put up the tents and prepare for the holiday. Susan was taken down the next evening and was glad of a cup of tea when she got there. In the next two weeks the party was visited by David, Harry and Fred on several occasions, and some of the young bachelors arrived. On Sunday, August 16, Susan wrote that, "Mr.

Stanhope arrived this morning before any of us were up. He made the fire and helped to get breakfast ready."

Susan describes an interesting little episode a day later!

"Mr. Stanhope and Mr. Pooley came this evening and remained all night. While we were sitting singing around the bonfire a sloop containing three young men anchored a short distance from the shore. They had a violin on board and accompanied our singing. Then they sang something which our young men encored, and so they continued for some time until finding that the tide was going out, and they were in danger of running aground, they sang 'Goodbye Ladies' and sailed for the wharf."

As the family grew older the engagements and marriages of her boys and girls were discussed in the diaries. Harry was the first to marry. When Susan reviewed the year that was ending on New Year's Eve, 1899 she wrote that Harry was engaged to Annie Carmichael. They were married on December 18, 1900. Fred's girl was Bella Duncan. They were married in 1906. It was the girls who gained the most attention in the diaries as they debated the proposals of the young men who came to dinner. It was Isabel who married first. Less than three weeks before her wedding, Isabel still was uncertain which of her two men she would marry. At the end of April, 1904 she decided to marry Percy Roberts who wanted her to accompany him to the Yukon where he was a captain of a river boat. The wedding took place in May so that Percy could get away to his work and Isabel could go with him. Susan was busy sewing. Indeed, all three girls were busy. "Minnie Skinner brought the girls some fashion books to look at this evening."

On the 12th of May, 1904, Susan wrote, "The wedding dress arrived. It is very nicely made and I hope will fit her. Beatrice and Zephie are working now at theirs and I am doing what I can to help. I have altered my grey silk and have had some trouble to make the sleeves wide enough."

Now that Harry, Fred and Isabel were married, and there was perhaps a bit more money to pay the bills, Susan gave more time to her writing and to her favorite group, The King's Daughters. In June of 1904 a convention of the King's Daughters was held in Duncan. Susan wrote:

"I have been busy writing my Address of Welcome to the delegates. I hope I may be able to deliver it in a creditable manner. I declined the office but Mrs. Maitland seemed to have set her mind on my giving the address so I have undertaken it and now I am rather glad, as it gives me an opportunity of speaking on several subjects which otherwise I should not have had." She gave her address and felt it was very well received and she was given compliments, "more, I fear, than it deserved."

In October of 1910 the cornerstone of The King's Daughters Hospital was laid. Susan took part in the ceremonies and was elected to the Board of Directors. A host of activities were put on to raise money, but Susan vetoed the sale of cigarettes at a sort of tea dance. She wrote that: "people thought she was 'old-fashioned'."

Susan's children did begin to feel she was old-fashioned in her ideas. On Sunday, February 3, 1907, she found that even the girls had disobeyed her. There had been some very cold days and the young people were anxious to get in as much skating as possible even if it meant doing this on Sunday.

She wrote:

"They all went down to the Somenos Lake and I am sorry to say, Beatrice and Phil as well as Harry, Annie and Fred went skating. They all seem to think my ideas are very old-fashioned, for I do not approve of this amusement on the Sabbath day. Then in the evening Beatrice and Zephie were too tired to go to church tho' Harry and Phil did. This is the first time I have known one of my girls to do what is so contrary to my wishes and I am very sorry for it."

With pretty girls in the house there were often young bachelors to supper. A Mr. Appleyard was one of these and on one of his visits he provided a good anecdote. On Sunday, January 15, 1910, he came for lunch and spent the rest of the day and the night.

"In his laudable wish to make us warm and comfortable, he made such a big fire in the drawingroom that in a few minutes the chimney was in a blaze. Then, to see that it was not doing any damage to the roof, he climbed to the top, but having on gum boots, could not get a proper hold and the next thing, down he came! Landing, fortunately, on his feet, none the worse for his toboggan ride!" Susan was rather unnerved so Mr. Appleyard offered to stay the night and she was glad.

Susan had a long life. She was still active in her seventies. One day she saw a picture in the Colonist of her old home in Victoria at James Bay. This led her to write what could be her epilogue:

'The pictures take me back to the days of yore when I was a young girl just beginning life and entering on an untried world; and now as I draw towards my close after seventy years of ups and downs I can see many mistakes and many failures and at the same time very many blessings. I trust my life has not all been lived in vain. I have brought up six children and put them on the right road which I trust with God's blessing they may continue in. One dear one has reached home before me, saved probably from many troubles, which even those who live the easiest lives have to bear, in one shape or another.'

Florence Kier (nee Monk)
(Mrs. George Kier)
1868-1960)
by her grandson Elden Kier

Born in Warrington, Lancashire, England, to Alfred and Annie Monk, Florence Monk came to Cowichan with her mother in 1882.

Her husband, George Kier, was the first provincial policeman in the district. It is recalled that he was late for their wedding on February 17, 1886, at St. Ann's church, Tzouhalem, since he was involved in a case, the double Dring and Miller murder case at Crofton. (One of the murdered men had been mistaken by an Indian, Quomlet, for the hangman who had executed his relative).

It was in Cowichan that she raised a large family of four boys and five

Mrs. George Albert Kier, nee Florence Sara Monk, 1868-1960.

girls. One son, Sidney, still lives at Youbou. She also has grandchildren and great-grandchildren living in the Cowichan Valley.

She and her husband were accomplished musicians, on piano and violin respectively.

Florence was noted for her excellent honey and won many awards for it in exhibitions. In 1931 she won first, second, third and fourth prize for her honey at the Vancouver Exhibition. During the 1930s her honey was placed on the commercial market under the title "Cowichan Honey."

After her husband's death at Somenos in 1934, Mrs. Kier left the district to live with her daughter, Anna Kier Patrick of West Vancouver.

Mrs. Kier died on January 6, 1960, at St. Paul's Hospital, Vancouver and is buried at Mountain View Cemetery, Somenos. It is of interest to note that that cemetery is land that her father-in-law, Archibald Kier, donated for a burial ground.

Lucy Kingston
1875-1952
by her niece Mary MacRae Stone

Lucy Kingston was born in Toronto, Ontario and at the age of three, came to San Francisco by rail and from thence by steamer to Maple Bay where her father met and took them to their new home on Lakes Road (presently known as Timbercrest Subdivision). Lucy was one of a small class that attended "high school" which was on the hill behind the present Government Buildings on Station Street in Duncan.

She was a good gardener and her interest was in collecting rare plants and seeds. She also was an excellent needlewomen, having learned the very difficult art of Irish Crochet from her friend Mrs. Stoker. Many a young girl was taught to sew, or knit or crochet by "Miss Lucy."

Nora Kingston (nee Kellor)
(Mrs. William Kingston)
1851-1931
by her granddaughter S. Mary Stone

Nora Kingston was born in County Kerry in 1851 to Colonel John and

William & Norah Kingston's home and barn in 1880, near Lakes Road.

Back row: Lucy, William Kingston, Fanny.
Middle: Jonathan.
Front row: Nora Kingston, Charlie.

Mary Kellor. When her parents were in Toronto, Upper Canada, her father was Colonel-in-Chief of a regiment in which William Kingston was serving. They met there and were married in Toronto in 1871. Very shortly afterwards he lost his hearing entirely due to a mastoid infection and was discharged, ending his career in the army.

He decided to visit his cousin in Oak Harbour, Washington, who asked him to take up land with him there. Nora, with their infant daughter, Lucy, returned to relatives in Cork to await word on this venture. But when William discovered Oak Harbour was in the United States he decided he could never live anywhere but under his Queen (Victoria). So in 1874 he

Nip and William Kingston.

set out for Victoria, British Columbia. There he heard about the recent discovery of gold in the Cariboo and he joined the rush. He soon returned, disappointed, to the Island, stopping at the Cowichan Valley. He saw the Somenos Creek with the beautiful mossy knoll and the grand old oak trees and beyond them the thick fir forest. (This is now Timbercrest Subdivision). This property reminded him so greatly of his parents estate in Cork that he decided that this was where he wished to start life anew and that he would bring Nora and Lucy out from Ireland to join him.

They arrived in 1875 travelling by boat to Boston, across to San Francisco by railway, on to Victoria by ship and finally to Maple Bay by a smaller boat. William met them there and took them to their new home, Lucyville, by wagon. Here Jonathan, Fanny, Madeline and Frank were born.

The first months in her pioneer home with a small baby and a stone-deaf husband, were very lonely for Nora and very terrifying because the Indians were not friendly. But as months went by this fear disappeared and in times of need the natives were very good neighbours. As time went on there were more settlers.

William had a little spaniel dog named Nip who was his constant companion, always at his side. When he was far off in the clearing and Nora needed him she whistled very loudly for the dog and Nip immediately began pulling and tugging at William's pant leg. Off in a hurry Nip and William went to Nora. This was a frequent experience.

When William first decided to settle here, he had their household effects shipped to Victoria and on to Maple Bay wharf. Word reached him that the boat was to arrive sometime around a certain date. So William hitched up the team and the wagon and made numerous trips, sometimes spending the night near the wharf waiting for his boxes. They came one night when he was not there and he was told by an Indian that the boxes had been unloaded and hauled away. With anger and great disappointment he returned with an empty wagon to Nora and little Lucy. One cannot imagine how Nora felt. Many years later Lucy was in an antique store in Victoria and purchased an old sewing box in-laid with mother of pearl. Yes, it was Nora's!

Lucy attended the one-room school where Arcadia School is now, and Jonathan and Fanny attended the elementary school on the corner of Indian and Maple Bay Roads.

In 1885 a diphtheria epidemic swept the community. On Christmas Eve Jonathan, Fanny and their two little friends, the Duncan children, were buried. Can you imagine the parents great sorrow and despair? They had no doctors, no medication and no idea when or where this dreaded disease would stop. Four little coffins were hastily built and neighbours dug these children's graves by hand. It all happened so suddenly. Five days earlier they were happy school children planning a school Christmas party and play. St. Peter's Church was only eleven years old and those four little graves were among the first in that cemetery.

Nora was a supportive member of St. Peter's Church and with other women of this parish they had their Women's Association meetings, and church suppers, et cetera. The Cowichan Fall Fair was an event they looked forward to each year. There was news of new babies, arrival of new settlers and exchanges of their experiences here in their new homeland. The Salvation Army Brass Band from Victoria played all the favourite old tunes with loud and lively rhythm and was certainly one of the highlights of the Fall Fair.

With only one post office and a very small store which sold only the necessary items for the home and fair, such items as gifts were not available. But there was one cheery little Chinese pedlar who arrived at the Kingston home before Christmas. He wore the traditional Chinese clothing of the time, a black tunic, wide baggy pants and a round black skull cap. He was short and stockily built and carried a wooden yoke on his shoulders. Suspended by this were two rice bags containing ginger, teas, silks, toys, china and many other interesting things. These he spread on the floor for all to see and buy. Many a time he was invited to stay for a meal and, if it was cold and late, to spend the night. I have among my most treasured gifts four cups and saucers my grandmother, Nora, purchased from this little man. I am sure the pleasure and excitement of his visits were shared by visitor and family alike.

Nora was a courageous, happy Irish lady. She had a strong faith and gave a cheery word and encouragement to all whom she met.

Eleanore Frances Elizabeth Macdonald (nee Smithe) (Mrs. Joseph Macdonald) 1874-1921 by her daughter Alma Y. Green

My mother, Eleanore Macdonald, was the only daughter of Martha and William Smithe. She was born at Somenos in 1874.

On November 17, 1890 she married Joseph Macdonald in a ceremony at St. Peter's Church. The couple lived in Victoria and then Kamloops for a time, where Mr. Macdonald died.

Eleanor Elizabeth Frances MacDonald, nee Smithe, 1874-1921.

Mrs. Macdonald spent most of her life in Cowichan and was identified with many women's activities. Perhaps her greatest interest was the King's Daughters, but she was also an active member of the Cowichan Women's Institute and worked hard for its Arts and Industries section.

In April of 1917, she was elected to the Duncan School Board, filling the vacancy caused by the enlistment of her brother, Ormond Smythe (the spelling he adopted soon after that). During 1917 and 1918 she was chairman of the Board, the first woman in Cowichan to hold that office.

She died in Duncan in January, 1921, and is buried in St. Mary's churchyard in Somenos.

Elizabeth McLay (nee Crawford)
(Mrs. Robert McLay)
1831-1908
by her great-granddaughters, Margaret Filion and Doreen Wilkinson

Elizabeth Crawford was born at Beith, Ayrshire, Scotland, in 1831, the daughter of Margaret Cunninghame Nairn and Robert Crawford, who owned a bakery in the High Street. She married Robert McLay who had been born in 1829 at New Monckland, Lanarkshire. He was the son of a successful coal mining contractor who had lost his fortune in the collapse of the Bank of Scotland.

Robert and Elizabeth set up house in Airdrie, Lanarkshire, where they owned a shop. Five children were born to them - Robert, John, Margaret, Mary and Robina. Elizabeth looked after the "penny-shop" where one could buy a pennyworth of tea, sugar, tobacco, thread, et cetera. Robert worked at the mines.

Early in the 1860s Robert journeyed to California and was so taken with the country that he went home to bring his family out. However, Elizabeth flatly refused to leave Scotland. In 1867 Robert decided to make another trip to California and wanted to take their eldest son, Robert, with him; but Elizabeth could not bear to see him go and the boy remained at home with her. Robert found employment in the coal mines at Mount Diable in the Sacramento Valley of California and sent for his wife and family to join him. Meanwhile, his son, Robert, aged eleven, had been drowned in an accident in the river Clyde. Elizabeth blamed herself for having refused to let the boy accompany his father. She still did not want to emigrate but she was devastated by this tragedy and decided that her place was with her husband. She and the remaining four children set off by ship for New York. She was very seasick on the voyage and had to rely on her eldest daughter, Margaret, aged ten, to look after the younger children.

They travelled by train from New York to California and settled in a home on a mountainside in Somerville. In this hot dry climate the lack of water was the greatest hardship. Water was hauled by a tank wagon from the Sacramento river from the valley below. These conditions, such a contrast to life in the valley of the Clyde in Scotland, also the wish to live under

4 Generations — Elizabeth McLay, nee Crawford, 1831-1908.
Standing: Margaret (McLay) Evans & Elizabeth (Evans) Castley.
Seated: Elizabeth McLay & Amy (Castley) Murton. c.1906.

the British flag, made the McLays decide to look elsewhere for a permanent home.

Robert travelled north to Vancouver Island while Elizabeth stayed behind, she had told him that she did not mind where he decided to settle as long as there was lots of good, fresh water.

The year was 1872 and Robert gave up the idea of coalmining for farming. He pre-empted three hundred acres of land at Koksilah, between the Cowichan and Koksilah rivers where there was ample fresh water. Part of this property is the site of the present British Columbia Forest Service

Nursery. Robert built a log cabin, and his second daughter, Mary (later Cavin), came up first to help her father prepare for the rest of the family. Elizabeth and the other children, including another daughter, Janet, born in California, arrived at the farm in 1873. They lived in the log cabin until Sayward's mill was operating at Mill Bay and then Robert bought lumber and built their permanent home; the first house built of sawn lumber in that district. Their youngest child, Robert, was born at Koksilah when his mother was forty-eight years of age. Elizabeth suffered complications which affected her health for the rest of her life.

The McLay farm was called Willow Brook because of the many willows growing along the small streams and sloughs which filled with water when the rivers were high in winter and spring. Elizabeth's wish for plenty of fresh water was fulfilled. Their nearest neighbours were Indian families with whom they always had pleasant associations. When the patriarch of the Mullock family came by their house, the old man would stop at the door for a visit. Elizabeth would produce tea and sweet biscuits. At first conversation was limited, but Elizabeth soon picked up a good knowledge of Chinook and was able to converse with her Indian friends with ease.

Her husband, Robert, never lost his wanderlust. Until old age he often was absent from home. Elizabeth was left to care for the family and to manage the large farm, which speaks much for her capabilities.

When the railway line was being surveyed in the early 1880s a representative of the company called at the McLay farm to discuss the fact that the line would pass very close to their barn. There was the danger of fire caused by sparks from the smokestack of the engine. He knocked at the door and when Elizabeth appeared he asked if Mr. McLay, the head of the house, was in. She replied, "No, Mr. McLay is not in. I may not be the head of the house, but I am certainly the neck and would not I do instead?"

There are many family stories of the close eye she kept on the proceedings when a butcher came to buy an animal, to make sure there was no mistake in the weight.

Elizabeth was an example to her descendants of the virtures of independence, thrift and honesty. She remained at Willow Brook farm for the rest of her life. By the year 1906 her health was failing and her eldest daughter, Margaret came with her husband, David Evans to look after the farm and to nurse her. She died at Willow Brook at the age of 77 in 1908.

Madeleine MacRae (nee Kingston)
1886-1955
by her daughter Mary Stone

Madeleine MacRae was the daughter of William and Nora Kingston and was born in their pioneer home on Lakes Road, now Timbercrest Subdivision. She attended the one-room school on the corner of Indian Road and Maple Bay Road. She loved music and took violin lessons from Mrs. Ashdown Green in her home which is now the Silver Bridge Inn. Many times she accompanied St. Peter's Church Choir on her violin and another girl

Duncan MacRae & his bride, Madeleine Kingston.

played the guitar. This was before the church had a "pump organ."

She loved horses but was forbidden to ride bareback or astride. In those days, women only rode side-saddle.

In 1908, Madeleine married Duncan MacRae and they raised two children, Don and Mary (Stone). For a wedding present they were given by her parents 25 acres on the corner of Lakes and Wicks Roads. This they cleared and after the First World War, they raised daffodils commercially for bulb and flower markets. Each Spring thousands of golden yellow blooms were shipped to Prairie markets. These she packed carefully between strips of green wax paper in rows and rows in large wooden boxes which were taxied early each morning to Duncan Railway Station.

She lived all her happy life on Lakes Road and contributed in many ways to her church and the community.

Mary Louisa Marriner
1872-1928
(from her diary)
compiled by the Researchers

Mary Marriner was born in Cowichan in September of 1872. Her father, Edward Marriner, had come to Cowichan by sailing ship ten years before. The ship had left England on August 8, 1862 and without calling at any intermediate port had sailed around Cape Horn, arriving in Victoria on December 27, 1862, a voyage of one hundred and forty-two days. Edward moved to Cowichan on January 21, 1863. Over the years he built up a large farm, producing butter, eggs, beef, hogs, oats and hay. He sold firewood and provided cartage services with his horses and oxen. However, in 1884, at the age of forty-one, he was killed when his team bolted.

This left his widow, Augusta, to support four children aged four to thirteen, and to operate the farm to earn a living. Mary was the eldest child. A brother of Edward's, Henry, had come out from England with him and also was farming in the area. He may have helped out, as may Indians and others who had been employed on the farm.

While farming Edward Marriner had kept a diary which provides valuable detail of his farm operation and costs, but tells almost nothing of his family, home life or life style.

And so it is not until 1894 when Mary Marriner, (known as Mardi), aged twenty-two, commenced a really informative diary that we obtain an understanding of the type of life lived by the Marriner family. Here again there are limitations, as Mary seldom expresses opinions; she does provide a detailed commentary on her farm life and the activities in the Cowichan community.

Throughout her life Mary was a devoted member of the Anglican Church. Her father, the son of a clergyman in England, had been a very staunch church worker at St. Peter's, Quamichan, and had made sure that his wife and daughters attended church regularly. Mary was active in church work, decorating the church, singing in the choir, providing flowers, cooking for church socials and being a useful member of the sewing circle

Mary Louisa Marriner, 1872-1928, Diarist 1894-1925.

and Women's Auxiliary. This was a large part of her life. She also cleaned the church, in some years receiving remuneration for this.

Farm and family finances were a problem, and Mary worked very hard to bring in additional income. She would walk from Cowichan to Duncan carrying eggs to sell at 25 cents per dozen. Chickens brought in 45 cents each, and the blackberries which she picked realized eight cents per pound when sold to the Duncan Bakery and hotels. People did give her rides when they saw her walking along the road. Later in life she rode a horse.

With the farm being close to Marriner's pool and the mouth of the Cowichan River, it was a popular place for fishermen. The Marriners took in boarders and rented sites for camping. A boat was rented for two dollars a week, and Mary would row for twenty-five cents for an afternoon. She repaired, caulked and painted the boat herself.

Mary did sewing, darning and dressmaking, both at home and working out. On one occasion she was paid 35 cents for knitting new feet to a pair of stockings. She cleaned house for families for twelve and one-half cents per hour, though in later years this was increased. She worked on tennis courts, weeded gardens, cut grass and tended children. When people were ill she would be called in to care for them. All this, of course, was in addition to her work on the farm where she ordered seeds and plants, worked on the flower and vegetable gardens, tended the chickens and sometimes milked the cows.

When ladies entertained at socials and tennis teas, Mary might be asked to help prepare and serve the food. She tells of being called in to houses to work while the Chinese servants were away.

Work, however, was only one part of her life. She enjoyed meeting people, going to community functions, attending theatricals and musicals, particpating in sports and travelling when the opportunity arose. She frequently visited homes, and visitors often came to her home.

Her diary seldom mentions her mother and sisters, though it does tell us that her mother was elected as school trustee in 1896. For the most part it covered her activities and what was going on in Cowichan with a smattering of commentary on world events, and gives an insight into the life style of her times. Reading books was a pastime shared by many. Books borrowed from friends or the library (the Cowichan Lending Library and Literary Institute was formed in 1871) were read aloud and discussed at home and at meetings known as reading circles. Sewing, too, could be social and women met in sewing circles. Many amateur theatricals were staged, the script sometimes written by local residents. Musical talent abounded and concerts were frequent. In 1896 the Nanaimo Amateur Operatic Society performed Gilbert and Sullivan's "Pirates of Penzance" in Duncan. An operetta staged in 1902 included Robert Service in the cast. Robert Service, later to become known as the Bard of the Yukon, at that time was thought of as the champion handshaker.

The community was very sports-minded. In winter there would be sleighing, tobogganing and hockey, as well as skating on Somenos and Quamichan lakes. In warmer weather tennis was the social game with the South Cowichan Tennis Courts, the Duncan Tennis Courts and many private courts active. The Polo grounds were just south of Duncan and the cricket pitch near where Rotary Park is now. Soccer was popular, especially the games between local teams and teams from the ship's companies of the British warships that called at Cowichan from time to time. A great many other sports, such as baseball, lacrosse and rugger were also played.

On the water there was canoeing, sailing and swimming as well as outings in power launches. The Cowichan Regatta drew large crowds each year. One year the ship City of Nanaimo alone brought four hundred people to the Regatta. There were many types of boat races, ladies' single and double sculls, and novelty events such as upset canoe races, greasy pole walking and log rolling. Of course, refreshments and parties followed the contests and sail past.

Perhaps to make up for all that she had missed in her earlier years, Mary Marriner participated wherever possible in the recreational activities of the day. She learned to swim and bicycle when she was 35. A few years later she was target shooting and playing croquet with teen-agers. At age 47 she took up badminton and the next year enrolled in singing lessons. At 50 it was ice skating. Later she learned to play golf.

Card games were popular, the usual ones being whist, bridge, bezique, five hundred and cribbage, with poker enjoyed by the men. At church fetes entertaining games were numerous: cake walk, fish pond, up Jenkins, Aunt Sally and Pinning the Tail on the Donkey. Waxworks and Silhouettes were enjoyed. Mary must have been a real bridge enthusiast as she speaks of walking from her home to Cowichan Station to play with a group there, a seven mile round trip.

Life had its problems, too. Flooding in 1909 covered the roads in places deeper than the axles of the buggy. Floating logs smashed the boat and boathouse. The pig had to be rescued by canoe. Later the canoe was smashed against a fence by the fast running flood water and Mary's brother and an Indian were thrown into the water. There were fires, sickness and injuries, but these were met as part of life and where possible shrugged off with a laugh. Mary speaks of being at a party where the chimney caught fire and of the hilarious time spent in pushing men up on the roof to deal with it. There was a more serious matter in 1924 when a couple of fast talking oil stock promoters sold her five hundred dollars of worthless oil stocks. That was a lot of money in those days.

Living so close to the Indian village of Clemclemlets, Mary got to know some of the Indians very well. Some worked on the farm or farmed nearby. They were good neighbours, helping out when emergencies arose. The diary describes their homes and ceremonials such as funerals and potlatches.

The completion of the Esquimalt and Nanaimo Railway in 1886 made travel much easier and Mary was able to attend recitals in Victoria to hear singer Madame Albani (1897 and 1906), pianists Rosenthal (1899), and Paderewski (1908), and actress Madame Sarah Bernhardt (1913). Mary also did local travelling and gives interesting descriptions of trips to Kuper Island Indian School in 1899, canoeing to the head of Cowichan Lake in 1905 and a trip to Seattle in 1920. She was in Victoria in September in 1924 for a visit of the large British naval squadron which included H.M.S. Hood, Rodney and Repulse and H.M.A.S. Adelaide.

Many inventions came into use around this time, though some were rather late in reaching Duncan. In 1897 Mary visited a friend to have the use of a sewing machine. In 1901 she visited Mrs. Corfield to hear a gramophone, and she saw moving pictures in 1905. The following year, while driving a horse, she was approached by the first motor-car that she had seen. Then the telephone, radio and succession of electric appliances which have so changed our way of life, came into the area.

Mary's mother died of pneumonia in 1916 at the age of 75. Three years later her brother, Arthur, was thrown from a horse, dying the following day. Parts of the farm were sold and the three sisters carried on. They did not marry. With Nettie's death the Marriner family of Cowichan passed into history. Mary died in 1928, Gertie in 1939 and Nettie in 1961. They share a plot in the churchyard of St. Peter's, Quamichan.

Excerpts from Mary Marriner's diary:

1916 July 28 Dr. Price came to see Mother and said that she had pneumonia. The only thing that relieved her was poulticing, which we did. A letter came from Aunt Elizabeth Elliman says that Walter has been released from Rheubelan Camp and has arrived in England well and safe. I read it aloud to Mother and she seemed to understand it - I'm sure she did. She died without any pain at about a quarter past one o'clock, a.m. on Saturday morning the 29th of pneumonia followed by heart failure.

July 31 the day of mother's funeral. Canon Leakey and Sumner came in the morning and had lunch with us. The funeral was at half past two in the afternoon. The pallbearers were: Mr. Corfield, Mr. Edgson, Kenneth Duncan, Cecil Walker, Mr. Hutchinson and Mr. Jaynes, Frank Kingston and David Alexander, Frank drove the coffin to the church in his buggy - we did not have a hearse. Mr. Keeling and Canon Leakey took the service. Mr. Christmas was there also as one of the congregation. Mr. Stephenson played the organ. We had "Lead Kindly Light" in the church and "Peace Perfect Peace" at the grave. Quite a number of Indians were there and many friends. There were a lot of lovely flowers sent. After the service Edie Sumner, May and Mrs. Edgson came and had tea with us. Mrs. Edgson will be staying with us for two or three days.

Shusann Menzies (nee Drummond)
(Mrs. John Menzies)
1833-1903
compiled by the Researchers

Sometime in the 1850s or early 1860s, Shusann Drummond arrived in Ontario with her family from Perth, Scotland, where she had been born in 1833. She married John Menzies in Ontario and had her six children, four girls and two boys, before they set out for Vancouver Island.

The family travelled overland by the Southern Pacific Railway to San Francisco, by ship to Victoria and again by sea to Maple Bay where Shusann's brother, Hugh Drummond was already settled. When they arrived in 1876 they set about looking for land to farm and John Menzies pre-empted one hundred and sixty acres to the west, in the area of what is now Menzies and Gibbins roads.

The property was densely treed so that when they first came to look at it and to see where to start a garden they became lost and had difficulty finding their way. There was a good creek through the property, later named Menzies Creek after the family, and Menzies Falls, named after John Alexander Menzies, a son. John Menzies camped in a tent beside the creek until a bridge was built and a road cut through to start clearing the land. Shusann Menzies and her children stayed at Maple Bay during this period.

It was 1881 before they were able to move on to the land and by that time Shusann, who was about 48 years old, had spent most of her adult life as a pioneer woman in Canada. She lived at Cowichan until her death in 1903.

Annie Monk (nee Brown)
(Mrs. Alfred Monk)
Pioneer Cowichan School Teacher
1843 - 1940
by her grandson Elden Kier

Mrs. Annie Monk, pioneer teacher, was born Annie Brown in Warring-

Mrs. Annie Monk, nee Brown, 1843-1940, Pioneer Teacher.

ton, Lancashire, England on September 25, 1843.

In 1875 Mrs. Monk, with her young family of two sons and three daughters, emigrated to Hamilton, Ontario, where some of her family already lived. About 1862 she had married Alfred Monk, also a native of Warrington who was a professional musician. There is no record of her husband having come to Canada. She taught school in Hamilton for a period of time before moving to British Columbia about 1882 to teach in a Cowichan schoolhouse at the corner of Maple Bay and Indian Roads, Quamichan.

This school was built in 1884 on land given to Bishop Hills, Victoria, in 1861 by Queen Victoria and was the first Cowichan schoolhouse built for that specific purpose. The land was given under the condition that it be used as a site for the erection of an educational institution but that if at any time the land ceased to be used for this purpose the ownership was to revert to the parish of St. Peter's Church in Quamichan.

As the school was not ready for occupancy when Mrs. Monk arrived in 1882, she taught for some time on Mayne Island. However, she found it difficult to adjust to the isolated setting of Mayne Island, particularly with a young growing family. In a letter to the Superintendent of Education in 1882 or 1883, Mrs. Monk lamented that there was no local store where she could buy some wool for the baby bootees that she was knitting for a new addition to the Superintendent's family. As a result of her letters to the Superintendent, she was granted a transfer to the new school in Cowichan on Vancouver Island at the end of the first school term in January of 1884. Her salary was then fifty dollars a month.

Quamichan School built on corner of Maple Bay and Indian Road in 1884 and where Annie Monk was the first school teacher. It was later converted for use as a Boy Scout Hall. It was destroyed by fire in the 1980s.

In 1884 Mrs. Monk became the first teacher at St. Peter's School, Quamichan. Before that, she had taught at a private school, the old Roman Catholic Mission School, which was at the corner of Tzouhalem and Maple Bay Road. This old school was in the heart of the Quamichan Indian country and parents were fearful for the safety of their children during the potlatches when many other Indians, strangers to the settlers, were in the neighbourhood to take part in unknown ceremonies. Indian Agent W.H. Lomas was aware of the problem so the school was closed about 1882 or 1884. Mrs. Monk was the first woman teacher in the Cowichan District and one of the first public school teachers under the provincial school system.

Mrs. Monk left a lasting impression upon her pupils. She tried to develop their personalities and characters as well as their minds. She was a fine singer. Although there was only one piano in the district at the time, she encouraged the children to give concerts and entertainments until the school managed to acquire an organ and she began teaching them music.

When the first Esquimalt and Nanaimo Railway train came through Duncan's Station, Mrs. Monk's school children sang a few appropriate selections to welcome the dignitaries to the Cowichan Valley.

Mrs. Monk was remembered by older residents for doing clever knitting and needlework for which she was famous in her younger days.

After her retirement, she lived with her daughter, Mrs. Edgar Bryan of Portland, Oregon where she died on 23 July, 1940 at the age of 97. One of her other daughters became Mrs. George Kier of Somenos.

Anna Ordano (nee Telefero)
(Mrs. Giovanni Baptiste Ordano)
died 1928
by her granddaughter, Isabella DesRosiers

To tell the story of my grandmother, Anna Ordano, I must say a little about the life of my grandfather, Giovanni Baptiste Ordano before they were married.

Giovanni Baptiste was Italian born. He started his North American life in San Francisco at the time of the gold rush, but soon found that packing for and supplying the miners was more lucrative than gold mining.

From San Francisco he went to the San Juan Islands, but left there on twenty-four hours notice when American troops occupied the Islands in 1859. At some time in these years he met an American Indian and married "by the custom of the country".

He brought his family to Genoa Bay where he fished and traded with the Indians. He sent his five children to the Sisters of St. Ann to be educated. After the death of his Indian wife he made a trip to Italy, taking with him an adult son and daughter. The three of them found spouses in Italy.

My grandmother, Anna, was a member of the Telefero family who had a villa at Cervo, Italy. When Grandfather brought his party back to Canada and to Cowichan Bay, besides his wife there were a son and daughter-in-

Giovanni & Anna Ordano, Michael & Angeline.

law, a daughter and son-in-law, and a nanny/cook named Caroline who was to help my Grandmother. So far as is known, they were the only Italian-speaking people in Cowichan at the time.

Grandfather had a flourishing store at Cowichan Bay and Grandmother kept herself busy helping in the store and with the thirteen children she eventually had. One child died in infancy. I have been told that for the first two, possibly three, births my Grandmother returned to Italy.

Anna Ordano was on very good terms with her step-children who must have been around her own age. She also was very interested in the Indians who were their nearest neighbours, the reserve being close by. As far as she was able, she helped them in sickness, delivered supplies to them from the store and, in case of need, gave them food.

Anna worked very hard in the store. Possibly because her husband was so much older, she took on the job of hitching up horses and wagon and driving to Cowichan Station to collect the orders that had come by train. The store got most of its supplies by steamer from Victoria, but perishables came by train as soon as that service was available.

Because Grandfather's sight failed in later years, Grandmother took charge of the store's business matters. My Grandfather set up his son-in-law, Peter Frumento and daughter, Antoinette in a hotel business at Cowichan Station. His son, Austin, died after a few years as a result of an accident, leaving his younger Italian-born widow with two small children. She asked her father-in-law to pay their way back to Italy which he did. Obviously he was a well-to-do-man. The local tradition is that he was a clever businessman. Equally obviously, his wife had been no hindrance in promoting the success of his enterprises.

Giovanni Baptiste Ordano died during the first World War of old age. About the same time a son was lost in the wreck of a naval ship, Galiano, off the coast of British Columbia. Two other sons were serving with the army overseas. Caroline had married a man named Sulli and was living in Nanaimo. The younger children in the family did not speak Italian, and with the older ones scattered, Anna Ordano was very much isolated. She lost the little English she had learned and reverted entirely to Italian. At some point after her husband's death, she moved to Victoria where she was even more isolated. In 1928 she died in her sixties.

Among her 13 children there was Maria, (known later as Mary), who married George Logan Robson in 1917 who had come out from Scotland.

The youngest Ordano daughter was born in 1906 and died in 1985. The Robsons had one daughter, Isabella, (the writer). Mrs. Robson the sixth child died in December 1985 at the age of 88 at Duncan, B.C.

Lily Pannell (nee LaFortune)
(Mrs. Owen Pannell)
1881-1957
and
Rose Gueffroy (nee Pannell)
by granddaughter and daughter Bunny Knott

The following is a description of life in the Cowichan Valley as experienced by my mother, Mrs. Fred Gueffroy, and by her mother, Mrs. Owen

Pannell, who was born in Cobble Hill near Mill Bay in 1881. Mrs. O. Pannell, who died in 1957, was the oldest of a family of seven children born to Mr. and Mrs. Joseph LaFortune (nee Frances Verdier); there were four girls, Lily, Ethel, Nora and Isabel and three boys, Joseph, Johnny, and Stephen. Mrs. Pannell's mother, Mrs. Joseph LaFortune, was also born in the area. Her mother, Mrs. Alphonse Verdier (Anne), was the daughter of Angus McPhail, a Hudson's Bay factor who settled in Saanich in 1851. I am transcribing the following just as it was given to me.

"The families of the district used to gather in winter on Pannell Hill (at the top of the long hill on Riverside Road) for bobsledding parties. They would hang lanterns all the way down the hill. The Doneys, Michelins, Pannells, Mowbrays, were some of the families who participated. There were a lot of people. They would start at the top near the Pannell house, about five or six to a bobsled, which were handmade by the families, and slide down the hill to the Koksilah bridge. It would be so cold. Mrs. Pannell would dress Rose in most of the clothing the little girl owned, several layers in all. They would also skate on the river when the Koksilah would freeze up; the weather was different in those days. One year Rose was sickly and the doctor told Mrs. Pannell that the location of the Pannell house - at that time located in a hollow near Shaw Road on Riverside Road - was wrong, that it was too damp there and that they should move to the top of the hill, (the house still stands there). The house had been built by Owen Pannell's father, Charles Pannell, who built many homes in Cowichan, including the Mills' house. They received help from the neighbours and with a team of four horses got the house on skids and started slowly moving it up the hill through the pasture. To the delight of the children, Rose and her older brother Bill (or Willie), they spent the night halfway up the hill at a decided slant. The kids had to help Mother cook dinner by holding the pots on the stove. It took two full days to get the house to the top and in its permanent position. Rose's condition improved right away and she became a healthy little girl.

There were many pheasants and other birds in those days. Once, when Mr. and Mrs. Pannell were not home and the children where pretty little, a large cock pheasant showed himself in the field. Bill got out the shotgun and shot the pheasant, although he could hardly lift the gun. He must have been about seven years old at the time.

The family lived off the land in those days. They had cows, pigs and chickens, plus a big garden but they also shot game which was plentiful. It was cold in the winter then you could hang the deer in the shed and it would stay frozen!

Pig-killing day was a big day for the neighbours would come but the kids were not allowed to hang around. They would kill the pig and fill a wash barrel with boiling water and dunk the pig into it to loosen the bristles. They would slide the pig onto a table and all would scrape the pig. They would put down the meat in brine for bacon and hams.

At Christmas, Mother and Dad would start off the day before (Christmas Eve) with the team and with hay in the back of the Democrat carriage, if the winter was green. If there was enough snow on the roads, they would use the big sled. Mother (Lily Pannell), would heat irons and wrap them in flannel and put them at the kids' feet. The would arrive at (Frances and Joseph LaFortune's), the grandparents house in Mill Bay and the whole family would gather from all over. The menfolk would cut a Christmas tree after the children were in bed. It was then decorated so that by the time the kids awoke it was finished and ready for them. However, they did not light the tree candles until two o'clock in the afternoon, just before dinner. In those days, children only got a handkerchief or something homemade from the aunts and uncles. It was rare that a child got a doll, even from the parents. A big treat was a Japanese orange in the stocking.

The children, Rose and Willie, went to Cowichan Public School at Cowichan Station. The school recently celebrated its seventieth reunion and Rose was present.

There were two halls in those days, the Cowichan Amateur Athletic Club (1914) hall and the older South Cowichan Public Hall (1887). They had dances during the war years. Sometimes the children of the district put on performances on stage in the hall. Willie and Rose were in one with Willie wearing his father's army hat. Mothers and fathers would take their small children and put them in the cloak room to sleep during the dances. They made beds of the heavy coats for the kids. Someone was always popping in to see how they were doing. The children used to play in there and have a whale of a time. People took the children everywhere with them as there were no babysitters in those days."

Anna Porter
Mrs. George Porter
1845 - 1891
by her granddaughter Jean (Porter) Graham

Anna Porter was one of the pioneer women of the Cowichan Valley. She was born on July 21, 1845, at North Cove in Suffolk, England, and married George Robert Porter on October 6, 1870, at Halesworth Church. In 1883 they decided to emigrate to Chemainus, British Columbia, on the glowing reports of Henry Croft, a partner in a sawmill in that area and whose father had a steel mill at Leiston, located a mile or so from their home at Hill House, Theberton. With a family of six sons and two daughters, Anna and Robert felt that Canada would be a place of opportuntity for their children.

On October 13, 1883, Robert and Anna with Alice, Ella, George, Frank, Alan, Harry, Bert and Walter set sail from the London docks on the ship Erin of the Allan line. They encountered a severe storm and two sailors were swept overboard. It was a very difficult trip for Anna, pregnant with their ninth child, who was a gentlewoman, not accustomed to coping on her own.

They travelled on the first emigrant train on the Northern Pacific. It was a trip of life-long memories for the children as there were Indians, cowboys and buffalo involved, as well as a crossing by ferry of the Mississippi River. They travelled only during daylight hours as the Indians often ripped up tracks or put obstructions on them as they believed the tracks crossed their land. In North Dakota a group of rowdy cowboys boarded the train but left when their curiosity was satisfied. Occasionally herds of buffalo thundered over the tracks and this was a sight to remember.

It was many days before Portland was reached and that evening at the hotel all the family enjoyed their first hot bath for many a mile. The following morning they boarded a boat which took them to Victoria, where they stayed at the Occidental Hotel. They left Victoria by the paddle wheeler Enterprise for their destination of Chemainus. There was snow on the ground when they arrived in Chemainus in November. During that winter they lived at Horseshoe Bay, and the older children attended school at Chemainus River. In the early spring they bought a quarter section (160 acres) of land from Mr. C. Blaney, who lived in a log house on the property which was located approximately three miles north of Chemainus. After selling for one dollar an acre, he moved farther north.

The family lived in the cabin and tents until their house was built; a two-storey structure, overlooking Stuart Channel. The lumber to build the house was brought by scow from the mill at Chemainus. On May 12, 1884, a son Leiston was born.

Before a school was built on property given by Robert and located on the Old Victoria Road, school classes were held in the Porter home. The teacher's name was Mr. Scott and he boarded with the family. The Indians were friendly and sold them deer for one dollar, and three salmon for 25 cents. They could dig for clams, collect oysters and get crabs from the beach in season. They had canoes and boats and caught salmon, blue cod, rock cod, flounders, skate, herring and perch. They soon acquired a cow, later two more, and some hens. Two steers were raised and trained as oxen, being driven with reins.

Gradually the land was cleared. There were many setbacks as wild mink twice killed all the chickens. They planted potatoes, peas and oats. Some seeds were sent out from England as both Anna and Robert took a great interest in the garden.

Clothing was hard to come by and most of it was sent out from England. At first all sewing was done by hand, until a wonderful day arrived when Anna got a sewing machine, quite a novelty in those days. New material was obtained from the Hudson's Bay Company but hand-me-downs were the order of the day.

Fuel was no problem, but water had to be carried to the house from the creek down the hill.

There was lots of game and they sold ducks, grouse and deer to the pursers on the ships at Chemainus. Guns were muzzle loaders, twenty-five yards the limit, and with powder smoke so thick that for a few moments nothing could be seen. Wild strawberries and blackberries, as well a huckleberries, salal berries, blackcaps and salmon berries were eaten and used to make jams and jellies.

It was some time before they had a horse. The roads were poor and at times impassable, so travel was mostly by water.

In 1885 clearing the right of way for the railroad began. The timber was cut by white men, the burning and grading by Chinese. The rails were delivered by a full-rigged sailing ship to Oyster Harbour at Ladysmith.

In October 1889, a daughter Ruby was born, their last child.

An excerpt from the diary of Rev. R.J. Roberts of the Kuper Island mission, dated May 30, 1891 recorded after taking the Bishop to Nanaimo, Mrs. Roberts and I went to Squire Porter's to offer our services in the nursing of his youngest son who was very ill with diphtheria, but the devoted mother, although slowly dying herself of cancer, would allow no one to attend to the child but herself. It was very late when we got home, and I had to go back to Chemainus to send off a telegram for Mr. Porter.

On June 1, the diary recorded:

Early this morning, Mr. Porter sent one of his sons to tell me the child died last night and to say that he wished him to be interred in our cemetery. I lent him our large boat to carry the body over. Percy (Mr. Robert's son) and Mr. Hanson dug the grave and in the p.m. I officiated at the burial.

Later that year, on October 9, the diary reported:

Heard Mrs. Porter died last night and it was her desire to be buried here. I went, therefore, along with Mrs. Roberts, to Sitwells on Thetis Island and then to Porter's and arranged for the funeral to be at 4 p.m.

On October 11, 1891, the diary excerpt read:

A great many people came from Chemainus, and after interment (they) remained ten minutes for refreshments which Mrs. Roberts gave to nearly all the people. We had an evening service. The little church was beautifully decorated with produce from the farm, fruit, flowers and roots for the Harvest Festival and was filled with an attentive congregation of whites and Indians.

Anna enjoyed music and many enjoyable evenings were spent around the piano. Her life was devoted to her family although she was also interested in the community. She wrote poetry and articles for religious tracts and retained a strong faith. She had true belief that Canada was the right place to raise a large family.

Edith Share, (nee Maitland-Dougall)
(Mrs. George Share)
1882-1969

Edith Share died on August 26, 1969 and her death should be marked by more than a brief obituary because she and her family were pioneers in this valley and for more than four decades were part of the fabric of this community.

Her father, Frederick Maitland-Dougall, a Scotsman, immigrated to Georgia in the 1870s, and in Savannah in 1880, married Bessie Hopkins, daughter of a cotton broker. There, two years later, Edith Share was born, and in 1886 the family came to Duncan to live on the Cowichan Bay Flats off Tzouhalem Road, near the Tennis Club corner. Her father had a bit of family money and besides being a farmer was what we today would call a developer. His principal venture was the purchase of a large tract of land at Koksilah at the height of the land boom in 1912. He paid what was then an enormous sum of money for it. At first, having no immediate plans, he

Mrs. George Share, nee Edie Maitland-Dougall, 1882-1969.

made it into the Koksilah Golf Club. This was not a profitable operation and he eventually sold the land at a substantial loss. Today the property is owned by Koksilah Farms Ltd.

Edith's mother made a notable contribution to this community. She founded the Scattered Circle of the Order of the King's Daughters, drawing inspiration from the founding of American Chapters of the Order. The Cowichan circle was the first in Canada. Under her inspiration, this circle established a convalescent home in Duncan which was staffed by members of the Circle who did nursing duties, aide duties, kitchen work and cleaning. The home ultimately grew into a hospital and Mr. Maitland-Dougall was the first president of The King's Daughters' Hospital Board. For 55 years, the King's Daughters' Hospital ministered to this community, a tangible expression of the devotion of Mrs. Maitland-Dougall and women like her. All her life Edith Share was a member of the Scattered Circle, a circle which, sadly, now is scattering.

In 1888 Edith's father invited a group of like-minded people to play tennis on property owned by A. Pimbury, now Tzouhalem Farms, just east of the Goldstream Sawmill on Tzouhalem Road. However, the Club outgrew this location and moved to property, also on Tzouhalem Road, which G.T. Corfield made available. When Mr. Corfield died he left the property on a perpetual trust for the use of the South Cowichan Lawn Tennis Club. Edith Share was an active member of the Club for about 50 years and an honorary member for an additional 30 years.

The Corfield family and Edith's family were neighbours and friends, both occupying large tracts of land on the Cowichan Flats. There were a

Edie Maitland Dougall & Billy Bundock at South Cowichan Tennis Court, 1910.

number of Corfield sons, a little younger than Edith; two of them were at her funeral.

In 1906 Edith married Stephen Phipps, son of a wealthy Wisconsin family. She went to Hudson, Wisconsin to live. Something went wrong, but what it was is not certain; it is entirely possible that she missed Cowichan and was unhappy. In any case she returned to Cowichan after an absence of a year and a half. Except for this absence, she lived on the family property from her arrival in 1886 until her death 83 years later, surely a local record.

In 1921 she married George Share, an Englishman of charm but little money. Indeed, for all her life, though she lived comfortably enough, finances were a problem and her father's unprofitable land investments denied his wife and daughter an inheritance which they might otherwise have had, but the family property was retained. Edith and George turned to agriculture and brought the property into intensive use which culminated in the asparagus farm for which they became famous in the period between the wars. Their marriage, an immensely successful and happy one, ended with George's death in 1959.

The record of Edith's friends and neighbours during her long life includes all the early Cowichan settlers and many Victoria citizens as well: Livingstons, Falls, Mutters, Marriners, Corfields, Leakeys, Duncans, Tyrwhitt-Drake, Days, Hassells - and many other well known Cowichan families. Robert Service who worked in the Corfield store and post office was a visitor and guest at house parties. Edith's house a comfortable and gracious home, built in 1900, was the scene of many early-day parties. The garden and grounds were one of the show places of the district.

But what of Edith herself? What was she like? She was a keen sportswoman. After she gave up active tennis she played golf and played well. She and her husband had a boat and were keen on yachting, travelling up and down the coast.

She liked people. There was no "side" to her; snobbery was utterly alien to her nature. She was very fond of her Indian neighbours. They were always her friends. One of them, Simon Charlie, was a pallbearer at her funeral. She and her husband and her father before that employed many Indians over the years.

She loved Duncan, or "Duncans", as she invariably called it, harking back to the old days when the name of the place was Duncan's Station. She loved her home, her property and the Cowichan Valley. She had a passion for gardening. Until two years ago she looked after her extensive garden by herself, requiring only someone to cut her lawn.

She was a familiar figure on the streets of Duncan and could always be identified by her clothes which were either green or yellow, her favorite colours, and by her wide-brimmed and floppy hats, also of the same two colors. She delighted in wearing large paste beads and brooches and bracelets, always of green and yellow. Above all, she could always be identified by her laughter.

What was her outstanding characteristic? The answer is simple: her sense of humour. She retained this literally to her dying day. She knew how to laugh. Her humour was not malicious though the foibles of human nature always amused her, but it was simple, innocent and spontaneous. She laughed at the trivial and silly things that happened to her and to people generally. It truly could be said of her that she saw the funny side of things.

We don't need to be sad about her death; she had a long and happy life, but nonetheless we are sad - all her friends will miss her - and the district has lost almost the last link with the early community; when the coming of the train was the big event, when people rowed from Saltspring Island to play tennis at Cowichan Bay on Saturdays, when people went to St. Peter's Church twice on Sundays and when the streams were full of fish and the woods filled with game.

AN APPRECIATION By David R. Williams, Q.C., Published in the Cowichan Leader following Mrs. Share's death in 1969

Agate Maude Smithson (nee Sutton)
(Mrs. Frank Smithson)
1882-1952
by her daughters Molly Pratt and Daphne Ryan

Our mother was the first white child to be born at Genoa Bay. This was when the former mill there was owned and operated by her father, the late Alfred Sutton.

Our grandmother was Margaret Alexander before her marriage, a sister of David and James Alexander, and of Mrs. W.H. Lomas and Mrs. Edgecombe. Through her brother David's wife, she was connected with the Mainguy and Prevost families.

Grandfather Sutton was accidentally shot and killed by a friend while hunting, and Mother (Agate) and Grandmother (Margaret) lived together in Duncan where Agate opened a tea room. The tea rooms were in the home which at that time stood on property extending from Station to Government Streets. In the summer meals were served in the garden.

In 1912 Mother married Frank G. Smithson, then on the staff of the Bank of British North America which amalgamated with the Bank of Montreal in 1918.

The couple lived in a house at the corner of Coronation Avenue and York Road which has since been taken down to make room for a service station on the new highway.

A newspaper tribute had this to say: "Mrs. Smithson's life was spent in serving the communities in which she lived. While in Cowichan she joined the Scattered Circle of the King's Daughters in its early days and was the first secretary. She continued her interest in Vancouver and received her 50 year citation.

She was a member of St. John's Ladies' Guild, Duncan, and took a keen interest in all church matters.

Mrs. Smithson took particular interest in caring for elderly people's needs and those in less fortunate circumstances."

1910 photograph of Margaret (Alexander) Sutton's home in Duncan and where her daughter Agate Maud (Sutton) Smithson opened her tea room.

SECTION III
THEN CAME THE RAILWAY
The Period 1887-1900
by Elizabeth Blanche Norcross

On August 13, 1896, Sir John A. Macdonald, Prime Minister of Canada, drove the symbolic last spike on the Esquimalt and Nanaimo Railway at a point near Shawnigan Lake. That was the day chosen for the inaugural run of a passenger train, (a freight train had been over the tracks several months earlier). The Prime Minister and Robert Dunsmuir, owner of the railway with their wives and various dignitaries were making this trip from Esquimalt to Nanaimo to institute, with appropriate ceremony, the new service.

The stations which would be served by the Esquimalt and Nanaimo Railway already had been chosen and Duncan's was not one of them. Cowichan residents, their ladies, their Indian neighbours, Sisters of St. Ann Mission children and the children of Mrs. Monk's school all turned out to hail and stop the train at Duncan's Crossing. Dunsmuir was forced

E&N Station in Duncan, built 1886.

Duncan Railway Station, 1896.

to listen to representations advocating that Duncan's Crossing should be a regular stop with a station for the new service. His words from the observation platform as the train drew away were, "You'll get your station, boys!" Naturally there was no acknowledgement of the female part of his audience.[1]

Hand-down history tells us that those two hard-drinking gentlemen, Macdonald and Dunsmuir, were kept under close surveillance by their spouses for the duration of the run and were not allowed to imperil the dignity of[25] the journey by indulgence of liquor en route. Nanaimo, end of the line, provided an oasis. Robert Dunsmuir, as the most important coal-mine operator on Vancouver Island, probably thought it appropriate to offer his guests a visit to a mine shaft -- with liquid refreshment at the bottom. The ladies did not care to follow the gentlemen there.

The effect of the building of the railway had been felt in the Valley well before the inaugural run. As early as 1883, when hope for a railway turned into certainty that it would soon become a reality, land values began to rise. New people started to come in, people with capital to buy land and the equipment and stock to work it. When the trains actually started regular service this third wave of settlement could almost be characterized as a flood.

The railway had much more effect on the life of Cowichan than did the road to Victoria which had been petitioned for in vain for so many years and finally cut through in 1884. Only the automobile and great improvements in the road would later make it truly useful and popular.

Flo Jaynes (Mrs. J.H. Whittome) and her uncle Percy F. Jaynes outside E&N Station across fromQuamichan Hotel, c.1889.

The effects of the railway on Cowichan women's lives were quickly apparent. The fact that there was an increase in the number of residents mattered immensely; the greater tax revenues from increased population resulted in more and better roads which enabled women to get about freely to meet with one another, both in a social way and for group activities. Probably the newcomers can be credited with bringing with them the changing feminist outlook that was sweeping the western world.

It was the "maternal feminist" wing of the movement to which Cowichan women were drawn. These feminists did not have as their goal a demonstration that women could do this, that or the other as well as men. They simply felt that they as women, being "obviously" morally superior to men, they would be better equipped to improve society if they had the vote.

Their maternal feminist bias was reflected most notably in the formation of a branch of the Order of The King's Daughters and Sons. Bessie, (Mrs. F.H.) Maitland-Dougall, a dynamic young woman, had brought the organization with her when she, her husband and little daughter arrived in Cowichan. The Scattered Circle of the King's Daughters was formed by her in 1887, only a year after their arrival, and was to play an important role in Cowichan life in years to come.

The next year St. Peter's Guild was formed. The minutes of the inaugural meeting (June 22, 1888) record: "A number of ladies met at the Rectory, Quamichan, to take into consideration what would be the best and most agreeable way in which they could help financially the Building and Repairs Fund for the Churches and Rectory in their District."[2]

St. Peter's Guild was only the first of a long line of church-related women's organizations. Early minutes of the Ladies' Aid of the Methodist

Church are not available, but minutes of the Board meeting dated February 8, 1897 contained this: "Communication received from Mrs. R.H. Whidden, secretary of the Ladies' Aid in Duncan, intimating that the Society of Ladies' Aid had paid the half-year's rent for the parsonage, but did not feel disposed to any further effort on that behalf."[3]

Obviously, the Ladies' Aid had been in existence for some time and was confident enough to take an independent line.

An account in Heritage of One Hundred Years tells us in respect of the Maple Bay Methodist Church, "The women swept the church .... the annual church scrubbing by Mrs. John Flett .... entailed hitching up the team to the democrat, heating water on the stove, pouring it into a barrel on the back of the wagon, driving it one and one-half miles to church, unloading and proceeding with scrubbing."[5]

In these post-railway years the Methodists built a church in Alderlea, the community that later came to be known as Duncan.

For the community as a whole, health service improved only slightly when Dr. J.H. Rowbotham took up residence in the Valley in the late 1880's.[5] He was retired, but there is at least one record of his prescribing for a sick man, Arthur Robinson, as recounted in Emilie A. Robinson's biography in this section. Women and their families still depended heavily on other women who had a little skill in the health field to assist them, whether in childbirth or in the illness of family members. On occasion a doctor was brought up from Victoria by special train at a cost of one hundred dollars.[6]

Recreational activities expanded with the arrival of the settlers who came in on the Esquimalt and Nanaimo Railway. In this same year of 1887 that Bessie Maitland-Dougall organized a branch of The King's Daughters, her husband, Frederick, organized the Cowichan Lawn Tennis Club, now the second oldest lawn tennis club in the British Empire. In this same period the Cowichan Bay Regatta became an annual event, enjoyed by everyone in the district.[7]

While the railway brought Duncan into being, eventually to become the Valley's trading centre, other hamlets grew up, clustered around the stations. (Duncan's Crossing or Duncan's Station did not become "Duncan" until incorporation in 1912). Cowichan Station, for one, had hotels, a general store, a post office and other amenities. It was populous enough that Canon Leakey of St. Peter's Church took services there at intervals, though it was many years before he mentioned a church.[9] It was the station where Ordano's Cowichan Bay store picked up most of its supplies.

Somenos, to the north, likewise became a small centre, with its post office and general store, a school, a brickyard and a hotel.

From the beginning Duncan's growth, though not startlingly fast, took the lead over other railway stations in the Valley. In 1888 the Agricultural Society built a new hall, replacing the Maple Bay original, on leased Indian land close to the station. A few years later the Municipal Government moved its meetings from the Somenos schoolhouse to this new Agricultural Hall and two or three stores and hotels established themselves in the station's immediate vicinity. Homes clustered around the businesses and the rising population necessitated the construction of a new one-room school, soon to be enlarged to two rooms, and at a later date, named Zenith.[10]

Women made a cautious intrusion into public life with Mrs. Wellburn serving as a school trustee in 1895,[11] followed by Mrs. Marriner in 1896.[12] Unexpectedly the influx of moneyed people into the Valley seemed to bring about a lessening rather than an increase of support for the Library and Literary Institute. Possibly these new people came with better stocked personal libraries than the "public" institution provided. At any rate, the number of members declined to an annual average of twelve, and the library was closed during 1895. When there was a strong revival of interest two years later, we find that women took a hand. A large donation of books from England, sent by friends of Mrs. G. Hadwen, was received, and Miss Duncan became librarian. Women had always held that post with its small honorarium.[13]

Settlement of a sort began at "the big lake", Cowichan Lake. To encourage it, the provincial government let a contract for the building of a "colonization" road through twenty miles of almost unbroken forest to the Lake, not without protest from the established residents of the lower valley who felt that the money could be better spent on improvement of roads within the already settled district.[14]

Prior to this, there had been a little logging activity at the Lake but now numbers of men took advantage of the new means of access to go in and take up land, only to drift out again, discouraged by the poor soil and the difficulties of clearing the heavy timber. Logging activity did increase but still only on a small scale. The tortuous and rapid Cowichan River remained the means of getting logs out.[15]

The pioneer Henry March farm was the only one to survive to the present day but there were other permanencies such as the hunting and fishing lodges. The Lake area acquired such an international reputation as a sportsman's paradise that on learning that rail would get them as far as Duncan in comfort, many of the titled and well-to-do felt that the rewards at the end of the colonization road made the rough part of the trip worth their while.[16]

In North Cowichan Municipality an increasing number of women, as a consequence of widowhood, were managing their own business affairs. In the minutes of the municipality for the 1890s there are several references to women appealing assessments and taxes, petitioning for the closing of an old piece of road (Mrs. Charley) and for a private road (Mrs. Smithe). Also in 1890 we see that it was resolved that three ladies, Mrs. Marriner, Mrs. Sumner and Mrs. Hales, should be exempt from real estate taxes and arrears. We know that of these at least Mrs. Marriner was a widow, struggling to support four dependent children (the population was still so small that it was not considered necessary to identify these women by first names in the minutes). By such means in that period the municipality extended aid without the stigma of "charity."

In the settled lower reaches of the Valley, farm women were the beneficiaries of a major labour saving device, the first to come their way; it was a direct consequence of the new capital and new business expertise that followed the inauguration of rail service. There is no indication that it was

144

particularly meant to impinge on or improve the lives of women. This new enterprise was the Cowichan Creamery, opened for business in 1896.[17] No longer would farm women have to perform the arduous chore of making butter for the market in their homes as a cottage industry. This was not seen by all as an unmixed blessing. Some women regretted the loss of financial independence when the "butter money" became part of their husbands' incomes.

Where there was any specialization at all at this time, the Cowichan Valley's mixed farms inclined to dairying with one notable exception. That was Arthur Robinson's strawberry farm and jam-making business, an operation which flourished for some fifteen years and was brought to an end only by Mr. Robinson's death.

In these last years of the nineteenth century we find women teachers replacing men in the one-room schools. This change reflected the facts that more remunerative occupations had opened up for men and that the population now included single, qualified women to assume this work.

Private schools for girls made their appearance. It was a genteel way for a woman to earn an independent income. There was Miss Edith Fry who operated a school for a year or two until her marriage, to be succeeded by Mrs. Monk, the same lady who had brought her children to Duncan's Crossing to sing a welcome song for the first passenger train. The Sisters of St. Ann continued their work with the education of the Indian girls of the district and the handful of non-native girls of the Roman Catholic faith.

The Cliffs, a private school which was destined to become a long standing institution, opened its doors in 1894. It catered to the young ladies and younger gentlemen of a wide area, taking in both day pupils and boarders. The Misses Wilson, the founders, had a considerable influence on the cul-

Cowichan Creamery, where the Caprice Theatres now stand, c.1912.

tural life of the community, both in their personal quiet support (for they were retiring ladies) and even more through their graduates. Retiring they might be but nevertheless they were forerunners of the independent businesswomen who made their appearance in numbers during the opening years of the next century.

Public education in Cowichan came to an end at Grade VIII, but there was a widespread practice of reading aloud in the home on winter evenings and our hand-down history tells us that the reading matter was of good quality. It was not a bad substitute, having in mind society's requirements at that time for the non-existent secondary school. For both women and men there were mainly unskilled or semi-skilled jobs that were open -- housework, retail clerking, road work, farm work and so forth.

Somenos became a centre for neighbourhood socializing, for parties in the larger homes and dances that went on until daylight.[18]

Old Sahtlam School — built in 1890.

Back, l. to r.: Lawrence & Joe Jordan, Walter Robinson, Charlie Jordan, May & Nellie Robinson.

Front, l. to r.: Pearl Jordan, Freda Payne, Henry Robinson, Allan Payne, Gilbert Robinson, Lily Robinson.

Teacher: Miss May Blake. 1896/97.

146

The economy was certainly in its most flourishing state to date, but residents could still claim that Cowichan did all its business on one ten-dollar bill, and add with wry humour that "there must be money in Cowichan, a lot has gone into it."

In the late 1890s the gold rush to the Yukon took many young Cowichan men off to the northern adventure. Others, prospecting closer to home, hit pay dirt on their own doorstep. From earliest years of white interest in the Cowichan Valley there had been the hope of mineral riches being discovered which never quite died. Mount Sicker proved to be the Eldorado. The question has often been raised as to the origin of this mountain's name; the answer seems to be that it was named for a John Jacob Sicker who in 1863 pre-empted two parcels of land each one hundred acres in Quamichan and in Somenos.[19] His name does not appear again in Cowichan's history. The prospects looked so good and certain that the municipality built a road to the mountain in 1898.

The ore mined consisted of various minerals of which copper was the most important. The world market for that metal was good at the time.

The twentieth century opened with something more concrete than hope for the Valley.

South Cowichan Lawn Tennis Courts
by Geraldine Weld

This is the oldest grass courts club in Canada and has won international recognition. Very early in the history of the South Cowichan Lawn Tennis Courts competitors from the United States northwest were coming to Cowichan to take part in tournaments. As time went on, they came from farther and farther afield, though almost entirely in North America. A brief history of the club was sent to the General Secretary of Wimbledon in England who is the honorary president of all English tennis. In 1984 he replied with a phone call and invitation to anyone of the club, if they were in England, to get in touch.

Responding to the invitation, Mr. Jeff Hunter got in touch when he was in England. The viewing of Wimbledon's centre grass court where so much tennis history has been made is almost a rite, you do not step on its immaculate turf.

Yet Wimbledon, for all its fame, is only eleven years older then the South Cowichan Lawn Tennis Courts.

This club came into being in 1888 with two courts on Augustus Pimbury's farm by the Pimbury bridge over the Cowichan River. The president was Mr. Maitland-Dougall. His daughter, Edie, then a child of six, later became Mrs. Share and kept a lifelong interest in the activities of the young club. Some of the names from a group photograph of an early tournament were: Bundock, Mrs. Leather, Miss Arrowsmith, Mrs. Elkington, et cetera. There were twenty-five or more members, most with nostalgic memories of formal gardens and the green courts of their homelands.

David Williams, Q.C. and British Columbia historian says that some

This picture taken in 1888 includes handwritten list of some of the members as follows:

Back row: Mr. Maitland-Dougal, Ainsley Johnston, Mrs. Leather, George Johston, Jack Musgrave, Mrs. Maitland, Mr. B. Johnston.

Middle row: Mrs. Johnston, Mrs. Elkington, Miss Arrowsmith, Robert Musgrave, Edith Ward, Mrs. Musgrave.

Front row: Mrs. Johnston, Mrs. Musgrave, Edie Maitland-Dougall, Mrs. Drummond, Kitty Johnston, Bob Barkley.

Inscription on frame reads: "Mrs. Share (nee Edie Maitland-Dougal), 1882-1969, was a long time benefactor and patroness of the club (S.C.L.T.C.). In the 1888 picture she is in the front row with dark hair and wearing a dark dress."

rowed across from Saltspring Island to play. Among these would have been Mr. and Mrs. Jack Musgrave, for whom Musgrave landing is named.

Did they row up the Cowichan River and tie their boats at the Pimbury bridge just a few hundred yards from the new courts? The river is tidal to this bridge. Then, the river was fuller and the tide flowed strongly in and out. There were just as many times they were swept gently down river and out into the bay when they were leaving the courts as there were when they bucked a rising current as they set out to row home again.

In 1901 the ladies of the club decided that an interesting thing to have would be a teacloth with the members' signatures embroidered on it. At this time Robert Service, most remembered as the Bard of the Yukon, lived in the Cowichan Valley and was an active member. His name with the date 1901 is in the centre of this first cloth. Others are: J.I. Mutter, C.S. Fall,

Follie, Roberts, Smythe, Elkington and many more whose names are remembered.

By 1905 the membership had outgrown the two courts on Pimbury farm. Mr. Corfield was asked if his two-acre property at the intersection of Tzouhalem and Cowichan Bay roads could be acquired for new courts. He agreed that the land could be used if the taxes were paid by the club, but he would not sell it. In the terms of the agreement it states that the land may be used, "so long as tennis shall be played." So even today the South Cowichan Lawn Tennis Club does not own the property.

When work began on these new courts one of the famous stand of giant maples had to be sacrificed to clear the ground; but the others were to flank the south end of the property and to shelter the new, very simple clubhouse. There was a kitchen to boil a kettle for tea, and a men's changing room with a shower, provided by a barrel in the attic filled with clear, cold water from the creek. A third small room was for the ladies to hang their hats and change their shoes. A veranda ran the length of the building. Saturday teas began on the early Pimbury courts and developed into a vital part of social week-end tennis. Everything was home-baked on wood stoves, and served elegantly by two women members.

Over these years two more tablecoths were embroidered with the signatures of many new members, Hadwen, Kennington, Mrs. Hassell, Miss H. Hook, Dobell, Hutchinson, Shaw, are just a few. Mrs. Edie Share was still a moving spirit and it was after her death in 1969 that these signed tablecoths came to the public notice again. By then of historic interest, they were framed and donated to the Duncan museum by Mr. and Mrs. Hamish Mutter in 1982.

The International Club, one of whose interests is to keep grass tennis alive, has given donations to help. Americans and many from across Canada who come here to play in the annual tournaments are a bit sentimental about this old club and also support it in a practical way. The decline of lawn tennis is due to the expense of keeping up the courts. Added to that, the South Cowichan courts are on land that is an extension of the Cowichan Bay estuary. They have faced flooding with attendant damage and debris. In spite of it all a core of determined men and women have kept it beautiful.

The competition in tournaments always had been keen, and after moving to the present location with more courts, inter-club matches increased. One trophy, a tall jug-shaped pewter cup, inscribed, "S.C.L.T.C. 1908", won by Mrs. Hadwen in a ladies doubles is owned by her daughter, Suzanne (Mrs. Alan) Stewart.

It was 1916 when I first remember being taken to tennis. There were other children, boys and girls, too young to play, but hopefully old enough to behave. The huge maples drew us like a magnet. Easy to climb, we played up there, talking 'pig-latin' and waiting for tea time. Very frequently an irritated parent would wave a racquet at us saying, "Be quiet, children!" A few years later we were seriously learning to play tennis.

It seems now that the sun always shone, except for the afternoon of an almost total eclipse. We stood under the maples holding our parents' hands as the world went dark. The men's white flannels and women's long white skirts were subdued by the shadow of the moon. When the rim of the sun slowly emerged, the players went back onto the courts and we went back to our perches in the trees.

Today the maples are trimmed of dangerous old limbs, but each winter takes its toll of the lichen-draped giants. There must have been dozens of children like us, warned to keep off the courts, yet who have played in them, right back to 1905.

A main social event each summer was the Bachelor's Tea and Tournament. Mr. Edwin Jackson may have been president of the club then, and his groundsman, Gerry Knocker. There was Mr. Colville, Corfield, Rutherford, D. Christmas and others who did the entertaining on that day. They had ice cream. I can remember a tub of it under the shade of the trees. I suppose it was packed with ice and rushed from Duncan. The mothers and girl friends of the bachelors were also expected to outdo themselves with a specially lavish tea.

The need for other than family contacts, a meeting place, a game of tennis where you could wear the long white skirt and blouses that were stored away; was born in the quite isolated lives of many early women settlers. Men had companionship in hunting and fishing together but quickly became interested in a club that would be recreation for anyone.

The seed of thought for those first courts on the Pimbury land must have been germinating for at least two years. Constant work for that period of time would have been required to have the courts ready to open in 1888.

So it would seem very reasonable if next year (I am writing in 1985) they took the years of preparation into consideration, they could hold their one hundredth anniversary club tournament in conjunction with Expo, 1986.

Enjoying a cup at a "Tennis Tea." Mrs. Rutherfurd and S. Rutherfurd at the South Cowichan Lawn Tennis Courts.

Making Strawberry Jam in Sahtlam
A digest of an article written in 1958 by Kate (Mrs. Gilbert) Robinson.

Mr. Arthur Robinson, who in 1887 had acquired a farm in the Sahtlam District of the Cowichan Valley, decided to grow strawberries extensively to take advantage of the good markets in Nanaimo and Victoria. Having cleared considerable land, he began to set out plants and to propagate more plants until eventually he had as much as six acres devoted to this crop.

In addition to the two main varieties of strawberries grown for the market (Woods and Warfield), Mr. Robinson also grew experimentally several other varieties of strawberries to try to develop plants which would produce the best all-purpose fruit.

Taking care of this project required the help of many hands. Along with the older members of his family, he employed both Indians and Chinese. The Indians were engaged to pick the strawberries, an operation which took several weeks, so they brought their families and possessions, even their dogs, and lived in a large shed. It was what might be called a "rancherie." They worked as families in the picking.

The Chinese lived in a cabin by themselves. These men took quite a professional interest in the success of the crop. One year, after looking over the acreage, one of them observed, "No muchee Wafell, hi-you Woods." (Not much Warfield, lots of Woods).

The family constructed the one-pound boxes and the crates to hold the boxes and the jam pails. To make the boxes, a strip of veneer was bent over a metal sheathed block of wood to form the bottom of a little box (hallock), and then another piece was placed around the mold. Next, tiny tacks were pressed into the veneer. Then the tacks were hammered against the block

Grandpa Robinson and members of the family picking strawberries in 1896.

and the metal sheathing turned the points of the tacks into hooks that held the boxes together. The crates were made mostly from wood prepared on the farm.

The shipping was always delayed each day to the last minute so as to get really fresh berries to the market. As the deadline approached, the horse was hitched to the loaded democrat and the race to the depot engaged the best efforts of horse and driver until the consignment was safely aboard the train.

Sometimes the market was not keen nor the weather favourable and the berries would have been a loss if jam-making had not been introduced.

A lean-to attached to the barn was the scene of the cooking operation. A complication was that no matter what expedient was used, the kettle would boil over. Mr. Robinson eventually learned the secret was to put a lump of butter into the boiling fruit. When the jam was of the right consistency, it was ladled into little wooden pails, and when cooled, wooden lids were fastened into place. The jam was sold both locally and to the wholesalers in the city, and shipped as far as Winnipeg.

"In the busy strawberry season," May Robinson Castley recalled, "my job was to weigh the berries as the pickers brought them in, and to check on the correct weight in the crates."

In June of 1900 when the season was at its peak Mr. Robinson shipped three thousand pounds of berries in one day.

The responsibility and management of the business was so onerous that after Mr. Robinson's untimely death in 1904, the whole project was gradually abandoned.

Mary Grace Allman (nee Colvin)
(Mrs. George Vernon Allman)
1887-1965
by her daughter Gladys Mary McCormick

The old farmhouse on Rosedale Farm where Mother was born is still standing in 1986. It was built about the same time as she was born in 1887. For many years it was the only proper frame house in that area at the end of Riverside Road, Cowichan Station. As most homesteaders did at that time, her father Robert Mouat Colvin had built a log house until her mother Jeremina arrived and they were married in 1886. Her parents were both from the Shetland Islands.

Mother worked on the farm and at home to help her mother. She was the eldest of the six Colvin children and as her father, a fisheries inspector, was away from home a lot of the time, she had to help raise the younger children.

As she grew older, she would take turns with her sisters, visiting the different ranches around the area for parties. Before her June wedding to George Vernon Allman in 1914, mother sometimes worked as a housemaid. After marriage, she and her husband lived at Rosedale Farm and that is where my brother, James Everard, was born in 1915 and myself in 1917.

Mary Ellen (Lillie) Baron
1881-1958
Compiled by the Researchers

On July 13, 1948, a Tuesday, one of Duncan's longest established merchants held a staff reunion to mark her fortieth anniversary in business. She was Mary Ellen Baron, known to her intimates as Lillie.

There were fourteen former and present staff members at that dinner held at the Alderlea Tea Room, the site of many receptions and special events.

Lillie Baron was born in St. Hyacinthe in the Eastern Townships of Que-

Lillie Baron, c.1948.

bec and came west to San Francisco with her parents. Later the family moved to Victoria where they lived for a time.

Miss Baron cared for her parents until their deaths and it was only then that she opened her business in Duncan. Prior to that she had trained as a milliner with David Spencer Limited in Victoria.

Lillie Baron advertised her business as The Bon Ton Millinery Parlours, and hats and fancy trimmings for hats were her main line of merchandise at the outset. Soon she was advertising the latest styles in ladies' dresses and Spirella corsets. As time went on, she concentrated more and more on infants' and children's wear so that the business popularly was known as Baron's Baby Shop. This part of her business was so important to her that any child born on July 13 received a gift from her. It was said that her first reading in the local paper was the "hatches, matches and dispatches" column!

Miss Baron was an enterprising businesswoman who did not neglect advertising in the paper or indirect promotions such as contests to guess the number of beans in a jar displayed in her window, or "dollar day" specials.

She was handicapped by one leg being much shorter than the other so that she had to wear a special boot to compensate. Therefore, whatever the prevailing fashion might be, she always wore long skirts.

In spite of this physical handicap and in spite of the demands of a thriving business, Miss Baron was active in her church. She sang in the choir of St. Edward's Church and was a charter member of the Catholic Women's League which succeeded the Altar Society of that church in 1944. In recognition of twenty-four years of service, she was given the title of Honorary President. "Her religion and her language meant all to her," said an old friend.

When she retired in January, 1952, she moved to Victoria, but was buried in St. Ann's Churchyard, Cowichan beside her parents.

Elizabeth Lovely Bell (nee Vallack)
(Mrs. Meadley Bell)
1863-1955
by her grand-daughter Helen G. Maltby

Mrs. William Bell, our great-grandmother, lived on First Street in Duncan possibly for fifteen years during the late 1890s or early 1900s. We know little about her, not even her first name or the year she died (possibly in 1912). We do know that she was very straitlaced and referred to a pack of cards as the "devil's prayer book."

She and her husband came from Yorkshire. Her children were born there and followed their parents to Vancouver Island. Apparently great-grandfather worked at Corfield Farm at Cowichan Bay.

The children were Meadley, our grandfather, Sam, David, John and Hannah; most of them lived in or near Duncan at one time.

In 1910 our grandmother, Mrs. Meadley Bell, came to live in the house on First Street. She came with her husband and family from Newcastle-on-Tyne. The family consisted of Harriet, twenty-four years, Lilyan Gladys, our mother, who was fourteen and Claude, aged nine. Three other children had died in England.

Grandmother's maiden name was Vallack and she was always called Lily. She was a very bright, cheerful, energetic little person. For a number of years around the First World War she kept boarders, and for ten years from the early 1920s to early 1930s she helped her husband in his stationery store which was situated where the Greenhaven Cafe is now. Grannie was a wonderful cook, one who never measured; she just simply seemed to take handfuls of this and that! We still talk of her Sunday dinners with roast beef and Yorkshire pudding or leg of lamb with mint sauce; not to mention her cookies, applesauce cake and scones with currants inside and icing on top.

When we stayed with her we were served tea in bed in the morning and in cold weather a "pig" was placed in our beds at night. The "pig", a stoneware bottle, flat on one side and thought to resemble that animal, was warmed on the oven door of her wood stove then filled with hot water.

Grannie had a very good alto voice and loved to sing, especially hymns. She went regularly to St. Andrew's Presbyterian Church next door to her home and always invited visitors in for tea and music after the evening church service. She would give us Scotch mints during the service and always placed one on the collection plate for Mr. Tom McEwan when he took up the collection.

In her later years she loved to play cards, especially cribbage. She also knitted socks for her grandsons and grandsons-in-law.

Grannie had a wonderfully alert and active mind until the time of her death at age 92, in 1955. She had a delightful sense of humour and was a very happy and pleasant person; we all loved to visit her.

Hatty Alice Bevan (nee Pryor)
(Mrs. Herbert W. Bevan)
1870-1945
by her daughter Dolby (Bevan) Turner

Hatty Alice was born to Robert and Molly Pryor (nee Moscript) in St. Joseph's, Missouri on July 17, 1870 while her parents were visiting there. She was their only child.

When Hatty was three years old her father was drowned and later her mother remarried, a Mr. Carmody. He was very strict, highly educated and a perfectionist to the point that Hatty was allowed to play only one-half hour a day after school, the rest of her time being devoted to studies with him.

In 1885 at the age of fifteen, Hatty graduated from high school, the top in her class, and that summer she married Lewis Herrnan by whom she had two daughters, Lulu, who was born on April 27, 1886, and Lola, born on October 16, 1888. Lewis was killed in a runaway carriage accident when the girls were four and two years old.

Hatty Alice Bevan, nee Pryor, 1870-1945.

On May 25, 1899, Hatty married Herbert Walter Bevan, an Englishman who had opened a chicory factory in Omaha, Nebraska. Later they moved to Colorado Springs where their first child, a daughter, Laura Edith, was born, August 7, 1902, and then a son, Hubert, born on April 6, 1904.

Mr. Bevan, who had hunted from childhood in England, taught his wife to ride and they did his version of fox hunting in America by running 24 Irish wolfhounds. They did not chase the fox, but followed wolves and coyotes.

In 1906, Hatty wanted to move to California where her mother was then living. Her husband, agreeing to check out the possibilities, took a train to Seattle and spent a night there before heading south. He ran into an old friend who, upon learning of the search of new pastures, said, "Bevan, you cannot possibly move south until you have seen something of the country-side around here." The outcome was that Mr. Bevan joined Mr. Stilwell and together they journeyed to Duncan.

156

One weekend and one hundred and twenty brace of pheasants later, Hatty received a wire, "Forget California, we are settling on Vancouver Island." Hatty later said she tried to find the spot on the map but could not. It might have been Timbuktu!

Herbert Bevan had bought the old Thomas Skinner farm consisting of four hundred acres on Quamichan Lake, and re-named it Happy Hollow.

The family arrived by ship from Seattle to Victoria and then by train to Duncan with three freight car loads of furniture, three hunters, 24 hounds, a cat and a parrot.

The Bevans stayed two or three months at the Tzouhalem Hotel until the existing house on the property was re-organized and they could move in.

At this time Mr. Bevan became a partner wih Francis Leather in the firm known as Leather and Bevan, Real Estate and Insurance.

Country living and a place to farm was Herbert Bevan's dream, and he raised a prize herd of Jersey cattle and owned the top line bull, "Brampton's Pride." The H.W. Bevan Memorial Cup for the prize yearling bull still is competed for at the Cowichan Fall Exhibition.

Two more daughters were added to the family, Mary Maude on June 3, 1908, and Dolby on March 1, 1910.

In the summer of 1912 the old Skinner farmhouse burnt to the ground when the Japanese cook, Tomoshi, put a handful of gumwood into the kitchen stove while preparing dinner for the twenty expected guests. Hatty was in the bath at the time and called to her son to tell the gardener to stop smoking his pipe under the window because it was choking her. (The chimney had caught fire and the old shingle roof, covered with moss, was

Interior of "Happy Hollow" — home of H.W. Bevan family.

ablaze). Suddenly realizing what was happening, Hatty threw on a dressing gown, grabbed Mary under one arm and Dolby under the other and ran towards the wooded point and so to safety.

The dinner guests arrived, and with four husky farm hands rushed into the house to save what they could, of all things salvaging the piano, ignoring what could have easily been carried out. A Guarneri violin, two Butt's bows, Jacobean chests, Persian rugs and priceless paintings were left to burn. Fortunately, the dinner table was set with silver and Edie crawled through a diningroom window, folded the four corners of the table cloth and dragged it out just before the roof fell in.

The big house above the Maple Bay Road was half completed at that time. Mr. Bevan took Edie to stay with his family in Sussex, England, while his wife with Hubert, Mary and Dolby went to California. They remained there until the house was completed.

Hatty Bevan and the children returned to their new home at Happy Hollow when it was finished and fully furnished. So began 17 wonderful years. The living room was large enough for dances, and accommodated two hundred guests plus Mr. Heaton's five-piece orchestra from Victoria.

Mrs. Bevan who loved to entertain, was in her element putting on cabarets at least twice a year, held mostly at the Cowichan Agricultural Hall. John Galsworthy's niece, Doris, took part in one of these. Edie Bevan had a clear, sweet voice, trained under Eva Hart, so her mother always had a star for her shows. Edie was also a very beautiful girl and a good dancer. Once she and Ronnie McBain performed a spectacular Apache dance which gives a little suggestion of the shows that Mrs. Bevan put on.

The Bevans' social activities took many forms. In 1918, for instance, when the original barn on the farm was pulled down and a new one erected, they celebrated by giving a barn dance for which Mr. Bevan fiddled through the night. The dance ended only when breakfast was served to all of the 15 guests.

It should be noted that the dress that night was an exception to the rule pertaining to the dances normally held in Cowichan. Fully 80 percent of the men would dress in white tie and tails, mostly tailored in Bond Street, while the other twenty percent wore dinner jackets, the women's gowns would rival any of those in New York or London. All women were wearing long white kid gloves and carrying programs.

No one missed Mrs. Bevan's teas at the Cowichan Lawn Tennis Club when it was her turn to supply them. Her meringues, filled with whipped cream from the "Happy Hollow" cows, were the piece de resistance.

In those years, Cowichan became home to many noted names and the flow of relations and friends from the "old country" usually filled their hosts' spare bedrooms. Canada was "dry" at the time. When the visiting British naval officers were guests, they were doubly welcome for they arrived with quarts of Scotch, brandy, gin and rum by the suitcase load.

Hatty had other interests. She became an avid fisherwoman and although she could not swim and terrified her family, she was out rowing, trying her luck at every opportunity. Among her feats as a fisherwoman, she caught a record-breaking salmon. When it was weighed twenty-fours hours after the catch (no one thought to do this at the time it was landed), it tipped the scales at sixty pounds; fresh caught it probably weighed more like seventy pounds. (The Field and Stream quoted seventy-two pounds. It started the competition for the largest salmon.)

Hatty also made jam and jelly, though she insisted it was a mystery to her why the good Lord had been so misguided as to allow fruit to ripen at the height of summer. When she stood and stirred for hours over a hot wood stove she would say, "It would have been a pleasure when it is cold, with snow outside."

After the preserving, it was hunting season. Mr. Bevan and Hubert with 18 to 20 friends spent the days tramping through the fields and woods after local game, and the evenings sitting before the twenty-four by twelve-foot blazing fireplace, telling stories and reminiscing.

In 1923, Mr. Bevan's eyesight began to fail. He died on the operating table during an emergency operation.

In 1925 Edie married R.E.G. Gore-Langton. Mary was in nurse's training at St. Joseph's Hospital in Victoria and Hubert was away at work, leaving just Mrs. Bevan and Bolby in the big house, very much alone. They, in 1929, sold to an English family, Mr. and Mrs. de Las Casas who had five children. When Mr. de Las Casas died shortly afterwards, that family returned to England.

The house was rented many times until it was sold and became a nursing home for twenty-two guests. It remained a nursing home until recently demolished. The land was subdivided, leaving no record of the happy times and happy years that the Bevan family had spent at Happy Hollow.

Mr. Bevan had thought the day would come when there would be a street car service between Duncan and Maple Bay and he had envisioned the growth of the Cowichan Valley and the influx of families, but it is doubtful he could have foreseen a future where so much lush pasture land would be subdivided into suburban lots.

For Hatty Bevan, born and raised a city woman with a telephone beside her bed, Quamichan seemed the last outpost to her. The only thing she could not stand was to be bored and so, as we have seen, she created her own interests and amusements. She was a woman of great charm and had a gift of making everyone or anyone feel at home. As Mr. W.H. Haldane, Q.C. said in later years, he could understand a young man falling in love with an older woman. He first came to Happy Hollow at the age of 21 and for the first time in his life a woman (Hatty) made him feel interesting and important. It was a gift she had and it is not yet forgotten.

Margaret Blair (nee McDowell)
(Mrs. John Blair, Jr.)
1873-1938
by her daughter Mary Peck

Margaret McDowell, daughter of Annie Munro and William McDowell, was born in Victoria. Her father had come from Ireland to Ontario in the 1860s and then to Victoria where he met Annie Munro. The Munros had originated in Scotland.

The family lived in Victoria but Margaret became a teacher and came to the Sahtlam log school in 1891. It was at Sahtlam that she met and married John Blair, Junior, in 1895.

Though not fully completed at the time, the school was considered fit for use and it is probable that Margaret McDowell was its first teacher. She returned to Victoria and taught there for approximately two years.

The Blairs had four children, Anna (Pipe), Jean (Grumbach later Anderson), John, and Mary (Peck).

Clara Bernice Castley (nee Dodds)
(Mrs. William James Castley)
1886-1969
by her daughter Lorna R. Mainguy

Clara Bernice Castley was born in the small town of Aylmer, Ontario, in the year 1886. Early in her life her parents, Clara Arletta and William Dodds, moved to California to join relatives who were farming in Sacramento. William Dodds spent much of his time there training and handling horses, and during these years the family lived also in Roseville and in Lincoln. My mother loved California and often told us about her delight in the mountains, the eucalyptus trees and the beauty of the wild flowers.

Eventually my grandfather William Dodds, sustained a bad injury to his hand and had to find a new occupation. At this time there was great excitement over the discovery of gold in the Yukon so he made up his mind to move north. Having reached Seattle he chanced to meet one of the Castley brothers from Cowichan who persuaded him that Vancouver Island had much to offer. So it was in the year 1899 that the Dodds came to Duncan. Jim Castley was with a small family group waiting at the railway station in Duncan to welcome the Dodds. This must have been the beginning of a romance for three years later Clara Bernice Dodds and William James Castley were married in the little church of St. Mary's, Somenos.

The Dodds family had settled on a property just north of Duncan adjoining the Cowichan Lake railway and the Old Island Highway. My father bought property also bounded by the highway and by Holmes Creek from David Holmes just across the railway from the Dodds. He first lived there in a small cabin while he cleared the land and built a home on the hill overlooking the creek. This was Inglewood and my father and mother lived there for 62 years. It is still standing, a tribute to my father's skills as a carpenter.

My mother loved her home and sang while she worked. How many children today have mothers who sing while they are washing dishes or dusting? She sewed many of our clothes and spent long summer days canning and preserving. Even so she was never too busy to welcome friends, young or old. As children we were always bringing our playmates home after school and mother made us many a tea-party, with special dishes from the best china cabinet and her latest bread and scones.

In a sense she raised two families. The first three girls born were Hazel,

Helen and Clara. Helen died at the age of seven from polio for which there then was no treatment or vaccine. Then came the Great War and my father was overseas for four years. In the 1920s the family was extended by the arrival of Lorna, Colin and Denise.

At the turn of the century, daily life had its challenges and hazards. In Duncan there was no hospital before 1911 and medical care was not what it is today. Mother nursed some or all of us through scarlet fever, whooping-cough and pneumonia. My sister, Clara, became ill with bronchitis when just a tiny baby. Fearing that she might not live my parents had her baptized at home. Mother's best crystal bowl served on this occasion! Hazel, who needed minor surgery as a small child, was dealt with on the dining room table by the doctor who carried all of his equipment with him.

There were many anxious times. During the war years my mother must have dreaded the news of war casualties. It seems a miracle that my father returned home safely, although he nearly died in the flu epidemic before leaving England on his way home.

He had established greenhouses at Inglewood as a commercial venture before the war, but these had to be abandoned after he left. Subsequently my mother rented a house nearer to town. She was trapped here by the historic snowfall of 1916. Men from the 88th Battalion who were stationed in Duncan were sent to dig out the families who needed help. They went to Inglewood and shovelled several hundred yards of driveway, only to discover that there was no one there. However, they went on to clear another long driveway and rescued my mother and two small girls who considered it a very exciting day. Their food supply must have been short by that time, but Clara remembers that the men were served tea and bread and bottled pears before they went on their way.

Our earliest water supply was from Holmes Creek, brought into a tank on the top of the hill by a "ram" which sat on the edge of the stream. The water was forced up pipes by a pressure and lock system as the water flowed through the base of the heavy iron installation. It made a pleasant click-snap sound day and night and seemed to create a cool and relaxing atmosphere. It was a stubborn device in winter when the running water supply sometimes froze. That was the signal for everyone to haul water in buckets and wait out the siege!

By 1927 power lines were extended to our home and we had our first electric light. Soon after this we had a well and a gas-powered pump to fill the water tank. A good supply of water was a major concern of early residents; that and a constant vigilance against fire. I can recall when a fire on the roof of our house was successfully extinguished and the time our gas pump caught fire and almost destroyed the pump house. Our worst fears materialized one hot day in July of 1938 when our home was totally destroyed by fire. This was a serious setback, but my father immediately set about clearing up the ruins and by early winter had built a new home on the site of the old one. The house still is there and is occupied.

It is hard to re-adjust our thoughts now to the time when nearly everyone worked a six-day week. Saturday night was shopping night. The stores were open until nine o'clock and the town was busy with people buying their weekly supplies. Butcher shops were open air, screened on all sides, and the meat hung from large hooks or reposed on heavy chopping blocks. There were no supermarkets or serve-yourself outlets. If my mother needed a new pair of gloves she went to the Cowichan Merchants' store, and sat on a stool in front of a polished wooden counter while the saleslady brought out different styles for her choice. The gloves were carefully tried on to be sure they had a good fit. Miss Baron, a milliner, had a popular shop for the ladies; besides buying their new hats there, often my mother and grandmother would buy lengths of ribbon and bunches of silk flowers to re-trim their old hats.

Sunday was a time for church, visiting, reading, or relaxing. On Sunday afternoon my mother would change into her best dress. I can remember her standing before her dresser curling her hair with the curling tongs which she had heated over a coal-oil lamp. In winter she would often sit down to read a book of poetry or the Bible, or The Family Herald and Weekly Star. In summer, sometimes there were picnics at the "Riverbottom" or just in our own woods. My father, a very understanding man, made a clearing in our woods on the hill where he built a picnic table and benches under the cedar trees and make a place for a hammock. This was designated as a retreat where mother could get away from the children and household chores. There was a fireplace built of rocks where we could boil a kettle. It was a cool and peaceful place where we could take our afternoon tea.

As a family we all found much pleasure in music. My mother sang and played the piano; in his younger days my father played the violin. As a young couple they often went to the old-time dances at Vimy Hall, west of Duncan, in the Gibbins Road area. There were musical evenings at our home when friends and neighbours would gather to sing and visit. Each would have "just happened" to have brought along his or her music. I have memories of lying in bed and hearing the sentimental strains of "My Little Grey Home in the West" or "It's Quiet Down Here," or the lively lilt of "The Kerry Dance," or perhaps "Who is Sylvia?" Then there was talking and laughter and refreshments for all.

Throughout the years there was always a playhouse in our yard, situated not too far from the house. The one my father built for us (the younger members) had a stone fireplace in it. This served as a retreat for us and I'm sure that it provided another safety valve for Mother. We were also fortunate to have our Grandma Dodds nearby, for it was always a pleasure to visit Grandma who was so good to us. My grandfather Dodds died around 1924; after that my father built a cottage on our own property in 1926 for her. She was a great support to my mother, too, always taking a lively interest in our interests and entertaining us in her own way.

I find it hard to give a progressive account of my mother's life. The contents here seem more like a piece of patchwork or piecework such as she and my grandmother used to make. There were dark times and bright ones, but they make up a personal pattern which was her way of life.

Mother laughed a lot. She had a lively sense of humour and found joy in many ways. She once said to me, "When I die you must not grieve for me because I have had a full and happy life". I believe that this was so.

Eliza Castley (nee Steadman)
(Mrs. Henry T. Castley)
1841-1890
by her granddaughter Doris (Castley) McEwan

The history of our grandmother, Eliza Castley, is very sketchy. We do know she came from Rosgill, Westmorland, England, in 1887. She was from a farming family and lived with her husband, Henry, on his father's

Edith Margaret Castley, 1880-1958.

farm. Eliza and Henry were married in 1866. After his father's death the family continued to live with the mother.

After the mother's death and when the estate had been settled, they found that after years of working the family farm, that it was the oldest son who inherited and not Henry and Eliza. By that time they had a family of nine children: Thomas S., John H., Elias, Mary Elizabeth (Campbell), Annie E. (Munro), W. James, Joseph, Edith M. (Grassie), and Timothy.

A decision was made to move to North America as more opportunities for a young family were reported to be there. Why they chose the Cowichan district we do not know, but in grandfather's prayer book the name of "Norcross," Somenos, is written in pencil. By that we presume contact was made and Grandfather and sons, Tom and Elias, came here and stayed with the Norcrosses until they found a farm.

Jim & Lizzie Campbell, James McLeod Campbell & his wife Elizabeth (Castley) Campbell.

They bought property which was originally owned by Charlie King and then later by Jim Auchinachie on Cowichan Lake Road. On the land was a shack in which they lived until the new part was built in 1897.

Grandmother Castley followed with the rest of the family later in that year of 1887, except young Timothy who died in infancy. I am sure she would have been a true pioneer here looking after her family with nothing much to work with. It was a blow to them all when she died suddenly with a stroke in 1890. The youngest girl, Edith, would then be eight years old and it was up to the oldest girl, Lizzie (Campbell), to take the reins and raise the family. Although Eliza Castley never lived to see the result of raising a big family, they would have made her proud as all married, raised families and all lived in the Cowichan district except for a married daughter.

Eliza and her husband, Henry, are buried in St. Peter's churchyard in Quamichan.

May Dorothy Castley (nee Robinson)
(Mrs. Elias Castley)
1881-1971
by her daughter Edna Green

May Robinson was born in Chicago, Illinois, a daughter of Arthur and Emilie Robinson.

In 1887 the family, consisting at the time of three daughters and a son, moved to the Cowichan Valley to a farm in the Sahtlam area.

May remembered the first big outing of her life in Cowichan a few weeks after their arrival. This was to attend the Fall Fair, held at Maple Bay. Travel with the team and wagon was slow, so the family took lunch and made a day of it. The following year the Fair was held on leased Indian land, where a City of Duncan parking lot now exists. The Fair was one of the greatest events of the year, not only for May but for the whole district. It was where everybody met everybody.

The twenty-fourth of May was another occasion for a big picnic with family and friends. For several years the Robinsons' chosen site for the picnic was the Riverbottom area.

The older Robinson children walked to school in Somenos (about seven miles away) but in 1890 a school was provided at Sahtlam. Among May's recollections of her girlhood were the dances held in the log schoolhouse to raise funds for interior finishing. "Admission for men was one dollar and the ladies were admitted free but were requested to bring refreshments." There were violinists to play for the dance, May and another girl, Edith Castley, assisted by chording on the organ.

May was a busy child on the farm. As the oldest child she often was sent on horseback to Somenos Store and Post Office to do errands. By the age of nine or ten she was helping to milk the cows and feed the calves. In the summer holidays she helped with such outside work as hoeing and weeding and with the haymaking and the picking of the fruit. At the end of the holidays there was always the treat of a family picnic on Maple Bay Beach.

Left to right: Edna Green, Ina Talbot, Dorothy MacLeod, May Castley (nee Robinson), Florence Waldie, Bertha Corbett and Gladys Castley.

Schooldays for May Robinson came to an end when she passed the high school entrance examinations in 1896. There was no high school in Duncan and no money to send her to Victoria, so she stayed at home, helping on the farm.

Soon after her sister Emily was born in 1897, her mother and the baby went on an extended visit to Mother's parents, near Chicago. They stayed for the winter. "I was left in full charge to run the house," said May, "having to cook for nine people, including the school teacher and the hired man. My father helped on wash days, turning the washing machine. He also helped me with the making of butter and bread."

This responsibility was excellent training for the future which young May Robinson fortunately could not forsee.

In 1901 she married Elias Castley whom she had known for many years. Elias had a 40 acre property on Castley Road, a few miles west of Duncan, and he had a new home on it ready for his bride, "one of the best built houses in the district."

The babies, six little girls, Dorothy, Florence, Edna, Gladys, Ina and Bertha, arrived almost annually. Mrs. John Evans, a near neighbour, assisted the doctor. "She was a Florence Nightingale for the whole community."

In 1904, Elias obtained the position of agent for the British Columbia Telephone Company and so it was necessary for the family to live in town. Again they built their own house, this one at the corner of Craig and Ingram Streets, with space for an office. In addition to running her home and caring for the young children, May Castley acted as an unpaid operator while her husband was out of the office on maintenance and installation work. In 1907 the Company provided for a full-time, paid operator.

"On Christmas Day, 1909, Mrs. May D. Castley's whole world came crashing down upon her. Her loving husband, Elias, died on that day from fatal injuries received two days previously whilst performing a voluntary favour for the local Fire Department. On that day Mrs. Castley and her six little daughters, the eldest only seven years old and her youngest one year, were left to face the world alone. She was only twenty-nine years old."**

For a short time Mrs. Castley was made chief operator, at a salary of $30 a month. The Company purchased property at the corner of Kenneth and Craig Streets, appointed a new chief operator, and informed May Castley that her services were no longer required. Along with her job, she lost the income from an outside building which had been rented to the Company for $25. a month.

The story of how she coped is almost incredible. She took in boarders and roomers, did the laundry and cleaned house for Miss Clack, the kindergarten teacher, in return for the children's tuition. In 1916, when the soldiers were stationed in the Agricultural Hall, she washed and mended clothes for six of them.

Her brothers assisted with food from the farm and to some extent financially. In late 1917 she was again working as an operator with the B.C. Telephone Company at one dollar a day.

Somehow in those strenuous years she managed to turn out all her little girls in starched white frocks on Sundays.

Remembering how her own education had been cut short, she was determined this should not happen to her daughters. One by one they were sent to Victoria to take secretarial or Normal School training. Money was borrowed from their uncle for tuition fees, and they worked in friends' homes for their room and board.

The Castley daughters in order of age are -- Dorothy (Mrs. D.W. McLeod), Florence (Mrs. E.M. Waldie), Edna (Mrs. Claude Green), Gladys, deceased in 1949, Ina (Mrs. L. Talbot), Bertha (Mrs. W.O. Corbett).

** From an eulogy to his mother-in-law, by Claude A. Green.

Bella May Chapman (nee Cameron)
(Mrs. William T. Chapman)
1879-1954
by her daughter Mrs. Mabel Fleetwood

Bella May Cameron was born in 1879 at Pictou, Nova Scotia. Her eldest brother, William, was born in 1875 and soon after the birth of her younger brother, Archie, in 1881 her mother died.

In 1884 her father, John David Cameron, decided he would come west, and came by sailing ship from Halifax, around Cape Horn to San Francisco and so to Victoria that year. In August of 1884 he took up 160 acres in Shawnigan district on what is now the road bearing his name, Cameron-Taggart Road. He built a small house, cleared enough land for a garden and then went to work on railway surveys.

In 1888 he sent for his three children who had been living with their relatives at Pictou. The children travelled across Canada by train to Vancouver and then to Shawnigan. Although never a robust child and being frail all her life, Bella May became the housekeeper for the family, cooking, washing and doing all necessary chores.

In 1907 she married William Thomas Chapman, Jr., son of William Thomas and Sarah Chapman, who had come from Chatham, Ontario, to Telegraph Road, Cobble Hill in 1885.

After the death of her father in 1920, Bella May and her family moved to Cameron ranch which she inherited. There they raised sheep, hay, vegetables and fruit to support the family. She sold the farm in the early 1940s, moving to Cobble Hill and, with the death of her youngest daughter in 1951, moved again, this time to Cowichan Station. She passed away in 1954. Her husband had pre-deceased her in 1944.

In spite of ill health, Bella May Chapman overcame the tremendous obstacles that confronted a woman of that day who was on her own. She was known district-wide as honest and kind, a real pioneer.

Verna Beryl Coates (nee Macdonald)
(Mrs. Ralph Coates)
(also Smithe and Kier families)
1895-1983
by her daughter Eleanore V. Coates

I recall my mother, Beryl Coates, telling of one experience. In 1921, with two babies and a nurse, she took a job teaching at Eagle Bay on Shuswap Lake near Salmon Arm. There was a shortage of teachers and Mother taught in a one-room school for four months. She had about eight students, children of immigrant Germans, who had never been in school. One of the families gave her accommodation. Provisions were brought in by boat and ordering was one week for subsequent delivery the next.

When Mother "came out" at Christmas, with her children and nurse, she came out in a sled across the frozen lake to Notch Hill where she caught the train. It must have been quite an experience as she did not return to this area!

My mother was the only daughter of Eleanore Frances Elizabeth Macdonald and Joseph Macdonald. She was born in the Cowichan Valley, at Somenos, in October of 1895. Her mother, my grandmother, was the only daughter of Martha Kier Smithe and William Smithe, also of Cowichan who became the Premier of British Columbia, 1883 to 1887. Her maternal grandmother, Mary Jane Towers Kier, was possibly the first woman settler in Cowichan when she arrived at Somenos in 1862 where her husband, Archibald Kier, and eldest son, James, had taken land.

Shortly after my mother was born her parents went to Kamloops to live. They returned to Cowichan when she was four years old. Living in the Okanagan in the early days in the country meant using gasoline and coal oil lamps, hauling water from the well, et cetera. She never mentioned whether the family had these inconveniences in Somenos, possibly they had.

Prior to her marriage at St. John's Anglican Church in 1919, to my father, Ralph W.S. Coates, farmer, apple orchardist, and dairy farmer, Mother taught school at Abbotsford, Agassiz, Powell River and Duncan. She re-entered the teaching profession after my father died in 1936, teaching school in Langley until 1958 when she retired. When teaching, Mother was always involved with students' activities, sports days, and May Day pole dancing. She enjoyed teaching and took a keen interest in the students' later achievements.

My mother was a good cook, knitted clothes for the family and always was interested in the Anglican Church. She enjoyed gardening and entertaining friends. Naturally I am biased, but I believe my mother was a good citizen and with my father's involvement in our pre-teens years, brought my brother and myself up to be a good citizens too.

Mother would wish to be remembered as Beryl, not Verna, she never did like the name Verna.

After Mother's retirement, she took an interest in the Conservative Party, serving as Treasurer of the local organization.

Margaret Ann Dirom (nee Carter)
(Mrs. Andrew Dirom)
1875-1958
by daughter Edith McKnight and son, Gavin A. Dirom

I always felt Mother was a strong person with a mind of her own.

My mother, Margaret Ann Dirom, was a young woman of eighteen years when my dad brought her as a bride to Vancouver Island. He was section foreman for the Malahat section of the Esquimalt and Nanaimo Railway. Her first home was at Fitzgerald's Camp, a rather isolated spot near the summit of the Malahat mountain, in 1893.

I can remember Mother telling me that she was given strict orders not to let any strangers into the house when my dad was away (at camp) on the line. There were several occasions when men did show up on her doorstep asking for food. She would give them some of her homemade bread and send them on their way.

A gun was always kept in the house for protection as well as for hunting for meat. Mother learned how to handle guns as a girl of fifteen when she had come out from England to Port Orchard, Washington, United States.

My parents moved from the Malahat to Duncan in 1894, known as Duncan's Station then. The section house was originally situated on the side of the tracks where Buckerfield's is now located.

Mother had two miscarriages before the family of eight were born. All of these children were born at home. The three youngest children were born in a new section house on the other side of the tracks, now levelled. Her children were named Albert, Olive E., Rachael M., John J., Margaret A., Gavin A., Florence M., and Edith C.

Mother had the assistance of a midwife for most of the births. She timed her pains by the Canadian Pacific Railway clock which hung for years on the wall in our home.

As with most large families the older children helped the younger ones.

By today's standards my mother did not have very many conveniences. In the early days there was no electricity and water came from a well. Later on she did have a wooden washing machine with a wringer attached. The handle of the wringer was turned with one hand while guiding the clothes through with the other, being careful not to have too much thickness or else it would jimmy-up-the-works!

The very soiled white clothes would be soaked overnight in a tub and then boiled for a while in a boiler on top of the woodstove. The handkerchiefs would always soak overnight in salted water. All then were put in the washing machine. Mother would use Fels Naptha soap and the work clothes would be scrubbed on a wood scrub-board by hand. Blueing would be used to whiten the clothes and would be put in only on the last rinse.

During the winter months and on rainy days, the clothes would be hung to dry above the kitchen stove on a rack which could be raised and lowered. Mondays was always wash day and the following day, Tuesday, was ironing day. Flat irons were heated on the kitchen stove.

When the first fine days of spring arrived Mother would start her spring cleaning. Down would come the winter curtains, to be replaced by more sheer ones. Perhaps this was a custom she carried with her from England. Mother always took pride in her curtains, especially those that hung in the sitting-room, a room that seemed to be used only for company. The dining room was always where the family would gather in the evenings.

The blankets would be washed and often laid out on the grass to dry. The pillow cases would be washed while the goose feathers would be laid out on sheets to air in the sun. The rug would be beaten with a broom.

My dad had a large garden to feed the family and Mother's summers were taken up with preserving - jams, jellies, fruits and pickles. Mother and Dad always entered produce and bottled fruit in the annual Cowichan Fall Fair. Mother would enter her baked goods, too and one year she won a McLary range for her prize bread. This stove was still in use at our home until the late 1930s. (It was like an old friend and I shed tears when it was replaced by a new sawdust burner.)

The foods I always associate with my mother are rice puddings, which she made on Mondays, by simply pouring good, rich milk over grains of rice, with a little sugar and sprinkling of salt. While the pudding cooked slowly vanilla flavouring was added just before it thickened, along with a dash of nutmeg. For Sunday supper Mother would make a chocolate fudge layer cake or a coconut cream layer cake with a cream filling and a white butter icing. The top and the sides were rolled in toasted coconut. The fudge cake was iced with a dark chocolate icing and decorated with walnut halves.

Another of mother's favourites was a spice layer cake with a lemon filling. There was also the "wartime" cake which was made without eggs, johnny cake, gingerbread, gingersnaps and hermits.

Mother always believed in good, wholesome food and lots of it for her large family. She did not scrimp and nothing was wasted. Her philosophy, which she still had until her death at age eighty-four, was that no matter what problems came along, one could cope better on a full stomach!

Another of her philosophies was that there was no shame in having to wear clothes that were patched and mended, providing they were clean.

Church played a big part in my mother's life and she regularly attended the United Church both morning and evening services on Sunday. She lived by her principles and would not countenance criticism by hearsay of another. She would say, "I speak as I find," and refused to listen to gossip. She believed Sunday should be a day of rest. Mother did not approve of Sunday sports, not even swimming when I was very young, but later reconciled herself to the idea that there were far worse things one could do on that day. Card playing was not allowed in our house on a Sunday, and gambling was frowned upon at anytime.

Though reserved by nature, Mother did have a sense of humour. Often something would tickle her funny bone and she enjoyed a good joke.

I've not made any mention of the years after my dad's retirement from railroading in 1932 at the age of sixty-eight. I was fifteen and, of all the family, felt the depression years worst, I think. I was the last one to leave home.

My mother had her heartaches. My two sisters, Marguerite and Florence, were bedridden and died at the ages of twenty-six and twenty-seven years of tuberculosis before I was married in 1940. My brother, Johnny, was killed a month before in a railroad accident.

In her later years when she was no longer physically active Mother became an avid reader. She told me once that she had always wanted to be a teacher. Before I was born she did teach Sunday school at the Methodist Church.

Like all mothers she sacrificed for her family. I remember the day the piano she had purchased arrived from Nanaimo in a big wooden box. Not having had the chance to study music herself as a girl, she wanted this for her children. All five of the girls took lessons at one time or another from the music teacher, Miss Lillian Clack. As the youngest in the family, I was given the family piano, a sturdy Heintzman upright, when I was married in 1940, along with all the receipts showing how much mother had paid for it, $625 at twenty dollars each month. She requested that I not sell it at any time. I never have.

Edith Margaret Grassie (nee Castley)
(Mrs. Charles R. Grassie)
1880-1958
by her daughter E. Grassie

Edith was born at Rosgill, Westmorland, England and arrived in Cowichan with her parents Henry and Eliza Castley in 1887. They had been encouraged to come by their friends, the Norcrosses.

Edith attended school at Sahtlam. Her mother died when she was twelve

Charles Robert Grassie & his bride, nee Edith Margaret Castley, married in 1902.

years old so she took over the household chores, cooking meals for her father and brothers.

In 1902, she married Charles Robert Grassie and moved into a small house on the corner of Ingram and Jubilee Street, site of the present day post office.

Four children were raised there; Evelyn, Iris, Sidney and Vernon. Edith made all the girls' clothing while they attended school. Although she was a good cook, she enjoyed being out of doors more. Gardening was one of her joys, in particular pansies, of which she had a beautiful display each spring. She was also a keen golfer, playing at the Trunk Road golf course.

Margaret Grassie (nee Simpson)
(Mrs. Robert Grassie)
1856-1927
by her granddaughter E. Grassie

Born in Aberdeen, Scotland, Margaret came to Canada with her family to settle in Hamilton, Ontario. There she married Robert Grassie in 1874. They had four children, Alice (Pitt), Minnie (Hattie), Charles, and Agnes (Peterson).

In 1890 they travelled by train in a Colonist car that had a stove at one

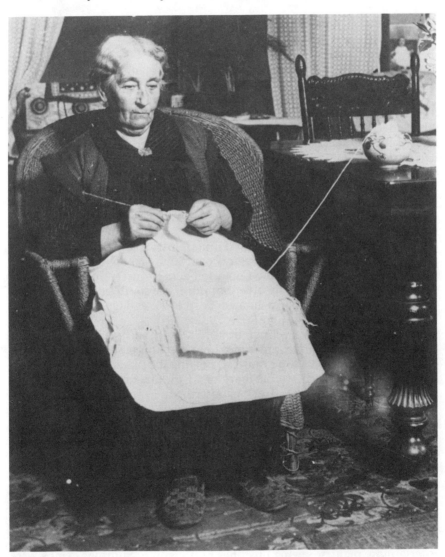

Margaret Grassie (Mrs. Robt. Grassie), nee Simpson, 1856-1927.

end on which to cook their meals. They settled in Cowichan where her husband started a blacksmith shop. Margaret was a staunch member of the Presbyterian Church.

Upon the death of her husband, she took in boarders to assist the family income.

Her grandchildren loved visiting their Grandma Grassie. She was usually sitting in her chair patiently knitting. She would tell them to help themselves to the large cookies that were stored in a big jar in the pantry.

Constance Clara Augusta Green (nee Dumbleton)
(Mrs. Ashdown H. Green)
1852-1937
by her grandson, J.W.A. Green

Constance Dumbleton came from England with her parents to visit family members living in Victoria. As her father, Henry Dumbleton, liked the city he decided to stay and had a large home built at 1750 Rockland Avenue. In 1888 Constance married Ashdown H. Green, a civil engineer who had settled in Duncan in 1869 and whose first wife had died leaving two children, Ashdown T. and Caroline. Because of his employment as a surveyor for the Indian Department in earlier years, Mr. Green was away from home a great deal, at times maintaining a home in Victoria.

The Green's home in Duncan was close to the Cowichan River, the house later becoming the nucleus of the Silver Bridge Inn still operating in Duncan. At that time the river flowed much closer to the house than it does now, and completely removed a tennis court one night while in flood. The gracious, two storey house stood on a ten-acre property, mostly meadow with large maple trees with the river bounding the south side. Mr. and Mrs. Green had two sons, Arthur Ashdown, born 1891, and Geoffrey Ashdown, born 1894.

Mrs. Green was an active member of St. Peter's Church as an organist and assisted with the choir sometimes holding choir practices at her home. Both she and Mr. Green were musical, playing the piano and harmonium, and he the violin as well. In the diary of a Cowichan resident, Mary Marriner, a party on January 1, 1897, is described:

"Mama and I walked to Mrs. Green's party in the evening. About fifty people were there. The house outside was prettily lit with Chinese lanterns which were hung on the veranda. Coffee, claret cup and cakes were served in the drawing room and more substantial refreshments in the dining room. Old Mr. Haynes played the violin and Mrs. Green the piano for the dancing for which the room upstairs was used."

Six weeks later there was a larger affair at which Mr. Haynes again played, but Mrs. Green, Mrs. Prevost and Mrs. Mutter took turns on the piano.

Life seems to have been a social whirl what with hosting tennis teas, entertaining, picnics, sewing meetings and visiting. Summer camps were held at Cowichan Bay and there was boating and fishing. Like many families at the time the Greens had a tennis court and also played croquet and ping-pong.

At the 1900 Agricultural Fair, Mrs. Green took prizes for her roses, geraniums and potted plants.

As her step-daughter was now of marriageable age, Mrs. Green took Caroline to many social affairs. In 1901 and 1902 there was the Fireman's Dance, the Somenos Bachelor's Dance, the Agricultural Ball in Duncan, the Hospital Dance at Chemainus, and others. In December of 1902 Caroline was married at St. Peter's Church to John Norie of Somenos.

In 1913 John and Caroline Norie emigrated to England and the Greens moved to Victoria, selling their Duncan property to Frank Price except for a cottage at 131 McKinstry Street which was retained as a summer home. In 1914 the cottage was given to Mr. Green's son, Ashdown T., as a wedding gift. At the present time (1985), the cottage stands very little changed since 1914.

The Greens lived in Victoria, in 1915 moving to the Dumbleton family home which Mrs. Green inherited. The 1918 death of their son Geoffrey, serving with the Royal Flying Corps in France, was a severe blow to his parents.

In 1927, Mr. Green died, Mrs. Green living on in Victoria until her death in 1937.

Ellen Green (nee Hills)
(Mrs. Mark Green)
1858-1933
by her granddaughter Betty Mellor

Ellen Hills was born July 1, 1858. She was the second of three daughters of James and Mary Hills of Ely, Cambridgeshire, England. Her father was a basket maker. Ellen Hills was a quiet person and it must have been very hard for her to leave her family, and England, to journey by herself to Canada. She left her home for Liverpool on May 21, 1890, and sailed for Canada on May 22, on the ship Sardinian. After a fairly uneventful trip she landed at Quebec. In a very brief account of her trip she wrote of Quebec as, "loveliest sight eyes have every beheld." The train journey across Canada was beautiful and the mountains spectacular.

Mark Green met her in New Westminster and they were married June 8, 1890, and came to his farm on Herd Road. After several owners the farm now belongs to Ellen's granddaughter and husband, Betty and John Mellor.

Ellen Green had four children who lived all or a good part of their lives in the Cowichan Valley. May Ellen (Nellie), then Mark James, Hannah Elizabeth (Bessie), and Dorothy Louise.

She kept house, looked after her family, baked, sewed, mended, but did no outdoor chores. The winter evenings were often passed playing cards.

The neighbours were friendly and visited as often as distance allowed. She lived here until about 1908 or 1909 when they moved to Hayward Junction. Part of this place is now owned by her grandson, Stan Green.

Ellen Green, nee Hills, 1858-1933, Mrs. Mark Green, c.1890.

Ellen next moved to Banks Road, off Gibbins Road, where she lived until her death in September of 1933. Her husband, Mark, had died about three weeks before.

Mary Ellen Guns (nee Henderson)
(Mrs. Edwin Guns)
1873-1952
by her daughter Helen Payne

It was in 1895 as a new bride that "Nell", Mary Ellen Guns, came to the Cowichan Valley from Northumberland, England. Her husband had pur-

Edwin & Mary Guns Wedding in 1896. Mary Ellen (Nell) Guns, nee Henderson, 1873-1952.

Edwin and Mary Ellen Guns with firstborn, Edwin, resplendent in 1897 wicker carriage.

chased one hundred and sixty acres at Kelvin Creek, Helmcken Land District, about two miles from the existing road. They lived in a log cabin for a time where the Indian women would sometimes come during the day and stare at Nell. Somewhat apprehensive, she would retreat to the cabin and hide under the table that was covered with a long cloth. The women also would peer through the window, eventually leaving her alone.

Nell and her husband lived at Lake Cowichan for some time and also at Mount Sicker where her second child, Elsie, was the first white child born there.

After living in Victoria they returned to Cowichan to manage the Pemberton estate at Fairbridge.

Nell raised four children, Edwin 1897-1917, Elsie (Herd) 1902, William 1902-1980, and Helen (Payne) 1916.

The Misses Hadwen of "Amblecote"
by niece Suzanne (Hadwen) Stewart

The five Miss Hadwens, along with their mother, younger brother, Seymour, and their aunt, Sarah King, followed their brother, Gaylard, to the home, Amblecote, which he had built for them in 1892, on the shores of Quamichan Lake.

Gaylard had come to Canada in 1885, first to study at the Guelph Agricultural College in Ontario, then to Vancouver Island to start a new home

The Hadwens of Amblecote, Quamichan Lake.
Anne Hadwen, nee Harrison, wife of Gaylard Hadwen. Came to Cowichan
Valley in 1892.
Group photo shows:

Seated front: Sybilla born 1875.
Seated middle row: Sarah King, nee Harrison; Anne Hadwen, nee Harrison;
and Bertha Hadwen, b.1865.
Standing back row: Ethelinda Hadwen, b. 1863; Gertrude Palmer, nee Had-
wen, b.1872; Agnes Hadwen, b.1867.

for the family following the death of his father. They were a Quaker family, able to trace their ancestry on the family tree to Thomas, a yeoman and clockmaker born in 1686. During the girls' younger years the family had moved to Lille, France, where they received their schooling. Their birth dates were: Ethelinda in 1863, Bertha in 1865, Agnes in 1867, Gertrude in 1872 and Sybilla in 1875.

The eldest, Ethelinda, did not accompany the rest of the family because she had already started a secretarial school for young gentlewomen in Edinburgh, a rather unusual profession for a women in those days; she came to Amblecote in about 1905.

c.1907 Hadwen house (A.M. Stewart). 6325 Lakes Rd.

The two youngest, Gertrude and Sybilla, went to San Francisco to become nurses in 1895. While there they experienced the great earthquake of 1906. This was a great worry for the family at home because of poor communication in those days. It was more than three weeks before all at Amblecote could relax with the knowledge that they were safe and had been very busy helping those less fortunate. Sybilla stayed in the United States with various nursing jobs and became Director of Women at Oregon State University. She specialized in dietetics, writing and teaching, and in 1934 published a cookbook entitled, "Good Foods for Better Health," which became well known to the hostesses and housewives of Oregon. She returned to Duncan in retirement and died in 1938. She and her mother, Anne, and Aunt Sarah are all buried in St. Peter's churchyard.

Gertrude, the only one of the girls to marry, became the wife of a widower, Richard M. Palmer, and brought up five step-children. They built a home on the westerly slope of Cowichan Bay, naming it Cedar Chines. Mr. Palmer, who served in the Tolmie Government of British Columbia, as Deputy Minister of Agriculture, and all their family became prominent in the Department of Agriculture or in developing the horticulture of Canada. Beatrice, the youngest, who still, in 1985, lives at Cowichan Bay, specialized in hybridizing lilies, and had customers throughout the world.

Agnes and Bertha remained at Amblecote providing a home for their brothers. Gaylard had various interests, one being the breeding of Hackney horses, some of which were shipped to the Boer War. An interesting sidelight to this was that by this time his brother, Seymour, who had studied veterinary medicine at McGill, was serving in the army and was able to look after the animals as they arrived in South Africa.

The Misses Hadwen's home on Jubilee.

The two sisters lived very gentle lives, providing a happy home for all who came to Amblecote. In those days there were a surprising number of relatives who came to see how the family was enjoying their new life. Also there were many young immigrants eager to start learning how to become farmers on the fields of Amblecote.

Bertha loved water-colour painting, and there are still many examples of her paintings in homes in Cowichan. Her favourite subject was the dogwood trees in their spring glory and also in their bright red autumn colours. Every Sunday she would row the family boat across Quamichan Lake to sing in the choir at St. Peter's church.

Agnes was always interested in trees and was responsible for helping Gaylard to plant many of the specimen trees which are prominent in the grounds and fields. The brother and sister started some of the holly trees which today are the ancestors of the present two thousand tree orchard well known throughout Canada. When Gaylard married Helen (Nellie) in 1918, Agnes and Bertha moved to the city where they lived out their lives at Edgewood, a splendid house on Cavell Street overlooking the town of Duncan. Ethelinda died in 1940, Bertha in 1942, and Agnes in 1946.

Gaylard and his wife remained at Amblecote until their deaths in 1951 and 1957. Now their daughter, Suzanne, with her husband, Alan, sons Gaylard and Ronald, and four grandchildren can be proud of nearly one hundred years and five generations at Amblecote.

181

Sybil Heppell (Nee McKinnon)
(Mrs. Edward Heppell)
1891 -
by her sister Flora Gowe

Sybil Heppell, the second daughter of Angus and Hannah McKinnon is a native daughter, as well as a pioneer of the Cowichan Valley. She was born when her father was operating a saw mill and living by Holmes Creek in 1891. She does not remember anything of her life there as her parents soon moved into town and lived on Station Street. She has vague memories of living in town as the family again moved on to the farmland that had been bought just north of Duncan.

Her memories actually began there. At that time gold had just been discovered in the Yukon and there was much talk of the hundreds of people who would be rushing to mine for gold. She persuaded her little brother to join her in pretending to be gold miners. At that time their mother had just been given a five dollar gold piece by visiting relatives. That was a wonderful gift at one time. So the two children "borrowed" the gift and a couple of spoons and went to dig for gold. There was a gravel pit in front of the house where they buried the coin, marked the spot, then went away and came back later and dug it up.

They did this a couple of times and then forgot to put in the marker. Dig as they would, the money was never found. Their mother was in such a state of shock that she probably could not punish the children anyway, but Sybil was discouraged from ever wanting to mine for gold again. Perhaps at some future time someone may find that money and wonder where it came from.

Another memory was of nearby graves of some Chinese workers who died while working on the railroad, building the Esquimalt and Nanaimo Railway. Occasionally a friend of one of the dead men would come to put food, et cetera, on the graves, but marauding animals soon took care of these gifts. A few years later the same men came to dig up the remains to send them back to China to be with their ancestors.

When Sybil was six years old she started school in the school house on the hill (later known as Zenith). Her first teacher was Miss Annie Carmichael, who became Mrs. Harry Holmes, and lived in the district for the rest of her life. The school was then one room with a bell tower. A big bell was rung twice every morning, once to warn the pupils that they had best hurry, and again at nine o'clock to remind them where they had best be.

The little girl liked school very much but some things were tiring for a six year-old child. The walk there was about one and a half miles and had to be made again in the afternoon. School benches had the old slatted seats and they were all of one size whether for a beginner or for a sixteen year-old boy.

With several grades for the teacher to handle, and the upper grades studying so many subjects, the little ones could not get much teaching time. This meant that those little ones had to spend a lot of time in those big seats busy doing work and dangling their legs, so they would sometimes get very cramped and numb. Sybil was lucky as Clara Duncan, one of the older girls who sat behind her, sometimes took her slate and tried to teach her a bit or show how to do things to keep busy.

After a few years another classroom was added. That made things a lot easier, for even though there were more pupils attending, having the extra teacher left time for the little ones to get more attention.

Those big classrooms were heated with one big stove in the centre of the room, so the heat was not evenly distributed. Each room had two entrances, one for girls and one for boys. There the coats, overshoes and lunches were kept. On very cold days the lunches could be brought right into the rooms, and if anyone forgot to do this it meant a very cold lunch. There were no playrooms or basements so on cold days when everyone stayed in at recess and lunch hour it became very noisy for the teachers, but they were usually patient.

There was no library and no extra reading books except for a big dictionary. There were maps and blackboards and a large picture of Queen Victoria, and one of King Edward VII was added later. The curriculum for the upper grades was very heavy, as to pass into high school it was necessary to write a government examination on eleven subjects. If one failed in one subject it meant repeating the whole grade. In spite of minimal equipment and busy teachers, Sybil and many others passed the whole course with no setbacks. There was no high school in Duncan then so this finished her formal education, but she always kept her interest in current affairs.

For the next few years she did not have the best of health so she stayed at home to help on the farm. She was very fond of animals, especially the young and helpless ones. She was a good nurse to any that were sick. One day she found a cold and weak little chicken that had lost its mother so she wrapped it up and kept it warm. Everyone told her that it was a hopeless case and would die, but she insisted she would raise it until it was grown up and sell for 60 cents. It did grow up and became a big rooster that was king of her yard and always did answer to the call of "60 cents"! Then she sold him for $1.25.

In her later teens she had to undergo a major operation, but then her health started to improve and she went out to work. Sybil was in the drygoods department in the Duncan Trading Company, a store on Station Street. She made many friends while working there for she was a pleasant and obliging clerk. A few years later she went to work for the British Columbia Telephone Company as an operator.

Sybil liked this work very much as this was more informal than it is now. She spent most of her time on night duty and she would often get calls from children checking on the time so they would not be late for school, or from someone wanting a 4:00 am call so he could go fishing.

It was thought that she was the second person in town to know the armistice had been signed on November 11, 1918. The telegrapher at the station got the news in the night and immediately telephoned Sybil and asked her to spread the good news, starting with the mayor. When she tried to telephone her own family she got no response. It was a party line with several parties on it and their own signal was six long rings. Before she finished everyone but her own family on that line had answered to see what the trouble was! Her family did not get the message until she got home in the morning. Her mother had died a few months earlier and though Sybil liked her work she left because she was needed at home. Life went on routinely for a few years until a disastrous fire destroyed all the farm buildings and it took the summer crop of hay as well.

Soon after that, Sybil received a severe burn on her hand which took several months to heal. When it was healed the fingers on that hand were inflexibly drawn up. She was still able to use the other hand to some extent but many of the things she liked to do were impossible.

Sybil continued on the farm until 1936. Until this time most of her life had been spent caring for others, but that year she married Ted Heppell who a few years before had bought twenty-seven acres of uncleared land at the end of Grieve Road and extending down to Crosland Creek. They had one son, Terrence, born in 1938.

Sybil and Ted still live in compatible retirement in their home they have occupied for the last 48 years.

Lucetta Maud Jaynes (nee Flett)
(Mrs. Philip Jaynes)
1893 -
Her own story

I was born in Somenos, 1893. My father was first station master at So-menos Station, that was before the Duncan Esquimalt and Nanaimo Rail-way station was built. When I was ten days old my parents moved to Victoria as Father then worked for the Provincial Government. My parents had land at the north end of Quamichan Lake and later on Father built a cottage there. Grandfather, John Flett, had come to Maple Bay from Victoria in March of 1870, and bought land on Herd Road. When my brother was in poor health he and I came to stay at the cottage and I looked after him. I was seventeen years old. Our parents left Victoria to come and live at Quamichan Lake after Father built the house which still is standing.

It was so pretty on the lake and around Stamps Road area. All the Quamichan hillside, where W.P. Jaynes had his farm, was beautiful, covered with oak trees. I used to walk through the trail to Woods' store on Herd Road. Mrs. Woods kept everything so clean. We used to skate on the lake and sometimes swam there in the summer. My school had been in Victoria, later I attended Columbia College in New Westminster, then took a course in typing and shorthand in Victoria, but I did not work at all.

On the farm I used to drive the horse and democrat to take eggs to the Creamery in Duncan. Sometimes, about the top of Alexander Hill, I would meet Lennie Bonsall with his delivery cart and team coming up the hill. My horse would get excited and dance backwards, the road was not very wide and he did not want to pass the team. I had to give him a flick or two of the whip to get him forward again.

One day I had overalls on while working in the barn where I was grooming the horse when Philip opened the door looking for my father. I was so embarrased I hid -- I did not want to be seen wearing overalls -- so that is

Lucetta Maud Jaynes, nee Flett.

how we got acquainted. We were married in Victoria in July of 1914 and just got back from our honeymoon and quite soon realized that there was going to be a war in Europe. The two brothers went but Philip did not have to go, only two of three sons were taken.

Before I was married, Campbell's clothing store in Victoria was where I bought my clothes. We went down on the train although the smoke and cinders used to make me quite train-sick. We always ran into Jaynes store on the corner of Canada Avenue and Station Street for peppermints to help me feel better.

After I married I had my clothes made by a dressmaker, Mrs. Colliard, I think. Miss Fraser made the children's clothes. She would come to my

The W.P. Jaynes home (built in 1882) is a local landmark at Tzouhalem and Jaynes Roads, essentially unchanged since this 1910 photograph.

This photograph of Jaynes home was taken in 1985, 75 years later.

home in the morning and spend the whole day while she worked on the sewing.

I had been brought up strictly Presbyterian and had not gone to dances when single but afterwards went to the Fireman's Ball occasionally with my husband. We lived quite close to Duncan as my husband worked there, but we did not entertain very much. I am not fond of large groups.

The photograph was taken of me a few months after I was married, by C.W. Sillence, photographer, in Duncan. The dress was a lovely soft wool in a gold shade with black trim. It was one of my favourite dresses.

Jessibelle Johnston (nee Herd)
(Mrs. Robert Johnston)
by her granddaughter Sharon Davis

Jessibelle Herd was born in the home of her parents, William and Susan Herd, during a snow storm in the late 1800s. She was delivered by Mrs. John Evans (Ruby Evans' mother) who walked the 4 or 5 miles from Auchinachie Road and back again, as the new father was not home and could

Family of William & Susan Herd c.1916.

Back row, l. to r.: Jeannette Marsh, Winnifred Van Norman, Marion Pickard, Ivy Johnston, Hazel Hodding.

Front row, l. to r.: Effie Thorpe, William Herd, Susan Herd, Jessibelle Johnston.

not accompany her. Jessibelle was named by her father both after his mother Isabelle and Susan's mother Jessie. She was the 4th of 7 daughters: Winnifred, Marion, Ivy, Jessibelle, Effie, Jeannette (Nettie) and Hazel.

It was a busy double household as William's brother Alec, his wife Jeanne and their 2 children Muriel (Peep) and Tom also lived with them. When Susan's mother died her father Joseph Salmond came to live with them until he died.

The large home was filled with many bedrooms, long stairways and long hallways. It sat on 350 acres of lovely woodsy land. Neighbours were not close but the Browns and Greens were the nearest. Cousin "Peep" was Jessibelle's best friend until she left home. None of the girls ever lacked for a playmate as there was always someone among the sisters who was willing to play. They enjoyed baseball and hiding in secret spots in the woods.

As this was a Methodist home, they were encouraged to learn to play hymns on the piano and organ by William, who was a loving but strict disciplinarian. Religion played an important role in the Herd household. Christmas was an austere and puritanical religious celebration, and so New Year's became a time which the girls came to enjoy more. Susan would decorate the house with beautiful green boughs, then entertain friends and neighbours.

The girls had many household and farm duties. After school they had to roam the fields searching for grazing cows. For three weeks in the summer they cocked hay. Jessibelle also picked strawberries for 30 cents a week, but money was never an important part of her childhood. In the summer the girls stayed with their favorite aunt, Jessie Thompson, in Cowichan Station, where they swam a great deal in the Koksilah River.

Jessibelle attended grammar school at Maple Bay School, then at Duncan High from the age of 13 to 17 years. Her own dream of becoming a milliner was set aside to comply with her father's wish that she become a teacher. In 1914 she attended Normal School in Vancouver for 6 months to receive part of her teaching certificate, transferring to Victoria from January to June of 1915 to complete her training.

After earning her certificate she taught school in Lake Cowichan for a year. She had 15 pupils of all ages who loved nothing more than to climb into her lap for a motherly hug. For half of the school year Jessibelle biked from Duncan to Lake Cowichan. The remainder of the year she caught the logging train at 4:00 a.m. The engineer blew the whistle in Duncan giving her the signal to be at the Hayward Junction. Her father would trot along beside the train to see her safely aboard. Since oil lamps were the only source of light she still cannot bear the smell of a lit match as it meant she had to "get up and get going."

After she left Lake Cowichan she taught at Johnston Road School in Sullivan (White Rock) near Vancouver. While there Jessibelle boarded with the Turnbull's whose daughter Maggie became her best friend. Together they attended many dances but not with the approval of the Turnbulls! The girls enjoyed listening to "Alexander's Rag Time Band". The clothing fad at the time was peg top skirts which were tight at the bottom and wide at the hip.

Dating was always done with a group, there was never any pairing off. At this time Jessibelle met neighbours by the name of Johnston who had 2 daughters and 2 sons, Bryce and Bob. Jessibelle soon started to date Bob with Bryce always in attendance. This dating consisted of leisurely drives in the country and attending concerts. Jessibelle's sister's fiance was killed in the war. To help ease her pain, Jessibelle invited her - Ivy Annette (Nennie) - to stay for a month. Soon Nennie was dating Bryce Johnston. The four of them, Bob and Jessibelle, Bryce and Nennie were nearly inseparable. Fortunately the war soon came to an end and the Johnston brothers and the Herd sisters had a double wedding at the Herd home (now on Green Road) on 2 October 1919. Jessibelle and Bob settled in Sullivan, White Rock and raised 5 children whose names were Tut, Lorna (Baker), Joyce (Rutledge), Maureen (Gay) and Marion (Graham). Sadly a young son Murray had died at 2 months of age.

Bob and Jessibelle moved back to the Cowichan Valley in the 1960s. Jessibelle is now alone after Bob's death in 1976 but lives in Duncan enjoying her family.

My grandmother, Jessibelle Herd Johnston has filled our lives and hearts with such love and laughter. How lucky we have been to know such a strong, dignified lady.

Hattie Vian Kier (nee Evans)
(Mrs. William Kier)
1890-1975
by her son Elden Kier

Hattie Vian Evans, the second oldest daughter of James and Hattie Evans, pioneer Cowichan residents, was born in a log cabin on what is now First Street, in Duncan. This part of the present Duncan was a portion of her father's land.

From this home Hattie, as a young girl, walked to the Duncan Elementary School located on the hill behind the present Courthouse. The school was later known as Zenith School and has since been demolished. The teacher at that time was a Miss Carmichael who married Harry Holmes.

In 1906 James Evans built a farmhouse at the corner of James and Garden Streets, North Cowichan. Hattie left this home in 1911 to marry William Kier, Provincial Constable, at St. Andrew's Presbyterian church.

Like many other young people of that time, Hattie and her groom travelled by the Esquimalt and Nanaimo Railway to Victoria where they spent their honeymoon. Upon their return the young couple built a home at what is now 2525 Alexander Street, North Cowichan.

Mrs. Kier's land, a part of the James Evans estate, is now the site of the North Cowichan Fire Department, the Community Centre, baseball diamonds and the Cowichan Agricultural Society lands.

William and Hattie Kier had four children - one son, Elden, and three

Mrs. Bill Kier, nee Hattie Vian Evans, 1890-1975.

daughters, Dorothy (m. Fiander), Verna (m.1 Ployart, m.2 Maher) and Aileen (m. Andrews).

Hattie Kier died in Vancouver in 1975.

Annie Lamont (nee Robinson)
(Mrs. John Lamont)
1869-1929
by her daughter Kate Robinson

Annie Robinson was born in Lambton County, Ontario, in 1869. Her father, Thomas Robinson was from Ireland and her mother, Mary Robinson, from Quebec. Mary Robinson's parents were United Empire Loyalists who had emigrated from the U.S.A.

Annie Robinson married John Lamont in 1898, and her husband came out to Duncan where he had relatives. The following year Annie Lamont travelled to join her husband. Their first house was at the corner of what is now Evans Street and Boundary Road, where they lived for two or three years. The next house was on Gibbins Road, Annie Lamont being the first white woman resident on that road. The Lamonts had three children - Alex, Kate (Robinson) and Ida (Cotsford).

Annie Lamont had been a teacher in Ontario but adapted to farm life, milking cows and doing other chores. She was active in the King's Daughters, the Women's Institute, the Presbyterian Church and was on the Girl Guide Committee.

She passed away in Duncan March 14th, 1929.

Jeannette Laurenson (nee Mebius)
(Mrs. Edward Laurenson)
1872-1929
by her niece Beatrice Cooke

Jeannette Laurenson, nee Mebius, School teacher in Cowichan 1892.

I remember Aunt Nettie (Jeannette) as a tall and blondish, kind and fun loving lady, but as she taught in various places away from Nanaimo, I did not know her as well as her sister, Lucy Aylmer Mebius, who taught continuously in Nanaimo. Jeannette won the Governor General's Medal in 1888 at Central High School and I have a volume of Wordsworth's poems awarded to her in 1888 for mental arithmetic. Illustrated with quaint old fashioned drawings by Henry Dell, it is a very posh book with a padded cover showing a vase of flowers, treated with varnish.

In Somenos she stayed with a Norcross family, a young son of which was Edward whom she was enjoined to address as "Mr. Edward." The distance of several miles on wagon trails to Maple Bay did not deter her and others from walking there for picnics. Later she taught Oscar Brown who became a well known builder, at Duncan and Basil Kier still later at Lake Cowichan and Youbou. When I asked the latter what he remembered about her he said, "She was strict."

At one time she taught at Nakusp in the southern interior where she said the sun went down at four in the afternoon because of the high mountains. She also taught at Beaver Creek near Alberni which was where she met the man she married, Ted Laurenson.

Ethel Leather (nee Simpson)
(Mrs. Frank S. Leather)
1862-1957
Compiled by the Researchers

The following biography of Ethel Leather has been drawn from several sources which include the first volume of her diary, a newspaper interview conducted near the end of her life, and an interview with her niece, Miss Peggy Simpson.

Ethel Leather, nee Simpson, was born in Chester, England. She is remembered by her niece as a tall brunette. It was an artistic family so Ethel gained most of her artistic training at home.

In May of 1888 she and her husband, Frank, together with her sister Gaynor and brother Harry, left Liverpool for Quebec, arriving in Victoria on May twenty-ninth.

The first volume of the early diary which Ethel Leather kept after her arrival on Vancouver Island is in the Provinicial Archives, and most of the following notes are taken from that.

The Leathers spent several days in Victoria while preparations were made for their trip to the Cowichan Valley to search for a farm. They appear to have had good connections as among their invitations in Victoria was one: "tennis at the home of Sir Matthew Begbie." Ethel describes the famous first Judge of B.C., knighted in 1885, as a "fine, good-looking and pleasant man."

On June 11, 1888, the Leathers arrived at Duncan's Station. The family's temporary home was a camp, consisting of three tents and a kitchen built with boards, on Colonel and Mrs. Matthew's property. The large tent was

Early rectory at St. Peter's Church from a watercolour by Mrs. F. Leather.

where the meals were eaten and where Harry, Pat and Dennis slept. Of the two smaller tents, one was for Gay and Hannah, the other for Frank and Ethel.

Over the next few weeks the party struggled with constant rain. Fir boughs were spread on the floor to improve the damp conditions and ferns were used as tablecloths. The Matthews supplied blankets and chairs, the Cargills provided quilts.

Neighbours were kind, supplying food, including milk and butter from the Matthews and preserves sent by the Cargills. Their meat which was venison, hung on lines from the trees, a practice not without its drawbacks for one night a cougar made off with the lot!

Considering the circumstances under which the Leathers were living, they seem to have had quite an active social life. The diary records a ten-mile walk to Somenos Lake, tea (with strawberries) at the Matthews, church, a walk to the Cowichan flats and a visit to the Johnstones who had a farm near Somenos Lake.

Frank continued to look for a farm and Ethel commented "people want awful prices for their land." They lunched one day at Mrs. Marriner's, viewed the property, but decided the three thousand dollars she asked was beyond their means. They eventually found a property in the Cowichan Bay area. In the interview with the Cowichan Leader late in her life, Mrs. Leather refers to this property as "the old Comar house."

On June 28 the couple went to the first meeting of the tennis club which was just being organized. A ride home with a Bay resident prompted the comment, "Society is mixed here. Mrs. X is a kind, unpretentious woman from somewhere near Chester."

The diary mentions many food-gathering excursions, including fishing for trout and salmon, shooting sand-hill cranes, grouse, teal, grebes, pigeons and gulls, and picking red currants. The preserving of apples, pickling of mushrooms, while putting some aside for ketchup, making butter and learning to milk are all part of the life of the early months.

On July 12th the new property is first mentioned and by August 16th preparations are being made to move from the tents to the farm. In October the house is described as being "slowly constructed".

Social activity continues with Dr. and Mrs. Rowbotham calling. Ethel, who could be frank in her diary, refers to them as, "Dr. and Mrs. Pomposity." Mrs. Ward hosts picnics and dances and many young ladies from Victoria come, such as the two Misses Dunsmuir, Miss Charles, Miss Pemberton and Miss Hills. Other visitors include Mr. and Mrs. Mainguy, Mr. Elkington (who later married Gay Simpson), Mr. Dwyer and Mrs. Maitland-Dougall.

The diary records a view of Indian homes when they were in the transition period. In quest of a "clean woman" to smoke her salmon, Ethel visited an Indian barn. In the darkened barn, she found one corner filled with shelves holding crockery. A shrivelled-looking woman was warming her hands over a fire which burned on the earth floor.

A piano arrived on the 25th of October, thus providing greater diversion from the chores of setting up a home.

While the Leathers generally stayed in Cowichan, there was a period of two years which they spent in Sooke, on the southwest corner of Vancouver Island, care-taking a sheep ranch. Sooke was then a remote backwoods with only one other white family there, three miles distant at that.

Peggy Simpson, a niece of Ethel Leather's, was sent to her aunt and uncle from New Zealand for reasons of health in 1911. By this time, Frank Leather had established a real estate and financial business (1907) in which he was joined by H.W. Bevan in 1910. Peggy Simpson made her home with them until their deaths, becoming a substitute daughter for the child they had lost, an infant son who died in England. At this time the Leathers were living in their home, Mereside, on Indian Road where they remained almost to the end of their days.

Ethel Leather had many hobbies, most of which produced some much needed income. She became famous in the district for her knowledge of horticulture. She was a Fellow of the Royal Horticultural Society, and her garden reflected that knowledge. Lavender was one of her specialities and she found a sale for it all across Canada. Generally she sold it by the pound but often she made it up into little sachets. Almost to the end of her long life she was still stitching these little bags. A variety of spring flowering bulbs were also an important product of the garden.

Another product Mrs. Leather marketed all across Canada were flies for fishermen. She ordered her supplies from England, and as a fisherwomen herself, she had a sound idea of what fish liked. (Sometimes she was relegated to the role of oarswoman for her husband and a friend.)

When these occupations did not keep her busy enough she sketched Cowichan scenery and painted in water colours. These paintings also produced some income.

Miss Simpson recalls that her aunt and uncle used to drive into town to the Farmer's Market with the buggy piled high with baking and garden produce.

Ethel Leather was still painting at the age of ninety-five when the Leader interviewed her. During her last years she lived in a succession of boarding homes, dying in 1957. Her husband had predeceased her in 1951.

<h3 style="text-align:center">Rose May Lovell (nee Evans)
(Mrs. Wilfred H. Lovell)
1894-1957
by her granddaughter Pat Feeney</h3>

Rose May Evans, daughter of James and Hattie Evans, was born in a log cabin on what is now Evans Street in Duncan on May 3, 1894. Unfortunately, the cabin is no longer there.

Rose May Lovell, nee Evans.

June 1913 — Wedding picture of Rose May Evans & Wilfred Lovell.

Back row, l. to r.: Hattie & Bill Kier, Emma & Frank Evans, George Lovell, Albert (Jose) Evans and Eddy Evans.

Seated, l. to r.: Alice Malbon with Violet on her lap, Henry William Lovell, Hattie Vian Evans, The Bride & Groom, Eliza Harriet Lovell, Jim Evans.

She was the fifth of seven children born in Duncan to James, who was then aged 54 and Hattie, who was 35. Her father was born in Berriew, Montgomeryshire, Wales April 10, 1840 and Hattie was born in Indiana June 25, 1859.

Rose attended school in a one-room schoolhouse on or near the Indian Reserve.

Rose was 12 years old when her father passed away. After her two older sisters, Hattie and Alice, were married, Rose helped out with housework, cooking and looking after her brothers.

Activities such as a ballroom dancing and sports were strong interests for her. She had won prizes for her dancing. She would sometimes travel by horse and buggy as far as Nanaimo to go to a dance and would stay overnight.

Before her marriage, she worked as a telephone operator in Duncan. On June 30, 1913 at age 19, Rose May Evans married Wilfred Henry Lovell, son of Henry William Lovell and Eliza Harriet Crossman, English immigrants then living in Vancouver. Wilfred, known as Harry, was working on the E & N Railroad as a steam operator with Rose's brother Frank, and so met Rose.

Rose and Harry moved to a rooming house in Vancouver as Harry had a job there. On January 14, 1915 their first born son, Roy Evans Lovell was heralded into the world by the sounds of firetruck bells clanging ... the rooming house where he was born was on fire!

In 1916, Rose, Harry and their infant son Roy all lived in a railroad car. Harry's job was to clear the tracks of debris from slides. He had to be ready to go at a moment's notice anytime of the day or night. My father, Roy can remember his mother saying that she never knew where they'd wake up.

It was in Burnaby that Rose and Harry raised their family of three; Roy Evans, Harold Wilfred and Audrey May.

Rose died on the fifth of February in 1957 at the age of 62. Behind she leaves a legacy of not only family, but of a family who reveres the past.

Hannah McKinnon (nee Berrigan)
(Mrs. Angus McKinnon)
1865-1918
by her daughter Flora Gowe

Hannah McKinnon was born in Goshen, New York of Irish parents who had immigrated from Ireland after the famine of 1849 and 1850. When she was in her early years the family moved farther west where there were more opportunities; railways were being built across the prairies and more land was being opened up for homesteading. When they were still in Minneapolis her father was stricken with a terminal illness.

With a growing family and a bed-ridden husband, her mother had to be the breadwinner. So she decided to file on a homestead herself and moved onto one at Hastings, Minnesota.

Here Hannah had her first experience at rugged pioneering. She had many stories to tell of winter blizzards when they were shut in for days and had to keep a rope strung from the house to the barn so that they could find their way to care for the animals. She recalled those families caught in the storms and frozen to death, or if they were fortunate enough to find a house, were taken in and kept until the storm was over, regardless as to whether they were friends or strangers. Sometimes a wife would not know for days whether or not her husband was safe. Against that she told of the cyclones and tornadoes in the summer when on seeing a certain black cloud in the sky everyone took refuge in the closest cyclone cellar.

It was a hard life, but in many ways a good one. Everyone was willing to help his neighbour. Winter was the time for socializing, and their main fun was visiting with a sing-song or dancing. Hannah loved dancing when she was young but never danced after she came to Cowichan, though she did go occasionally to visit with some of her friends there.

When she was asked how they could tolerate all those awful winters she always replied, "We always prepared for them." Those preparations must have taken up most of their summers.

They were very self-sufficient and she spoke of making their own candles sometimes of sheep tallow in an emergency, or of catching rain water for washing, (melting snow, too), as this was soft water and they could do their hair in it. The well water was hard.

One big drawback in their lives was the difficulty in getting much chance to go to school. The schools were far apart and the storms in winter kept the children home and in the summer they were needed on the farms.

Hannah's twin (and only) sister had died but there were five boys, some quite young, but some old enough to help their mother carry on. Hannah was now able to leave home and go to work. About the only work available was hotel work either as cooks or as waitresses. She worked as both. Grand Forks, North Dakota was the nearest town so that was where she started.

It was about this time that she met her future husband, Angus from Ontario. He was working at railroad building in North Dakota at the time. They were married at Valley City, North Dakota, in 1886 and shortly thereafter went up to Winnipeg to work for the Canadian Pacific Railway. Its western terminal was then at Port Moody but the line was being extended into Vancouver. They decided to come west and travelled by train to Port Moody and then by boat to the new city. Shortly afterward they were able to be present for the celebrations at the arrival of the first passenger train in Vancouver in 1887.

Hannah had a cousin who owned a hotel in Vancouver and she helped him for part of the two years she lived there. Angus had many jobs, mostly in logging. In 1889 he heard of a sawmill to rent in Duncan, he came to see it and rented it from the Reverend David Holmes. His wife stayed in Vancouver as she was expecting a child, and their first daughter, Anne, was born in October of 1889. She was five months old when mother and baby came to Duncan in March of 1890.

The mill was on Holmes creek just below the falls and not far beyond where Gibbins Road turns off from what now is known as Lake Cowichan or Trunk Road.

While there, mother cooked for some of the mill crew. She had one amusing story she used to tell about a little pig that she was raising. He soon got to know the friend was the person feeding him. One afternoon she started out to Somenos Road and was some distance on her way when she heard a squeal behind her. She turned and little piggy was close behind her. She took him home, put him in his pen and started out again. This time she had not gone very far when he was following her again. By the time that she had taken him home again and put him in his pen, she decided that her visiting would have to wait for another day and that he should have a stronger pen. Maybe he was just as lonesome as she was.

Before they left the mill another daughter was born, this one was named Sybil.

Her husband had some horses and equipment and they started freighting goods to Cowichan Lake over twenty-five miles of devious road. He had some very frightening experiences; one trip took three days just to reach his destination as the snow drifts were so bad that the horses were exhausted and the howling of the wolves terrified them. At home his wife and children did not know what was happening to him.

At this time, he was acquiring one hundred and twenty acres of land just north of Duncan which straddled the Esquimalt and Nanaimo Railway tracks. They built a small house on it and moved in with their three children. A son, William, was born while they were living on Station Street.

Then came their next struggle with pioneering. The house was so small and the water had to be brought up from the creek by the railway tracks. It was oil lamps now and wood-fired stoves. It did not matter how hot the weather was, the stoves had to be kept going most of the day to heat water, do baking, preserving and to heat irons for the ironing. There was plenty to do.

The land had to be cleared before crops could be planted so no money came until harvest time. Mother had to find an income so as soon as they could keep a cow and some chickens she did. As she was able to get some help from the school age children - and children learned early to help - she started to sell the surplus milk. If she had more milk than she could sell, she made butter from the cream and sold that too. The hens also provided a few eggs to be marketed.

In the course of a few years when more land was cleared and able to support more cattle, a larger house and farm buildings were built on the top of the hill near where the Extended Care Hospital is now. It was good to have more room but as winter came on a bigger problem arose. No water was available. It still had to be brought up from the same creek. Sometimes it was brought up in barrels by a team of horses and a wagon, but often carried by bucket too. When the town brought in a waterworks system, the water was piped right into the house and dairy.

Hannah was still finding ways to increase her income so she started raising ducks and geese. The geese were marketed at Christmas and the ducks were sold at the Chinese New Year. Also, when a sawmill was opened on the flats near Somenos Lake, she supplied many of the meals for the workmen.

The dairy business was growing and by the time the city was incorporated it was a family affair and a new method had to be found to market it. The idea of selling milk in bottles was new so a full set of steam operated machinery was installed to wash and sterilize bottles and dairy utensils. There is often fear of a new idea and so there was much opposition from many of the customers who thought it was impossible to treat bottles this way. In time the customers were convinced and accepted it, so the sale of milk in bottles began.

Hannah was a very good cook and her speciality was bread-making. She took many prizes at the fall fair shows, both at home and in Victoria. When Vancouver started having a fall show she started taking her bread there and was often successful. Going the round of those fall fairs was her annual holiday.

By the time the First World War started, a telephone was available and since her health was declining she got a great pleasure from being able to chat with her friends by telephone. She had many friends, for as many of her neighbours had a long walk into town they would often drop in when passing. They knew there would be a cup of tea to help them on their way.

She never did get home to Minnesota again but many of her relatives came to visit her. In the late 1890s, when her mother sold her farm and retired, she came out, too, and had a visit with her daughter.

The dairy was under Hannah's supervision until her death in April of 1918. She had been ailing all spring but had an acute heart attack and died quite suddenly at the age of fifty-three.

Her work was carried on after her death by her son, Lachlan, but in 1928 all the farm buildings with the crop of hay were destroyed by fire that fall and the dairy never really recovered.

There are three of Hannah's five children still living in the Cowichan Valley, all retired and they are: Sybil and her husband Ted Heppell, Flora Gowe, and Lachlan McKinnon. Also there are seventeen grandchildren and sixty great-grandchildren scatted through British Columbia, all carrying on in the tradition that Hannah set of industry, independence and citizenship. There are forty-one great-great-grandchildren who are being prepared to do their part when their turn comes to carry on the tradition.

Edith March (nee Wardroper)
(Mrs. Henry March)
1860-1943
by her granddaughter Sue Bolton

When my grandmother, Edith March, died, I was only about four years old so I never really knew her. She was apparently several years older than her husband.

Jim Wardroper, a grandson of my grandmother's brother (for whom Wardroper Bay on Cowichan Lake is named), is under the impression that his grandfather already was married when he came out to Vancouver Island. Jim Wardroper's father was born in Victoria in 1892 and there was possibly an older brother who died in infancy. It appears that Edith came out from England to help her sister-in-law with the babies. A story that I was told as a child was that Henry March used to row ten miles from his farm at Honeymoon Bay to the Wardropers on a Sunday, eat dinner with them, then stay until it was time to row home again. Finally one Sunday he rowed Edith out to one of the islands in the lake and refused to row her home until she consented to marry him.

I believe my grandmother spent her winters near Maple Bay where her two sons could go to school. Henry, meanwhile, went to work on the railroad to make money to further develop his farm. Steel was being laid in 1912 for the CPR (E & N) Railway branch line to Cowichan Lake. Edith March's first home as a bride was a log cabin, later replaced by a log house built in 1900 which is still standing.

There were two sons, John Owen (Jack), born in 1896 and killed in an accident in 1928. The other son, Charles, my father, was born in 1898 and died in 1977.

Isabella Allan Mutter (nee Morrison)
(Mrs. James Mitchell Mutter)
1849-1933
by her grandson Hamish Mutter

Isabella Morrison, daughter of Alexander Morrison, was born in 1849 at Kilmun, Holy Loch, Scotland. She was educated in London, majoring in

Isabella Allan Mutter, wife of Major J.M. Mutter, c.1912.

music under the direction of Symon Reeves. Returning to Scotland she became interested in medicine, assisting her uncle who was a doctor. She was particularly interested in the poor and underprivileged.

In 1873 she was married to James Mitchell Mutter in Glasgow and settled in Bowmore, Islay, where her husband and his two brothers owned and operated a distillery.

In 1889 she, her husband and six children (three boys and three girls) left the Island of Islay and stayed in Glasgow for a short time. It was there they decided to seek a colonial life in which to raise their family. They sailed from Glasgow to Montreal on the Buenesarian, three weeks at sea, then crossed Canada by Canadian Pacific Railway.

They chose Vancouver Island, settling on the two hundred acre farm which they purchased from James Kier at Somenos in 1891. Until this time Mrs. Mutter knew little if anything of cooking and such household chores. There were always servants at home, but it was not long before she learned this art and became a very good cook.

Other talents came to the front. She soon found out there were many settlers in need of help such as she was able to provide with medical aid, food, and clothing. In her own quiet way she saw to it that help was available.

After her family grew up she continued her efforts largely through St. Mary's, the Anglican Church at Somenos. Later on through her daughter Blanche (Mutter) Hamilton, a charter member of the King's Daughters'

J. Islay Mutter with his first car in Duncan, a 1910 Rover, right hand drive!

Hospital, Mrs. Mutter provided knitted wear and hospital bedding. During the first World War (1914 to 1918) her home was put to good use by the Red Cross in order to make up supplies, such as first aid kits and hospital clothing. She and her army of helpers met two days a week for four years to carry on this work.

In May of 1920 her husband, J.M. Mutter died. She retired from her very active life of helping the needy.

Blanche Louise Norcross (nee Hargrave)
(Mrs. Harold Norcross)
1882-1920
by her daughter Elizabeth B. Norcross

My mother's life illustrates the fact that you cannot put arbitrary dates on a pioneer period. Both her mother, Sarah Jane Hargrave, and my other grandmother, Maria Norcross, passed a portion of their adult lives in Cowichan in an earlier period than she did. Nevertheless, I think that she was most truly the pioneer woman of the three.

She was born in Melbourne, Ontario, and came out to British Columbia with her parents when she was six years old. Her mother was a native-born Canadian, her father English. They were widow and widower with sons

Mrs. Blanche Louise Norcross, nee Hargrave, 1882-1920.

from their previous marriages when they married.

The Hargraves lived briefly in Vancouver, then Victoria before settling at Burgoyne Bay on Salt Spring Island. While living there my grandfather, later with my mother manning a second pair of oars, rowed across Sansum Narrows to Maple Bay for supplies.

Later again, they moved to Maple Bay and lived in the first Agricultural Hall which had been converted to a house.

With her mother's health failing and her father an elderly man, my mother at the age of 15 took charge of the housekeeping and the garden, the latter with some assistance from her father.

When she married at the age of 22, her new home was a developing farm, a "stump ranch." She was a full partner with my father in the work of improving the farm and in the care of the livestock they raised in their mixed farming operation. This was not a hardship as the outdoor work was her delight. At the same time, she cared for the babies and the house, preserved fruit, made bread, sewed and knitted for the family like all pioneer women.

Her reading time came when she knitted. She could do both at once without missing a word or a stitch. She also found time for frivolous occupations like embroidery and lace-making.

My memories of her are mostly of the later war years when my father was still Overseas. At that time she had ploughing and haying to do, but still found time to blast out a few of those stumps.

When school consolidation was proposed, to begin in the 1919-1920 school year, she took time out from chores to drive about in horse and buggy, getting names on a petition to support the closing of one-room schools in the District and busing the children to the Duncan Elementary School.

A few years after her marriage, her parents had to make their home with her. My grandmother now required an increasing amount of nursing care until her death in 1910. When my father went Overseas, he insisted that Grandfather enter the King's Daughters' Hospital, then more a convalescent home than an acute care hospital.

There were two summers that cousins spent the school holidays with us, and the children from the motherless neighbouring farm spent most of their playtime with us. It was a busy life.

There were six children, Harold Hargrave, Iris Hope (Crabb), James Cedric, Elizabeth Blanche, Sarah Louise, and Charles Warren (died in infancy).

Maria Norcross
(Mrs. James Norcross)
1840-1920
by her granddaughter Elizabeth B. Norcross

Shortly after the Esquimalt and Nanaimo Railway passenger service was begun, James Norcross, my grandfather, arrived in Cowichan accompanied by his second son, Harold, then sixteen.

James bought a partly developed, one hundred-acre farm on Somenos Lake, the core of which property is now owned and occupied by Mrs R.H.M. Shaw. Father and son worked at readying the property for family occupancy. The next year, 1887, Maria Norcross and the three younger children joined them. (The eldest son remained in England to complete his education).

My grandmother, a few years older than her husband, was then a middle-aged woman, and I do not think it had been her choice to leave the comfort of a city home with the services of household help for pioneering life in Canada. She did learn to make butter, good butter, too, but I think she was happier assisting her husband with his books when he became North Cowichan's municipal clerk in 1892.

Grandmother departed so far from the model of a pioneer farm wife that she would not learn or allow her daughters to learn to milk. She argued that if the men were away from the farm on some business and knew that there was someone at home who could do the milking, then there would always be reasons why they could not get back in time for that chore.

The family came from Liverpool, England, where James had been headmaster of Liverpool Institute. There were five children, James Edward, Harold, Elizabeth Agnes, Norman and Irene (Rene) Maria.

Jessie Russell Norie (Nee Simpson)
(Mrs. Louis Fleetwood Norie)
1874-1971
by her granddaughter Barbara Elliott

In 1899 grandfather, Louis Fleetwood Norie, purchased property on the corner of what is now Howie and Koksilah Roads, on the road from St. Andrew's Church to Fairbridge. This was prior to his marriage. Part of the property on one side of the creek became the Burnett farm and the part across the road was sold to someone else.

His sisters, Eva and Rosie, lived with him at various periods before and after his marriage which took place in 1903. In 1910 Eva married Noel Souper, a teacher at Cowichan Bay. Rosie married soon after my grandparents, and her husband was killed in the First World War in 1916.

Grandfather came out from Scotland first to Arizona and then to the Cowichan Valley. Several other Norie families came out later, most notably Mr. and Mrs. Harry Norie (wife Lulu). It is not clear who suggested the Cowichan Valley.

The home my grandfather had prepared burned down while Grandmother was expecting her first child, my mother. The present house, Norns, was built in 1903 and 1904. My grandparents had married in Scotland in 1903 and, sadly, all the wedding presents were lost in this fire.

Grandmother had four daughters over a period of about fourteen years, which kept her busy. These were Marjorie, Ulrica (Buster), Joy and Elisabeth.

Family stories suggest that among the sights particularly strange to Grandmother were humming-birds and skunk cabbages. The former were rather fearsome and the latter deceptive in appearance since they are attractive until one has closer acquaintance with the scent!

Grandmother always had Scottish maids to help, young women who were sent out one at a time. Her sister interviewed in Scotland and then my grandparents paid the maid's way out. After a decent interval the ladies seem to have married or to have moved to something better. One went to the Dunsmuirs, a noted Vancouver Island coal mining family. There were Chinese for outdoor work and for a brief time one Chinese man served as indoor help (probably between maids).

Grandmother always loved going for long walks with children, pram and dogs. As a child, I also remember her still liking an afternoon walk.

She taught my mother and Buster before they were big enough to go to Phipps Road to a small school run by various ladies, Miss Lavington and Miss Hodges each for short periods and then Miss Ashdowne who called it Uppington School.

I believe Granny liked sewing generally and certainly did beautiful smocking. When Mother was little but dutifully knitting for Kitchener during the First World War, she suspects Granny would re-do the work to make it more acceptable!

Granny played the violin and along with Mrs. Gerry Knocker, and my grandfather singing or playing banjo, and with Mrs. Neel on piano would perform at Red Cross concerts. There were family and neighbour tennis parties at the Norns although Granny did not play at South Cowichan like my grandfather did. My grandparents played whist, then auction bridge and then contract bridge as those became popular. My grandmother continued to play bridge for many, many years. She sometimes walked to Lulu Norie's and Mrs. Fall's to play bridge. This would be at Hillbank area where the Nories and Falls presently live.

Before the younger sisters were born and while my mother and Buster were little my grandparents and the children made two trips back to Scotland going across Canada by train and then by boat. Granny's sisters visited Cowichan and other relatives came as well. There are several pre-1920 pictures of my mother and her sisters in fancy dress or costume in different years so there must have been children's parties as well as tennis and cards.

My mother lived at Cowichan until 1940 with the exception of a term at St. George's in Victoria which later was amalgamated with St. Margaret's. Buster went there, too as well as Joy who attended St. Margaret's School and Elisabeth to Queen Margaret's school in Duncan.

Unlike my grandmother, my mother loved animals and the farm and the outdoors in general. Granny was always tolerant or perhaps she just was of a different generation with different attitudes. Pictures show my mother with a dog which was nearly always an Airedale while Buster had a doll. Mother seems to have helped with gardening, farm chores, animals, the fields, hauling wood and she loved riding even as a little girl. In the 1920s and 1930s she was very active with horse shows and had a small dairy herd. She was also a Guide Captain and played tennis and a lot of badminton. Buster and Eric Leney were much better players, however!

Mother also taught Joy and Elisabeth during what must have been their elementary grades, and also taught one or two other district children. This was somewhere in the 1920s time frame.

I really have a number of female ancestors who lived in the Cowichan Valley prior to 1920, such as my grandmother, her sisters-in-law, my mother, three aunts and some cousins.

Grandmother was in her nineties when she died.

Hattie Owen (nee Whidden)
(Mrs. James Alfred Owen)
1888-1955
by her daughter Gwen Smith

Hattie Owen came to Duncan when she was a child of about two years. She grew up in the home on Ingram Street and attended public school at what was later the Zenith School. There was no high school. Before her marriage in 1910 she worked at Pitt and Peterson's store where Eaton's store now is located. After her marriage she lived for a short time in Prince Rupert and Nanaimo, then in Duncan on Garden Street, the house being next to Evan's field. When her husband went overseas in 1916 she and the three children went to live with her parents. When she was widowed in 1919 (her husband dying in England during the flu epidemic while still in the army), she made her home permanently with her parents until they died.

As a young woman she belonged to the Good Templars Lodge and after the war she was a member of the Methodist United Church.

The house on Garden Street was not an old one and life was not too different then, but one early memory is of Mr. Lamont delivering milk with the milk cans in a little cart. He measured the milk and poured it into a jug which our mother would take out when he arrived.

For a while from around the end of the war in the years 1919 and 1920, she drove the rural mail delivery to Maple Bay and also drove a "jitney" delivering parcels or taking occasional passengers.

For many years during her daughters' time in the Guide movement she was a faithful member of the Guide committee as it was known at that time. During this time the Guide Hall on Cairnsmore Street was built. She was given a thanks badge for her work which was quietly done in the background not holding office. She belonged to the Epworth League at one time.

She grew up in the Alderlea Methodist Church and later belonged to the Duncan United Church until her death.

Anna Jane Prevost (nee Fry)
(Mrs. Charles Prevost)
1853-1923
by her grandson Gerald Prevost

My grandmother, Anna Jane Prevost, came to Vancouver Island with her mother, Mrs. Henry (Jane) Fry, and the three older children from Devon, England, in 1864. Her father had preceded the family in 1862 and was managing a farm in North Saanich. In 1867 he went to San Francisco, leaving his family in Victoria. He returned in 1869 and the next year moved with his wife and children to a farm at Chemainus.

In 1873 Anna Jane married Charles Prevost eldest son of Admiral Prevost, Commander of the Pacific Fleet. The couple lived in Victoria until about 1895. Anna's pleasant life there as the wife of a prominent man came to an end when he fell afoul of the law. It was then that she moved to Quamichan Lake to a property known as The Barn, where she remained until about 1910. Later again she moved to McKinstry Road in Duncan.

She had a considerable struggle supporting her family single-handed until her husband was a free man once more. When her daughter Edna's marriage failed, she undertook the upbringing of her granddaughter, Winnie Calvert, who married Bert Gray. To her daughter's failed marriage was added another sorrow, that of the death of her younger son, Wilfred, in World War I.

A happy incident in my grandmother's life was a trip she made to the missionary settlement of Metlakatla (near Prince Rupert) in 1878 with her father-in-law, Admiral James C. Prevost. Since Admiral Prevost was largely responsible for the founding of the mission, the Indians provided a great

Anna (Fry) Prevost, 1853-1923.

welcome, which was described as follows in the Church Missionary Gleaner, 1879: "The village is gaily decorated with flags; the people, Tsimshean Indians, are gathered together in expectant groups. Presently a large canoe is seen approaching the shore, conveying an English naval officer and a lady and child. The tide being out, the visitors are transferred to a smaller canoe, which is instantly lifted up on Tsimshean shoulders and deposited on terra firma."

According to my Aunt Frida, the "lady and child" referred to were my grandmother and my father, then six months old. My aunt says her mother often spoke of this trip from Victoria with Admiral Prevost. She vividly recalled being lifted with him in the canoe which was a gesture of welcome for a visiting chief. She stated that she was so afraid that the bearers would drop her baby that she handed him over the side to the nearest Indian bystander. She also was horrified at the idea of consuming Indian food at the ensuing feast, and eventually the admiral got her excused by explaining that she had to watch her diet because she was nursing my father.

Grandmother was connected by marriage with two other well-known pioneer families as her sister Bessie had married Daniel Wishart Mainguy and her older sister, Edith, married David Alexander.

Edith Lucy Price (nee Booth)
(Mrs. Frank Price)
1872-1966
by her son Frederick A. Price

Edith Price was the daughter of George Booth who had retired from the Royal Navy, and Sarah Booth. She was born in Victoria on May 11, 1872 and was the second of their four children.

On May 2, 1899 she married Francis Henry Price of Cowichan Lake who, with Percy Jaynes, owned and operated Lakeside Hotel at Cowichan Lake. The hotel catered to the "quality" fishermen and parties. The new bride soon took her share in the management and proved herself capable.

In 1902 Frank built the Tzouhalem Hotel, named for a local mountain significant to the Cowichan Indian people, in Duncan and it was there on November 2, 1902, attended by Dr. Rolston, that Edith gave birth to her only child, Frederick Arthur, now living at Quamichan Park. Frank and Edith managed the Tzouhalem Hotel together with Edith supervising the catering, housekeeping and the purchase of supplies. With wholesalers situated in Victoria her work required considerable travel and correspondence.

As hostess for the hotel she had many ancillary duties such as meeting guests and visitors, and arranging banquets such as the special dinner at Christmas. From time to time prominent people stayed at the hotel, arriving usually by train. They were met at Duncan station by one of the Chinese staff who would carry the guests' bags.

In March of 1906 Prince Arthur of Connaught came by special train from Victoria to fish at Cowichan. In his party were General Kelly Kemp, Admiral Seymour, Sir Edward Hobart and Lord Redsdale. Prince Arthur's one day in Cowichan must have been memorable as he caught thirty fish. Lord and Lady Aberdeen also stayed at the Tzouhalem Hotel. With its

Back row, l. to r.: Mary Jane Price Marriott, Edith Lucy Booth Price, Francis Henry Price.

Front, l. to r.: Emily Booth, Fred Price, Augustus Pimbury, Ada Jaynes Price, & Muriel Price King.

capable hostess and her husband's management expertise, the Tzouhalem was considered the best hotel north of Victoria.

About 1912 Frank and Edith Price moved into their own home, the house which later became the Silver Bridge Inn in Duncan. There were two five acre parcels of land with lawns and a meadow with large maple trees. This provided a setting for colourful garden parties, entertaining and many fund-raising fetes held there during World War I.

Edith Price was a keen gardener and was known for her beautiful displays at local flower shows. She played golf at the Koksilah Golf Club and later at Duncan when the club opened on land close by her home and the hotel.

Mrs. Price also was active in local circles and was a charter member of

Tzouhalem Hotel c.1904.

the Imperial Order of Daughters of the Empire in Duncan. She also was a member, and served on the board of the King's Daughters who provided funds to build the first hospital in Duncan. During the first World War, she was with the Red Cross who supplied money, comforts, food and medical supplies for servicemen.

After her husband retired from business in 1919 he farmed in a small way on their land and they continued to live in the home until he died in 1943. A few years later Edith had a house built at the end of Price Place where she lived until March 22, 1966, when she died at the age of ninety-four.

Lillian Florence Roberts (nee Kier)
(Mrs. Henry Roberts)
1890 - 1982
by Elden Kier

Lillian Florence Kier was born at Somenos on August 8, 1890, to George and Florence Kier.

She attended Somenos School at the corner of Drinkwater and Somenos Roads and later graduated from St. Paul's Hospital in Vancouver as a nurse in the spring of 1915.

In April of that year she joined the Army Medical Corps Expeditionary Force. There were ninety Canadian nurses mobilized at Ottawa and they were royally treated during their three weeks stay in the capital, being presented to their Royal Highnesses the Duke and Duchess of Connaught and to Canadian General Sam Hughes.

In May of that year Lillian Kier sailed on the Hesperian from Halifax, bound for Liverpool. She served overseas in France from May of 1915 to August of 1919 with the Canadian Army Medical Corps. Among her decorations was the French Medal of Honour.

After her return from Europe she enrolled for a public health nursing course at the University of British Columbia and graduated in the class of 1920-21.

In March of 1920 Lillian was appointed school nurse for Duncan and Genoa Bay for the remainder of the school term. In January of 1921 she started her training in field work at the district health centre for the Cowichan District.

As a consequence of her wartime nursing she acquired a disability that required a warmer and drier climate and she moved to California about 1924 where she continued nursing.

In February of 1927 Lillian married Henry Roberts in Los Angeles. They lived at Senora, California, where she died on December 7, 1982.

Mrs. Henry Roberts, nee Lillian Florence Kier, 1890-1982. A Pioneer Nurse.

Emilie Annie Robinson (nee Baethke)
(Mrs. Arthur Robinson)
1858 - 1945
by her granddaughter Edna Green

My grandmother, Emilie Annie Robinson, was the daughter of John H. and Dorothea Z. Baethke, who emigrated from Germany to the United States. She was born in Chicago, Illinois. She and Arthur Robinson were married there in 1880.

In 1887 Arthur and Emilie Robinson came to the Cowichan Valley to seek a better life. I don't know why they chose the Valley. My grandfather, born in Derbyshire, England, had emigrated to the United States when he was nineteen and after more than one move, he settled in Illinois where he worked in a cheese factory. When he married, the couple's living quarters were above the factory and it was there that my mother, two of her sisters and a brother were born.

Grandfather, having bought the business, got into debt and had to close it

Arthur Robinson & Emilie Baethke. Wedding picture — 7 August, 1880.

up. It was then that he decided to start a new way of life in Cowichan, coming to the Valley in 1887.

By the time my Grandmother and the four children joined him some improvements had already been made to the farm that he had bought, and the tiny log house. The house had consisted of one large ground floor room with another large room above, reached by a ladder from below. The Robinson household was augmented by Mr. and Mrs. Robinson's hired girl and her husband.

Emilie Robinson always had help in the house. As the farming operations expanded, there were also hired men.

My grandfather had started with a mixed farming operation which meant chores for all the children as they grew old enough. When he concentrated on strawberry production after a few years, his strawberry acreage eventually expanded to six or seven acres. At the peak of the season there would be about 50 pickers, a few Japanese, four permanent Chinese employees in their own cottage, and many Indians. The Indians and their children had a longhouse on the hillside and lived there for about four weeks. On one occasion one of the women suddenly left the field to give birth to a child. She was back out picking within two days.

My grandmother had her anxieties, of course. The oldest child, May, my mother, was the one usually sent on errands away from the farm. In her reminiscences May recorded, "I remember having to go to Dr. Rowbotham's for medicine for my father when he was laid up with sciatica. Dr. Rowbotham lived on Jaynes Road and these trips would take me several hours. At this time I was nine or ten years old and my mother would often walk out to meet me when she became worried about my return."

Grandmother had three more children after coming to Cowichan, born in 1889, 1893 and 1897. In 1904, when the youngest child was only seven years of age, my grandfather met with an accident which led to blood-poisoning and his death.

With the help of her two eldest sons, Walter and Gilbert, Grandmother carried on the berry production. There was no will so it was not until the youngest child was twenty-one years of age that the property could be divided.

Emilie Robinson died in 1945, survived by daughters May (Mrs. Elias Castley), Nellie (Mrs. L. Bonsall), Lily (Mrs. W. Roseboom) and Emily (Mrs. D. Taylor), and her sons Walter, Gilbert and Henry.

Mary Skinner (nee Glyde)
(Mrs. Ambrose Skinner)
1843 - 1930
compiled by the Researchers

In 1872, Mary Glyde, eldest daughter of Mr. G. Glyde of Whitchurch, Dorsetshire, England, made her solitary way out to British Columbia. Her twin sister, Martha, followed her a year and a half later.

Mary taught school in Sooke and New Westminster before coming to the

Maple Bay school in 1873. She was the second teacher of that school.

In 1875 she married Ambrose Skinner, a son of Thomas and Mary Skinner. Martha Glyde married a Mr. Tait at about the same time.

Ambrose Skinner had property in Somenos at the corner of the Old Cowichan Lake Road and the Old Island Highway, (now Somenos Road) and there he took his bride to live in a log house.

When the telegraph line from Victoria to Nanaimo was put through in 1879, Ambrose got the contract to operate and maintain the line between Shawnigan Lake and Oyster Bay, the site of the present city of Ladysmith. Ambrose enjoyed the post very briefly, dying in 1880. Mary inherited the job as well as the farm. With a small daughter, Minnie, as well as herself to support, she needed income. Her sister, Martha Tait, had lost her husband at the same time and it seems she was even less well provided for than her sister. She came from New Westminster to join forces with her twin and it worked out very well. Martha took care of the house and Mary did the farm work while both brought up little Minnie. The farm work entailed milking several cows. Martha presumably could turn her hand to that also when it was necessary since Mary had assumed her late husband's contract for the telegraph line.

Maintaining the line meant riding through that rough country in all seasons to make repairs as necessary. The Oyster Bay end of the line was the worst with dense forest and the snow lying late on the ground.

By all accounts Mary Skinner was a splendid horsewoman and kept good horses. One admirer claimed that she could handle a horse better than most men.

Martha Tait was also a busy woman. From 1882 and for many years thereafter she worked for St. Peter's church as a collector for the Somenos district of pew rents and subscriptions for special purposes. When she gave up that work in 1902, the church committee records simply let her disappear from the scene without acknowledgement, a sign of the times, perhaps.

Eventually Mary Skinner sold her farm and bought a piece of the old Bell homestead where she lived until her death in 1930, active to the end.

A road in the area is named for her and her husband.

Rosamond Christine Spong (nee May)
(Mrs. Charles J. Spong)
1881-1979
by her daughter Frances Hopps

Rosamond May was born in Muskoka, Ontario. Her father, Nicholas May, a Methodist minister had come to Canada from England, as had her mother. In 1882 the family moved to British Columbia, settling at Maple Bay.

Rosamond attended school at Cobble Hill, probably riding her pony to school. At that time cougars were plentiful. Once, looking from the window of her home, Rosamond saw one prowling close to the house but there were no unpleasant incidents.

Leaving school Rosamond went to Victoria and became a professional dressmaker. Later, she moved to New Westminster where she trained as a secretary at the Columbia College.

In New Westminster she met her future husband, Charles John Spong, who was both a lawyer and an architect. They were married in 1905, living in Burnaby where Rosamond turned her hand to farming, both dairy and produce. They had five children, Victoria Herbert Spong, Helen (Grasly), Florence (Hopps), Marjorie (Welton) and Celia (Edwards).

Though some of her children and descendants still live in Cowichan she did not return, passing away in 1979 on the mainland.

Susan Stoker, (nee Harden)
1852-1936
by her goddaughter Mary MacRae Stone

Susan Stoker was the wife of Dr. R.N. Stoker (Indian Army Retired) and came to Cowichan in 1889, living each year for the winter six months at Maple Bay and the summer six months at Lake Cowichan in a log house. Here she collected wild flowers, plants and seeds from the higher mountains in that area. Her living room curtains always had small bags of seeds pinned on them where they were put to cure before sieving and then mail-

Dr. R.N. Stoker's home at Meade Creek, Cowichan Lake, built in 1889. It is now University of Victoria property.

Mrs. Susan Stoker

ing off to a seed firm in U.S.A. This she did for 50 years. She was a beautiful painter and produced water colour paintings of local wild flowers. This collection of paintings was given to the Museum in Victoria and from time to time it is displayed. This collection is particularly valuable since some of the plants included are now very rare.

Mrs. Stoker was a graduate of the Dublin School of Art, where she specialized in china painting. She had a large circle of friends and was very deaf but she owned an "ear trumpet" which she thrust at one and was able to carry on a good converstation.

When Quamichan Lake froze, which was more frequent in the early days, Dr. and Mrs. Stoker were host to all who were skating. They lit a huge bonfire on their lakeshore and served hot Ghirardellis chocolate with cinnamon buns! In those days women skated in long full skirts but enjoyed themselves nevertheless.

Harriet Ruby Thorpe (nee Symons)
(Mrs. Roland Thorpe)
1888-1978
by her daughter Bernice Brown

My mother's paternal grandparents, Mr. and Mrs. Richard Symons, Sr., were born in Cornwall. As a young couple they left England for Missouri, following a relative who had preceded them there. They arrived there in the 1840s. After a few years they left Missouri with their young daughter in a covered wagon headed for Grass Valley, California, hoping to find gold. En route their son, Richard Dunn Symons, Jr. was born in 1858.

Finding very little gold the family travelled north to Vancouver Island and reached the Maple Bay area by boat in 1870. Their farm, about three hundred acres in virgin forest, was bounded by what is now Stamps Road, Lakes Road and Herd Road.

After his father's death in 1883, Richard Symons Jr., my grandfather continued to clear and work the land until around 1912 when he sold a large part of the property to the Chapman family.

The Symons' kept a few acres for themselves and built a large house overlooking the fields of their former property. This house is still standing and occupied. The house my great-grandparents built, plus additions that the Chapman family made is still standing, but incorporated into a new house.

My mother's maternal grandparents, Mr. and Mrs. Joseph Mufford, left Cornwall with their son and daughter for Ontario in 1880. They stayed one year before heading across the continent and eventually settling in Maple Bay. Their son, William, taught school at Maple Bay for a while. Around 1885 the parents and William left for Langley.

Ann Mufford, Ruby Thorpe, Rossie Mufford, W.H. Mufford.

Around the time that the Muffords left Maple Bay, their daughter, Angelina, married Richard D. Symons. They had four children, William Francis Symons who lived most of his adult life in the United States, Harriet Ruby Thorpe, Pearl and Floss Symons. All were born in the original Symons farmhouse.

My mother, Harriet, attended the one-room school at the corner of Herd and Lakes Road, which was not demolished until the late 1940s. She wrote her high school entrance examinations at the school which was one of the first schools in Duncan on the knoll off the west end of Station Street. When Mother was a few years older she would have liked to find work away from home but her father would not hear of it. She put in long hours working on the farm, sometime milking as many as fourteen cows night and morning. She was organist at the little Methodist Church on Herd Road, close to the Symons farm.

It was at this Methodist Church that Harriet met her husband, Roland, who was in charge of the service one Sunday. They were married at the Symons home in 1911. All but one of the offspring were christened in the little church.

Our parents lived on Ypres Street in a new house built by our father. Their children were raised in that home and two of us, Myrtle and I were born there. In the summer of 1913 our parents travelled to England and several countries on the continent. They visited many relatives in England and attended the World Sunday School Convention in Switzerland. Both parents were very active in the Duncan Methodist Church which became the United Church in 1925. They both taught Sunday School. Our father was superintendent of the Sunday School for over thirty years and mother was in charge of the primary classes until 1925.

Mother also was a member of the Girl Guide Mothers' Auxiliary for many years and her daughters were members of the first Cowichan Guide Company. In the early years of the Hospital Auxiliary she acted as treasurer for six years and received a silver cake plate when she was no longer able to be active in the Auxiliary. Around 1949 when her son, Len, graduated from Northwest Baptist College with a Bachelor of Arts in Theology, Mother became a member of the Bethel Baptist Church and taught a primary Sunday School class until the age of seventy-nine. She passed away on December 24, 1978 at the age of 90 after five years of poor health.

Kirsten Marie (Mary) Thugerson (nee Hanson)
(Mrs. Charles Thugerson)
1874-1960
by her daughter Carrie Peterson

Mary Thugerson, as she generally was known, was born in Denmark. In 1900 for reasons of health she emigrated to North America and eventually settled in the Cowichan Valley to be with friends.

She married Charles Thugerson in Canada. Before emigrating, she had been a nurse in Denmark.

The Thugersons had one adopted daughter, Carrie, whom they had taken charge of in early childhood when her own parents died of tuberculosis.

Mary and Charles Thugerson bought a small property on Bell-McKinnon Road in the Somenos district. Mary always had a large area, probably one-quarter acre in front of the house which she planted in onions ("great, big beautiful globes") which she sold. All the money raised was given to the missions of the Methodist Church.

The onion crop was her special project for missions, but she was an active partner in most aspects of the small farm operation. The major source of income was the poultry and sale of eggs. They had a small incubator which was attached to the house where they raised the chicks which restocked the flock of Leghorn hens. For a time they also raised turkeys. Mrs. Thugerson, though she helped with these endeavours, described herself as primarily an agriculturist, and most of the fruit and vegetable production was in her hands.

She was adept at crocheting and other handwork. Her happiest time of the year was when the outdoor work had been largely wound up for the season and she could devote herself to these other interests.

A neighbour, living two miles from Mrs. Thugerson, tells a story which shows the type of woman that Mrs. Thugerson was.

The First World War influenza struck Cowichan in full force in the winter of 1919-20. In February of 1920 my mother had a baby that died 17 days later. Before she was fully recovered from the birth, Mother contracted flu. Out of concern for patients ill with other diseases, the hospital was then refusing all flu patients. The doctor refused to make a house call, saying that the road was too bad. Mrs. Thugerson, living two miles away and at the busiest time of year for her, travelled by horse and buggy daily to nurse my mother.

After Mother's death--it was said that no woman who contracted that flu shortly after giving birth ever recovered--we children, all except our oldest brother, came down with the disease. Again, Mrs. Thugerson harnessed up and came daily over that road which was too bad for the doctor to travel, to nurse us. I cannot imagine what our distracted father would have done without her.

Jane Roxborough Truesdale (nee Dick)
(Mrs. Lewis H. Truesdale)
1866-1942
by her granddaughters Margaret Filion and Doreen Wilkinson

Jane Roxborough Dick was born in 1866, at Hamilton, Ontario, the daughter of Scottish-born parents who had met and married after they emigrated to Canada. Jane was orphaned at the age of nine and then went to live with her mother's youngest sister, Margaret Simpson, who had just married Robert Grassie. In 1887, Jane married Lewis Henry Truesdale, the foreman of a flour mill in Binbrook, a village near Hamilton. Their eldest child, Harold, was born at Binbrook in 1889, and their second son, Walter, in 1891.

Her husband Lewis became ill with nephritis (a chronic miller's disease), and his doctor advised him to take a trip to California for his health. As the Robert Grassies had moved to Duncan a few years earlier, Lewis decided to pay them a visit and then continue south. However, the climate of Duncan in the summer of 1892 agreed with him so well that he abandoned the idea of California and decided to move his family to Duncan. He bought an unfinished house on Kenneth Street next to the present City Hall, and paid the owner to complete the building within two months while he went back to Ontario for his family.

The farm at Binbrook was sold, and the family set off for the West in October, 1892, travelling in rough weather from Hamilton to Port Arthur on a Great Lakes steamer. They then took the C.P.R. train to Vancouver, changing trains at Winnipeg. Jane had packed a lot of food for the trip, some already cooked, and some she could heat up on a stove at the end of the railway car. With two small boys scampering up and down the aisle, it could not have been an easy journey. From Vancouver, they took the S.S. Yosemite, a paddle-wheeler, to Victoria. The weather was rough, and Jane became very seasick. The old ship creaked and groaned from side to side, and she was afraid it was scraping bottom! They then travelled to Duncan on the E. & N. Railway.

Here they found that their house was still unfinished with nothing inside but the studding and 2 x 4s, and that the previous owner had left town with the money. However, they were fortunate to be able to stay with the Grassies for a few weeks until the house could be made habitable.

Jennie as she was called by family and friends, was dismayed at the view from her new home: she looked out to see acres of big, black stumps, with a blacksmith shop on one corner and a small shack on the other. She was so homesick for the beautiful fields and trees of southern Ontario that she made her husband promise that if she died he would not bury her among the stumps but take her back East. However, after a year or two, she was so happy here that she never wanted to leave, even for a visit. Her family increased by three more children: William, born in 1893; Blanche (Mac-Kenzie), in 1895; and Irene (Moore), in 1902.

The first years must have been rather a struggle; her husband could only find casual work as a teamster. Life improved when he found steady work on the railroad bridge crew and as a foreman framing timbers at the Mount Sicker mines. This meant he was away from home a great deal, and Jennie had the responsibility of raising the children and running the household.

After ten years in their little house on Kenneth St., they bought the Jim Flett property on Canada Avenue, between Evans and First Sts., where the Credit Union building now stands. There was a two-storey house, an acre of land, an orchard, duck pond and a small barn where they could keep the pony won by the boys in a raffle. Jennie was able now to cultivate a much larger vegetable garden and raise both chickens and ducks. There was a ready market for ducks at $1.00 each amongst the Chinese working at the Mt. Sicker mines.

Jennie attended the Duncan Methodist Church (now United) almost from its first opening, and she was a staunch member of the Ladies' Aid of that church.

In 1912, the family had built a fine new house on two lots at the end of Queen's Road, where the Regency Apartments building now stands. They had no sooner moved in than Lewis's health worsened rapidly, and he died there, at the age of 59, in 1915. There was more worry and sorrow in store for Jennie. Their sons, Walter and Will, already had enlisted and were serving in France with the Canadian Army where they both suffered lung damage from gas attacks. They returned to Duncan in 1919. Walter's lungs were so badly damaged that he died in 1922. Will had to spend many years at the Tranquille Sanatorium.

Jennie lived on in her home, keeping chickens and a large vegetable and flower gardens until she died at the age of 76 in 1942.

Orynthia Violet Tweedie (nee Lloyd)
1879-1967
by her daughter, Issa (Evelyn) Dobell

Orynthia or "Rynthie" (as she was called) Lloyd, third eldest of eight children, was educated at first by a governess, then had several years at St. Ann's Convent in Victoria.

Photo of Orynthia Lloyd.

In 1900 she was married to Henry F.M. Jones of Victoria, lately from Edinburgh, Scotland. With her husband, who was made government agent and policeman, she went to Quadra Island. There she had two children, Morgan and Evelyn (Issa). Happiness soon ended when Henry died of a heart seizure in 1907.

Rynthie brought Morgan and Evelyn back to her parents home in Westholme and later rented a cottage. In 1909 she was married to Reginald (Rogue) Gibbs and life was simpler.

When the First World War started in 1914, Rynthie showed how capable she could be. Nearly all of the men in Westholme went overseas and some wives went also. Rynthie and her children were really busy with chickens, a large raspberry patch and a garden. She sold fresh produce to the store which was nearby.

Later, when Rogue came home from the war, he built a new home on The Rock on Westholme Road. He and friends built it mainly out of old lumber salvaged from Lloyd's bunk houses at the Mount Sicker mill.

Delta was born in 1921 when they were living on The Rock.

Rogue died in 1937, and in 1940 Rynthie once again married, this time to Kenneth Tweedie. They moved to Duncan and had many happy years together until Kenneth died in 1956. Rynthie died in 1967 at Kings Daughter's Hospital and is buried at All Saint's Anglican churchyard, Westholme.

Edith Miller Vaux (nee Colvin)
1895-1978
by her daughter Edythe G. Long

Edith Vaux and her twin sister Margaret were born at Rosedale Farm, Cowichan Station in 1895 to Jeremina and Robert Mouat Colvin. Her parents had known each other in the Shetland Islands, Jeremina following Robert in 1886 when he was established in Cowichan.

Rosedale Farm, 480 acres of heavily treed land in the early days, was about two miles distant from the small community of Cowichan Station with few trails connecting them with neighbours. With bear, cougar and wolves prevalent in the area, it was not safe for the small children to attend Mrs. Haywood's Elementary School at Cowichan Station.

When the twins were old enough their parents sent them as boarders to the Misses Wilson's "The Cliffs" School in Duncan.

As Edith grew up she found plenty to do at home and around the farm and visiting other young people on neighbouring farms.

Following her marriage to William Henry Vaux in 1925, she lived in the Eagle Heights area, a short distance south of Duncan where her two children, Edythe Geraldine and William Dallas, were born.

Edith Vaux was an active member of the Koksilah Women's Institute until she died in 1978.

Edith Miller Vaux, nee Colvin, 1895-1978.

Clara Whidden
1885 - 1973
by her niece Gwen Smith

Clara Whidden came to Duncan as a small child. Her father arrived in 1889 and some time later her mother came with the two children, Clara and Hattie. Clara attended school in Duncan in what was known as the Zenith School. There was no high school in those days.

Most of her working life was spent as a telephone operator in Duncan, Vancouver, Victoria and Long Beach, California. She was chief operator in Duncan for many years until her retirement. Prior to her telephone days she did sewing.

Most of her growing-up years were spent in the family home on Ingram Street. Not having children of her own, she was a devoted aunt. As I think of my childhood I remember long Sunday walks to The Cliffs, the Misses Wilson's school, and hours spent by the piano as she played while we children sang.

At one time she belonged to the Good Templars Lodge but we do not know when that was, possibly around 1905 or 1910.

She grew up in the Alderlea, later called Duncan, Methodist church, belonged to Epworth League and played the organ in that church and in Mill Bay.

Robie Whidden (nee McNeill)
(Mrs. Robert Henry Whidden)
1859-1933
by granddaughters Mabel Sanderson and Gwen Smith

It would be about 1889 when Granny Whidden came clear across Canada from Nova Scotia to join her husband, Robert Henry Whidden, in Duncan.

The family lived for a little while in what was later the Main's house, where the Eaton's Garden shop is now. This was while their own house was being built by Robert Whidden. It was on Ingram Street about where the Trio store is now. Neighbours were bachelor Jimmy Murchie on the east side and Peterson on the west side. Another resident on Ingram Street was Dr. Watson Dykes who had his office in his home where the British Columbia Telephone building now stands.

As we remember it the house had city water but there was a pump in the back yard which was undoubtedly the source of water supply originally. There was electricity, but when we were children the power house was shut down at approximately 10:00 pm. for the night. There was no basement but a cellar was dug out of the earth, with an outside entrance. Here vegetables and canned goods were stored, at times a crock of homemade vinegar was made and sometimes a crock of eggs preserved in waterglass, a solution of water and isinglass. For many years there was a horse stabled at the back of the property and a chicken house with enough hens to supply us with eggs. As well as a vegetable garden there were a number of fruit trees including two huge cherry trees in front of the house.

Homemade soap was sometimes made to be used for cleaning and laundry. Perhaps from the days before the plumbing was put in we remember our aunt saying that she was always taught to count the cutlery before she put the dishwater in the garden. There were no J-cloths or plastic sponges in those days. Old rags were carefully saved. I can remember Granny saying how much a new bride appreciated her gift of a rag-bag full of cleaning cloths.

There were two Eastern maples in the back yard and each spring these were tapped and for a week or so the kitchen range was covered by large saucepans and pails of sap being boiled down to syrup.

Often Saturday supper was baked beans and Boston brown bread and this was warmed up for Monday's noon meal. Washday, always on Monday, was a big day. White things were boiled in large copper boilers and the washing was done with tubs and washboards in a woodshed adjoining the house. In rainy weather the laundry was dried in lines stretched across the kitchen ceiling. We stood on a table to hand them up. Spring cleaning was a very thorough affair with every inch of the house cleaned. Rugs were beaten with sticks while hung on a clothesline outside. No wonder the women wore dust caps in those days!

The first service of the Alderlea Methodist Church (later Duncan Methodist and later still Duncan United) was held in the kitchen of the Ingram Street house in 1890. From then until shortly before her death, Mrs. Whidden was a devoted worker in the church, her main interest being the Ladies Aid and the Sunday School of which she was the secretary for many years until ill health forced her to give it up. For a while she also had a group of teen-aged girls.

Around 1910 we have read in old Leader newspapers of her belonging to an Anti-Tuberculosis Society of which she was secretary and then treasurer. No doubt because of this she was always very concerned about the unsanitary practice of men expectorating on the streets. She also belonged to a Ladies Auxiliary to the Christian Aid Working Party. We do not know anything about these groups or how long they continued. She was also active in an organization meeting newcomers.

She was a very faithful member of the Cowichan Women's Institute and in this connection she worked hard toward the establishment of the health centre and the Queen Alexandra Solarium at Mill Bay. She was also a member of the Pythian sisters and the IODE. During the First World War she knitted tirelessly for the Red Cross. She was always interested in the government of Canada and of British Columbia, and in local affairs, especially when matters of welfare of local citizens were concerned.

She was very proud of the United Empire Loyalists in her background.

The Misses Wilson of "The Cliffs"
A School for Children
1891-1916
Compiled by the Researchers

For many years the two Miss Wilsons, Minnie and Maud, were part of the life of Cowichan in the late nineteenth and early twentieth centuries. They were members of an upper middle-class Scottish family of ten. A brother, Ronald, was the prime mover in bringing them to Vancouver Island. In the 1880s he first had tried his hand, unsuccessfully, at orange growing in Florida, then found his way to Cowichan where he was joined by his father, William. The senior Wilson was favourably impressed by the

The Wilsons — Minnie, Maud & Ronald.

tree crowned cliffs bordering the Cowichan River. He and his son bought land lying along both sides of the Cowichan River, bounded by Indian reserve.

Most of what follows has been excerpted from an article by Margaret Williams, published in the Colonist of December 10, 1961.

"The Wilsons first built a log cabin in the lower fields not far from where Queen Margaret's School now stands. To this humble place came Martha Wilson and two of her daughters, Teresa and Maud the youngest, in 1888.

On the high banks above the singing Cowichan, the Wilsons began building their home. The house was designed by William Wilson's son, Harry, and an odd rambling place it was. The huge fireplace in the original dining-room could have held six people, stairways twisted at odd angles, and off the upstairs bedrooms were numerous cubby holes where trunks full of fancy dress costumes and theatrical props were stored in later years. This house is still lived in, in the same Cliffs Road location close to Duncan.

Teresa Wilson soon returned to Scotland, and the family began urging another sister, Minnie, to come to Canada. Minnie was at this time teach-

The Cliffs Schoolhouse.

ing in Naples where she had been for some years. She loved Italy and it was with reluctance that she finally consented to come.

Upon arrival, Minnie taught for a short time in a private school in Victoria. When she came to Duncan, she started her own school in the log cabin, the family now living in the new house. Plans went ahead for the addition of classrooms.

There were four pupils at "The Cliffs School" on opening day. Soon more came, among them Philip Livingston who would later have a distinguished career as an ophthalmologist in the Royal Air Force and who eventually retired to Cowichan to spend his last years. At one time there were almost as many boys as girls. There were boarders among the pupils from Nanaimo, Chemainus, Victoria and as far afield as the province of Alberta.

Miss Wilson (Minnie) handled the teaching with some assistance. Later her sister, Maud, was the housekeeper, a delightful and gay person. When Maud first came to the district she did some private nursing and was to be seen driving around the country with young Dr. Perry in his smart buggy and fast team of horses. She was passionately fond of all animals and was never without at least one dog.

There were always horses at The Cliffs, of course. Miss Maud used to ride "Brutus", a bad-tempered but handsome beast. She took boarders on many a drive in the democrat. In later years she kept chickens and bred canaries. Her pot plants were on every verandah and window sill and were often unwelcome additions to the charming old drawing-room.

Maypole Dance at Cliffs School, c.1910.

Cosy fireplace and sitting-room of Misses Minnie and Maud Wilson, of "The Cliffs School".

In time when other schools for young boys had been opened in the district Minnie Wilson accepted only girls as pupils.

A note of some interest is that Teresa the sister who returned to Scotland, became secretary and a great friend to Lady Aberdeen, wife of the Lieutenant Governor of Canada (1893-1898). When the Aberdeens came to Vancouver Island, Teresa accompanied them and stayed at The Cliffs.

Minnie Wilson was a brilliant woman, well-read, and speaking French, Italian and German fluently. She was also an artist; her nieces still have a

A day for chores - Miss Maud Wilson and a helpful friend Miss Ligertwood at the bread mixer in everyday 1910 dress at the Cliffs.

few of her exquisite sketches and still life studies which she did in Italy. She never painted after coming to Canada. She said the great trees and mountains overwhelmed and depressed her, though she came to love the country.

She taught her girls drawing and painting, French, history, literature and fine needlework. It never occurred to her to prepare her pupils for entrance to university and evidently they were not interested in such a thing. Miss

The Hopkins at Cliffs School. Everald, Gwen, Ronnie, Margaret. c.1912.

Clack, a well-known music teacher in Duncan, came to the school to give music lessons. Good manners were important in those days and woe betide the girl at the dining-room table who had to be asked to pass the marmalade. One was taught to look after one's neighbour and the presiding mistress particularly.

Miss Wilson was an enthusiastic botanist, and if the girls did not know

Cliffs School c. 1905.

3 pupils of Cliffs School out for a ride in the pony cart.

an algebraic equation, they did know the Latin name of every flower and shrub that grew on the river bank. To them a shooting star was a dodecatheon and the easter lilies which grew there in such lovely profusion were erythroniums. Drawing classes were held outside and girls perched on the pathways leading down to the river, drawing from nature.

The Cliffs School became noted for the excellent plays produced. Some of these were put on in the schoolrooms and some, such as Midsummer Night's Dream, took place on the tennis court.

On Monday mornings Miss Wilson would read aloud while the girls did their needlework. She read The Water Babies, Kingsley's Heroes, Children of the New Forest and Black Beauty, and she scolded when a girl wept over this last story. One must not give way to sentiment!

Under Miss Wilson's rather stern demeanour was a soft heart. She was essentially rather a shy person though few would have believed it.

Miss Maud was deeply religious and was for many years a member of the Presbyterian Church in Duncan. Miss Minnie remained an Anglican. The pupils attended St. John's Church once, and often twice, every Sunday. Those girls with bicycles would sometimes be permitted to ride to St. Mary's, Somenos, for a third session!

Time brought changes. Financially the school did not prosper, teachers were difficult to get, and finally, Miss Wilson, Miss Maud and Mr. Ronald were growing older. Old Mr. Wilson had been laid to rest beside his wife Martha, in St. Peter's churchyard. In 1918 The Cliffs School closed its doors.

In the ensuing years all those empty rooms were filled by a succession of friends in need, visiting cousins, adopted grandchildren and paying guests.

The chests of beautiful silver brought from Scotland were sold to provide annuities and much of the lovely furniture went the same way.

Miss Wilson carried on her activities in the life of the community. She had always been a tireless worker for the King's Daughters Hospital, she had become a member of the Scattered Circle when she still was residing in Italy. She belonged to the Women's Institute, worked for the Red Cross and helped to found the Duncan Literary Club."

The sisters both ended their days in Victoria's Gorge Nursing Home, dying between 1951 and 1953.

Elizabeth Ann Woods (nee Cookson)
(Mrs. Willoughby Alexander Woods)
1855-1933
by her granddaughter Betty Mellor

Elizabeth Ann Cookson was born May 30, 1855 at Tarporley, England, the daughter of Thomas and Ann Cookson. She married Willoughby Alexander Woods on June 17, 1876 at London, England.

She, her husband and young children came to Canada about 1890. She had six children, four girls and two boys. The youngest girl was born after they came to the Cowichan Valley.

They first settled in the Quamichan area, near what is now St. Peter's Church. The children went to school in that area.

The oldest child, Annie, returned to England in 1901 where she married

Home of Elizabeth Ann Woods — Cheapside Store, Maple Bay Post Office, Herd Road.

and came back to Canada with her husband, Jack King, and two children in 1919.

The next child, Tom, went to school and sometimes had a ride along the way on a white horse belonging to an Indian. Other children were Rollie, John, Lilly and Fanny. Fanny was born after they came to Cowichan. They moved to property on Herd Road where they built a new house in 1904. Ben Woike now has a chicken farm there and the house is still in use.

They had a small store called Cheapside which was run from the house from 1906 to about 1912, and, for a short time, a post office. The grand-daughter, Fanny, helped in the store and post office.

Elizabeth Ann Woods did not do farm chores as many pioneer women did. Baking, housework, family and store kept her busy.

In 1913 she moved to Lane Road at Haywards Junction. Her husband died in January of the following year. Later she lived in Duncan with her daughter, Fanny, while her husband, Norman, was overseas.

Next she lived in a small house built by her son, Tom, on his place opposite Mount Prevost Road.

She suffered from heart trouble, so later her house was moved and joined on to Tom's. Here she lived until her death in 1933.

I remember the Sunday afternoons when she still lived in her own house, where we would be allowed to visit her. She always had peppermint candies - round white ones - and lemonade. She loved music and had a gramophone and would play her records for us.

Later on she liked to read children's stories and fairy tales until she would doze off.

Mary Ellen Woods (nee Green)
(Mrs. Thomas William Woods)
1891-1985
by her daughter Betty Mellor

Mary Ellen Green was born March 8, 1891. Nellie, as she had always been called, was the oldest child of Mark and Ellen Green. Her parents' farm was on Herd Road in the Somenos district. She had a brother, Mark James, and two sisters, Hannah Elizabeth (Bessie) and Dorothy Louise. After many owners the farm now belongs to her daughter and son-in-law, Betty and John Mellor.

She walked to school, a one-room school on Herd Road opposite Lakes Road, called Maple Bay school.

She always loved the outdoor and farm life. Mary Ellen soon learned to feed chickens, look after sheep, milk a cow and drive a horse. The farm fields were fairly small with stumps and patches of bush. The pastures were small clearings with lots of bush and trees. This meant hunting for cows and baby calves and lambs, things she liked to do.

Deer, grouse and duck were plentiful. She plucked duck and grouse but did not like this chore.

In the early summer Nellie would pick the little wild blackberries, some for the family and some to sell to a neighbour. This was her source of money.

The Mark Greens.

Front: Mark & Ellen Green.

Back: Bessie (Armour) Ogilvie, Jim Green, Dorothy Armour, Mary Ellen Woods.

A trip into Duncan was another exciting event, sometimes with the family and sometimes with a neighbour. On one of these trips she bought a little china tea set for her youngest sister, Dorothy, and was scolded for wasting money! In time Dorothy gave it to Nellie's daughter, Betty, then it went to Eileen, Betty's daughter, who still has it.

She told of watching her father make jars for jam out of bottles. He tied a string dipped in coal oil around the bottle, lit the string, and then plunged the bottle in cold water to break off the top.

In the fall the Indians would come to thresh the grain. This was a great improvement over the flail which had been used earlier. The men came with the women and children and lots of extra horses. The Indians were very fond of very sweet tea and bread with lots of jam on it.

About 1907 the farm on Herd Road was sold to Mr. Sprott and the family moved to Haywards Junction. While here Nellie worked at Crosland Brothers seed farm, weeding and staking sweet peas, and in the winter cleaning and packaging the seeds.

In November of 1917 she married Thomas William Woods, the elder son of Elizabeth Ann and W.A. Woods. For a short time they lived on Lane Road, then moved to their own place opposite Mount Prevost Road. She had three daughters, Betty, Margaret and Dorothy.

As busy as my mother was, she always had time for us and our friends and time to help others. She made home very hospitable and there was always room for one more at mealtimes. I remember her reading to us when we were small. Granny, my Dad's mother, lived with us when she could no longer live by herself. We usually went to her part of the house for the reading so she could listen, too. My mother looked after her for a few years until Granny died in 1933. My mother's mother and father died that same year within a month of each other.

In 1934 this farm was sold to Bergenner Brothers and we moved to May's Road, the old May place. This place was larger with an old house. A new house was built, complete with a housewarming. This was a mixed farm with quite a few laying hens which were her special project. My mother missed her old neighbours at first but the new ones were very nice. Art Vink now owns this property and lives in the house.

The next move was to Ford Road. Here she had egg customers. This was in 1945. They then moved to Sprott Road in about 1954 which was where my father died. She lived by herself for a few years with her cow and a sheep, a dog, cat and a few chickens. She sold eggs to friends and this meant a visit and a cup of tea. She had lots of people of all ages drop in, including children on their way home from school for a snack.

When she could no longer live alone she moved back on a trailer to her original home with her dog and cat. To her this was like coming home. Her daughter and son-in-law Betty and John Mellor live there now.She was a patient in the Extended Care Hospital and would have been ninety-four in March 1986. She died in late 1985.

SECTION IV
A COMMUNITY
The Period 1901-1920
by Elizabeth Blanche Norcross

Prospects for the Cowichan Valley had never looked rosier than at the turn of the century. Copper mining activity was proceeding on Mount Sicker with several companies involved. A town that in a few year's time would grow to be larger than Duncan was springing up on the mountain-side. Schools, hotels, and family homes gave it every appearance of permanence.[1]

In a letter dated June of 1903 to his mother in Cowichan, Fairfax Prevost, travelling and working in the United States, referred to a married sister's home on Mount Sicker. "They must be getting quite civilized," he wrote, "with their picket fences and lawns, gardens, et cetera." Obviously it was no rough mining camp that was mushrooming on the south slope of the mountain.[2]

It was on Mount Sicker that Cowichan's famous native son, Angelo Branca, was born. For many years he was a leading criminal lawyer in Vancouver. In 1966, he was sworn in to the British Columbia Court of Appeal where his carreer as a judge was recognized nationally. Had he ever made a sentimental journey home to his birthplace he would have found nothing there. Few mining towns have disappeared so completely. Some houses were substantial enough to make it worthwhile to move them to Duncan; in other cases lumber was salvaged from vacated buildings and put to use elsewhere. What remained rotted into the forest floor.

Mount Sicker effectively closed down in 1907. Before that happened it had spawned both a smelter on Osborne Bay and a town that was named Crofton. The smelter ceased operations with the abandonment of the Mt. Sicker mines, and the little town virtually died, though some limited life did remain. The ruin of both little towns was brought about by falling world copper prices combined with a major vein of ore running out.[4]

With the turn of the century, Duncan acquired a local paper, first the Enterprise which died and was revived several times over the next few years, and then the Cowichan Leader which had a continuous life from 1905 on.

Horse-drawn stages now served the Valley on a regular basis. During Mt. Sicker's boom years a stage met the trains at Westholme.[5] Stages also kept a regular schedule to Cowichan Lake and in 1913 there was a stage twice weekly to Maple Bay. These horse-drawn vehicles were replaced by motor stages before the outbreak of the war.[6] The fishing and hunting camps at Cowichan Lake continued to be almost the only industry there.

The influx into the Cowichan Valley of moneyed people began in the 1880s and continued on a grander scale in the early 1900s. This new class of resident naturally attracted equally moneyed visitors from afar who came for extended periods to enjoy the fishing and shooting, to take part in the tennis, polo, cricket and the regattas.

The chatelaines of the fine, architect-designed new homes were far from being stereotypical pioneer women. Not for them was the hauling of water by the bucket from a well, or doing the family wash with the aid of a scrub board. They lived the delightful life that had been the lot of a small, privileged society in Victoria half a century earlier and which it still enjoyed though now on a larger scale.

The polo-playing husbands did some gentlemanly farming with the aid of hired hands and, at least in one case, that of the Bevans, raised a notable prize-winning herd of dairy cattle.

The society which amused itself with balls in full evening dress, yachting, tennis, teas with damask cloths and silver tea service, existed side by side with the other older society which continued in its accustomed way, laboriously improving the farms year by year. The line between the two societies was blurred. While The King's Daughters looked for its membership in the main to the pre-eminently well-to-do, there were many women with less conspicuous money and even less leisure who also were welcomed.

Young remittance men who spent their days in overalls, doing labourer's chores while supposedly learning farming, turned out to the formal dances wearing correct evening dress and "smelling of cows and mothballs". "Remittance men", it should be explained were younger sons of well-to-do United Kingdom families for whom no useful place could be found in their country. Sometimes they were the black sheep of their families. In either

Duncan's first high school on Cairnsmore Street, destroyed by fire in 1946.

238

York Road School, built in 1912, was replaced by new construction along the Trans-Canada Highway about 1973.

case they received quarterly remittances from home until, it was hoped, they established themselves in their new country.

The Cowichan Library and Literary Institute announced proudly in February 1900 that after thirty years of existence it now had one thousand volumes on its shelves.[7]

The early years of the twentieth century were remarkable for the number of women who entered the business world, not as employees but as independent business women. Foremost among them by any standard of measurement was Miss Lillie Baron whose shop, Le Bon Ton, dealing in millinery, infants wear and a limited amount of women's clothing was an institution in Duncan for more than forty years.

There were many others at this time in not so long lived enterprises; they included a rival ladies wear establishment, Le Bon Marche (Miss Valedoss), a rival milliner (Mrs. A.C. Townsend), dressmakers in abundance, and tea shop owners -- the most prominent and best remembered of these was Miss Sutton's Tea Gardens, as well as seasonal tea shops at Maple Bay, (Porter and Boyd, Miss Anderson and Mrs. Springett). At Cowichan Bay Mrs. Lakes opened tearooms.

Then there were what might be described as "cottage industries," though most were conducted outside the cottage. Many rural women augmented their incomes by sales of home-grown products. Mrs. Leather advertised perennials. Other women offered such items as a rooster of prize-winning stock, cockerels, and setting eggs. Miss Muriel Herd must have been in a fairly large way of business for the times, having for sale setting eggs at eight dollars for one hundred. Springhurst Nursery, Mrs. H. Norcross, advertised bedding plants and hanging baskets; another woman offered to take in a paying guest. Some of the "for sale" items asked for such small amounts of money that apparently the newspaper did not charge for the advertisement.[8]

Another field in which a woman could make a living was education. The Misses Wilson continued with the school at The Cliffs, above the Cowichan River, just west of Duncan as the little town was to be called. Their work was supplemented by Miss Lillian Clack whose kindergarten extended to Grades One and Two. Like Miss Baron, she became a Duncan "institution". Her name lingers in the affectionate memory of every woman who lived in the city prior to 1940. In addition to her school for young children, she gave piano and water colour lessons.

Sharing as they did an upper middle-class background and reduced circumstances, Miss Clack and Misses Wilson became close friends.

In this pre-First World War period there were several women who offered piano and pianoforte lessons such as Miss Booth, Mrs. Legge-Willis, Mrs. Arnold B. Thorpe and at Cowichan Station, Mrs. Dunsterville, to name a few. These ladies all cited quite impressive qualifications.[8]

The extremely versatile Miss Violet Burkett of Westholme advertised private classes in singing, elocution, English Literature, Shakespearian reading and Swedish drill. Mrs. Sharp and Mrs. W. Bundock were also prepared to give singing lessons. Mrs. Wicks could give Esperanto lessons.

Miss Montgomery advertised in 1912 that she was conducting a small school at Cowichan and had room for one or two boarders. Two years later Miss V.E. Ashdown had succeeded her.[8]

Miss Lee "begged to announce" that she was giving dancing lessons at Maple Bay for both children and adults.[8]

It was in the summer of 1914 that that last advertisement appeared and in the same issue of the paper the prices of classified advertisements were

Maple Bay Regatta - was a popular annual event.

set out at 25 words or less for 25 cents per issue; four insertions for seventy-five cents; over twenty-five words, one cent per word.[8]

With no local high school until 1910 and then with all subjects taught by one teacher, there was a good market for private "extras."

The advertisements for "Work Wanted" and "Help Wanted" reflect the times. We have a "gentlewoman" and a "lady help" seeking work, also "lady help wanted." These "lady help" were women who could become a comfortable part of a middle-class family. There were also "mother's helps" advertising for work, and this suggests a different category.

In her diary (1894-1925) Miss Mary Marriner records a host of activities by which she earned her modest income. She tells of baby sitting, home nursing, helping at parties, knitting to order, rowing sport fishermen about Cowichan Bay, picking wild blackberries and selling them as well as farm produce to Duncan hotels; at one point she did housework for twelve and one-half cent per hour.[9] Quite possibly there were other women similarly employed.

Women's organizations expanded, the church-related groups, the Women's Institute of which a Cowichan branch had been formed in 1912 and, of course, the King's Daughters, going on from strength to strength. With help from the Provincial organizations, the King's Daughters had succeeded in getting their convalescent and emergency hospital opened in 1911. St. Edward's Altar Society, later known as the Catholic Women's League, gave strong support to their church before a church building existed.

In a 1926 review of the women's work for St. Edwards, a former president, Mrs. Edna H. Swan, said, "At that time with a Catholic community of not more than fifty families, it is doubtful whether the proposed new St. Edward's Church would ever have become a reality but for the tenacity of the weaker sex." And, giving credit, "With the best will in the world their objectives could never be reached without the sympathetic support and material help of their non-Catholic friends in and around Duncan."[10]

The pioneer spirit in which all helped to build one another's churches, was still alive and well in the twentieth century.

The Pythian Sisters and Ivy Rebekah Lodge, the Choral Society and the Dramatic Society (these last mixed groups) were active in pre-war Cowichan. All these organizations, secular and non-secular, were in the business of raising money for a variety of causes and it is amazing the amounts they did raise, especially considering the modest price of tickets. The St. Andrew's Ladies Guild for instance, put on something billed as an "Irish Supper," priced at thirty-five cents.[11] These fund-raisers also had a value as social events, binding the community together.

The Cowichan Leader came to recognize the important role that women now were playing in the Valley and from giving full reports individually of their activities graduated to a regular feature, "Women's Work."

Women were active participants, too, in outdoor sports. In 1912 the Leader announced the scores in Ladies' cricket, made reference to the Ladies' hockey club, to Ladies' basketball and to ladies taking part in a gymkhana held on the Koksilah Golf links.[12] Women played golf, as well as tennis. The latter sport held tournaments at Somenos and Duncan as well as in South Cowichan. These recreational activities did not vanish from the scene when war work took up so much of women's energies.

In the happy, prospering pre-war years, the little hamlet that clustered around Duncan's Station had expanded greatly with more businesses and more homes. The residents felt themselves distinct from the surrounding farms, having different problems and different interests. They petitioned, with success, for incorporation as a city municipality, and on March 4, 1912, the City of Duncan received its Letters Patent.[13] The city status did not change anything for Cowichan's women.

Cowichan Lake came into the mainstream of the Valley's life when regular passenger rail service commenced in 1913,[14] and the stages mentioned earlier continued service.

The care-free days, fun-filled for so many, came to an abrupt end with the declaration of war in August of 1914. Cowichan, with its strong "home" ties was probably more immediately affected than any other part of Canada. It was not just the men, young and not so young, whose lives changed overnight. Their homes lost the head of the house for the duration, many forever. The war wrought great changes in less direct ways in the lives of women.

The Cowichan Women's Institute, incorporated so recently, now took the lead in organizing volunteer war work. Immediately following the declaration of war, they called a general meeting of all "ladies" of Cowichan, (the term the Cowichan Leader favoured in those days), a meeting which attracted one hundred and fifty persons. Practical plans were made for providing comforts for the men in the Esquimalt camp. A committee was formed to gather up donations of fresh fruit and vegetables to supplement the men's diet. Also appointed at this meeting was the Friendly Help Committee which was to give support to soldiers' families.[15]

This general meeting set the pattern for war work, women's groups uniting again and again in a variety of efforts to raise funds for the Red Cross and the Blue Cross, whether from dances, tag days or the making up of parcels of "comforts" for overseas. All these activities represented traditional women's work, but as the war dragged on, taking almost all Cowichan's able-bodied men, women had perforce to step into the men's shoes.

When the secretary of the Canadian Council of Agriculture spoke to the United Farmers in 1917 and advised them to get their wives and daughters involved, he spoke to the converted.[16]

The Cowichan Leader of May 16, 1918, ran a lengthy article reprint from the Vancouver Province on the part Cowichan women were playing in the war effort. It spoke of one farm, operated by the younger brother of a soldier, where a sister of the absent soldier helped with the milking of 18 cows. It noted with surprise that young girls could be seen driving teams of horses and heavily loaded wagons into town. "Scores of farmers' wives," the writer said, "are doing half the work of a man in addition to their own not inconsiderable work in the home" and "the everyday peacetime labours have not been lost sight of in the war. The King's Daughters still conduct a spring and summer flower show."

In spite of the great drain of manpower from the Valley's farms, the article also could say, "It seems incredible, but the biggest fall fair in British Columbia last year, in point of all-round entries and stock exhibits, was the

The H.W. Bevan home on Maple Bay Road was a fine example of a 1913 substantial family home.

Cowichan Fall Fair at Duncan."

Coincidental with the declaration of war, a new Agricultural Hall was opened in Duncan.[17] It had been completed in time to serve as temporary army barracks for a period during the war years. Before that happened the Cowichan Fall Fair of 1914 celebrated its new, larger quarters with its first ever trade exhibit section and a prize for the best dressed store window.

In November of 1914 a Farmers' Market was established in Duncan, with women exhibiting both farm produce and baked items.

A young woman, Miss Dorothy Geoghegan, served for two of the war years as a churchwarden at St. Mary's, Somenos, a very unusual role in that period, to say the least.[18]

With patriotic fervour at a high pitch, this was an appropriate time for the Girl Guide movement to come on the Cowichan scene. The first company was formed in October of 1914[19] and on a Saturday in June of 1915 the company, now twenty-two strong, conducted a stall at the Farmer's Market. They raised $37.00 toward the fund for Canadian Prisoners of War in Germany. In March of 1920 another Girl Guide Company came into being at Cowichan Station.[20]

Women everywhere had been keeping the farms in production. As time went on they took their place in decision-making bodies. In February, 1917, a Mrs. Troughton was reappointed to the executive of British Columbia Beekeepers Association.[21] She was also on the executive of the Cowichan Valley Poultry Association.

Women had at last become visible in many areas of life. Even when the war was over and the men returned home, farm women did not slip back into the shadows. According to the Cowichan Leader, Mrs. C. Doering was elected a director of the British Columbia Jersey Breeders Association at a

Vancouver meeting.[22] The Leader noted that a shipment of goats had arrived for Mrs. Bradley-Dyne, "who is going in for the goat industry."[23]

The Leader also reported that "local poultry-men had entered into a government egg co-operative and Mrs. G.A. Tisdall had the honour of signing the first agreement."[24]

Without losing sight of the primary objective of winning the war, women pursued their long-term goal of winning equal political status with men. The slow progress of previous decades to that goal became a great leap forward in the war years. The gains came piecemeal, but quickly. The Church was first to grant equality in voting. The Cowichan Leader of February 8, 1915 announced on page one that the Anglican Synod of British Columbia, at its Easter meeting, would grant women the right to vote. While it is true that in September of 1916 the Conservative Party went on record as opposing Women's Suffrage and Prohibition in an interesting juxtaposition of concern, on September 14, a mere twelve months later, the local Conservatives were voting to have women on the executive.[26] The Liberals were ahead of them by a few weeks and had endorsed a new constitution and bylaws which provided that women could be admitted without a fee.[27] Now they were more equal than men! By this time a provincial referendum had approved the vote for women by a heavy majority.

Cowichan women took their new rights and responsibilities seriously. In late 1916 the Women's Institute heard a paper on parliamentary procedure. A few months later Maria (Mrs. Gordon) Grant of Victoria, President of the Political Equality League, talked to the women on the subject of rights and responsibilities, an address which was reported at length in the Leader of April 5, 1917. "Women were entering upon many new duties," she said in her Cowichan speech, "and events today have shown that women are equal to every demand made upon them...Within a few days the women of British Columbia would become citizens." The main theme of her address was that women must be equal partners to men. "It was a question, then," she summarized, "would women live up to the ideals men had of them, would they be able to do something to purify public life, or would they mar it? It should not be a question of 'How good are we?' but of 'What good are we?'"

For many years, commencing in the nineteenth century, Cowichan had been electing women to the School Board, and in 1915 the Board in turn elected a Mrs. Henderson to the chairmanship. (Note: The Cowichan Leader does not give her initials, but the 1920 Voters List shows a Mrs. Nellie May Henderson, married woman).[28]

In October of 1918 a new Provincial Voters' List was prepared and Edith (Mrs. E.F.) Miller the incumbent mayor's wife, was the first woman to put her name on it.[29]

A poem published in the Leader on February 6, 1919, furnished an old-fashioned bit of nonsense as a counter-weight to all the serious talk of the implications of female suffrage. The last verse runs, "Fools tell that love is blind...Not mine, come fly with me...In very truth I want to get her to the polling booth...Ere she can change her mind."

In May of 1919 the City of Duncan fell into line and conceded that

244

William & Noran Kingston's 2nd house built on the same property in 1905.

women might pay road tax and be allowed to vote. No discrimination here![30]

The Cowichan Women's Independent Political Union was formed in February of the same year.[32] In October, with a provincial election pending, the women met and elected officers.[31]

The Valley in these early years of the 1920s was no place for a faint-hearted lady. The occasional appearance of cougars in built-up areas was a reminder that the wilderness was still close at hand. The Leader reported that on Boxing Day, 1916, Mrs. C.H. Townsend had had a close encounter with one of the cats. It was broad daylight and she was near Mrs. Nuttall's gate when the animal appeared. "She backed through the gate," the newspaper account states, "...and the panther leisurely followed her for about ten yards...She made noises and waved her basket, the animal was unconcerned. She called for Mr. Nuttall and he and Mr. Forrest came with guns. In the meantime the animal had slid quietly through the gate and disappeared. Mrs. Townsend did not feel so much fear at the time as she did after the encounter."[32] This appears to have taken place in Duncan.

The big issue for Cowichan women in 1919 was school consolidation. The Women's Institute had introduced the subject in September of 1917 with a motion to be sent to the Conference of Vancouver Island Institutes being held the following month. "Whereas we believe that the country child is entitled to every whit as good an educational opportunity as that enjoyed by the city child, we beg the Minister of Education to consider the consolidation of schools in rural districts by establishing central boards of trustees."[33]

It remained for parents, mostly the mothers, to follow up on this. The North Cowichan Municipal Council was reluctant to implement consolidation; they had just built a new one-room school. The rural mothers got out horses and buggies and drove up and down the country roads, getting signatures to a petition requesting consolidation. Accommodation of the rural children would be no problem, the city had an eight-classroom building standing half empty. The North Cowichan Council gave in to overwhelming popular demand. All that remained was to work out the mechanics of transporting the scattered rural children to town.

A ramshackle fleet of buses was assembled, consisting of a retired stage line bus, a truck with wooden seats built in and canvas roof and walls built over, nicknamed the "Chicken Coop"; and a touring car designed for seven passengers, now considered adequate for thirteen children.[35]

September of 1919 saw the closing of all the small, ungraded schools in North Cowichan.[34] Hindsight suggests that the timing of consolidation was poor in view of a fact which no one could have foreseen. The killer postwar flu, the Spanish flu as it sometimes was called, struck in Cowichan with its most extreme force in the winter of 1919 and 1920. For months all public meetings, as well as many organization meetings, were cancelled. Hospital visiting was banned. No flu victims were admitted. Schools were closed off and on through that winter.

Undeterred by the epidemic, an auxiliary to the Great War Veterans Association was formed in January of 1920.[36] However, it was not until December of 1920 that they held their first fund-raising event, a concert, the delay due to the flu epidemic.[37]

While women voted in the provincial election of 1920, that did not mean blatant sexism had died. Edward, Prince of Wales, on his world tour, made a brief stop in Duncan in this year. The school children were marched down to the railway and then were assembled in a reserved area where they might have a good view of their future king. The smallest children were naturally placed in front, but the boys in each class stood in front of the girls.

Two girls private schools that opened in the last years of our pioneer period must be mentioned. One was conducted by Miss Dorothy Geoghegan in her parents' Somenos home. She had taken over the pupils of a Miss Young, also of Somenos, who had died. The other school was Miss Norah Denny's, operating in rented premises in Duncan. These two young women joined forces to found Queen Margaret's School which has grown "beyond all dreams" to be the institution we know today, situated on Duncan's western boundary.

It is impossible to draw a hard line between pioneer and modern times. Cowichan had changed greatly in the period between first white settlement in the 1850s and 1900, but even by the turn of the century there were many women still struggling with few household conveniences.

The story was different for the next two decades. While the year 1920 did not mark any clear break with the past, there were many signals that the pioneer period in Cowichan's development had ended. Cars began coming into general use even for farm families, and children no longer received their education in one-room schools. More and more women were put in touch with friends through the magic of the telephone. Admittedly electrical service for the back roads of the rural areas had to wait until after another world war, and farm wives continued to cope with coal oil lamps or, perhaps, gas lamps, and continued to do the family wash laboriously by hand or by gas fueled washing machines. The end of the war, the return of the men from overseas, not to mention the end of cumbersome long skirts, in many ways changed the slowly evolving character of the Valley. It had become recognizably the same as it is today, one hundred and twenty-five years after white settlement began.

THE KING'S DAUGHTERS AND THEIR HOSPITAL: 1911 to 1920
by Jo Ann Whittaker

The King's Daughters Hospital (KDH) served the Cowichan Valley for the years 1911 to 1967. Then it was replaced by the present Cowichan District Hospital on Gibbins Road. During those 56 years the building perched upon Hospital Hill, overlooking Somenos Lake. It underwent many changes, finally becoming too old to be of service and the old buildings were eventually torn down. Today, the Extended Care Unit of the Cowichan District Hospital occupies that site.

The King's Daughters Hospital founded by women and run by women is unique in British Columbia history. At that time for the most part women played a secondary role in hospitals, usually in the auxiliaries. They raised money and did volunteer work. Men ran the hospitals, served on the boards of trustees and made the decisions. However, the hospital came into existence at a time of expansion in Canada and in the Cowichan Valley.

Between 1896 and 1914 more than two million immigrants came to Canada. By 1911 over one-half the population lived in urban areas. Industrial expansion sustained this population growth and rural - urban shift. At the same time, there was a spirit of social reform. The evils of industrialization and urbanization threatened the social order. Interest in such issues as public health, better water and sanitation, housing, prostitution, The City Beautiful, alcoholism, "pure milk" and "to build a strong and healthy race" became the focus of the reformers, mostly members of the middle class. One of the manifestations of this interest and growth was the increase in the number of hospitals.

Hospital care improved after the discovery of microbes and the development of techniques to prevent infection. Hospitals became places for curing; no longer were they a last resort that could only end in the death of the patients. Medicine became a profession with an increasingly rigorous educational regimen and standards of practice. Nursing grew as well, copying medicine in its attempts to set standards of education and practice.

Concomitant with this growth, women were becoming more involved in the public sphere. They banded together in literary clubs, sororities and secular charitable organizations, groups which enabled them to expand their influence from the family to the public sphere. As well, it was here that women learned to conduct meetings, express opinions in public and to organize all areas in which they very quickly became expert. For the women of the Cowichan Valley, one such group epitomized this phenomenon. This was the Order of the King's Daughters and Sons.

In 1886 in New York City, Margaret Bottome, the wife of a Methodist clergyman, founded the Order of the King's Daughters. Another renowned Protestant clergyman, Edward Everett Hale, advised her to found a sisterhood for wealthy women.[1] Hale was in the forefront of the "Social Gospel" movement in the United States. Mrs. Bottome and other middle class and upper class women who founded this new group were also members of the leading Protestant churches in the United States.[2] One of them contributed the new group's name.

It was Marie Louise Irving who contributed the name. When the Reverend Theordore Irving was president of Helmuth College in London, Ontario, Marie Louise bestowed the name King's Daughters upon a group of female graduates. She wanted them to carry the name as an inspiration for their future life. They were God's daughters on earth to do good deeds for Him and to set a good example in their daily living. After her husband died, Mrs. Irving moved to New York City and worked as the principal of a large girls boarding school, St. John's where she continued the practice of bestowing the name King's Daughters upon her graduates. The name suited the purpose of this new sisterhood.

It was a non-affiliated, secular religious order whose purpose was to do good in God's name in a society that was seen as increasingly disordered. Their numbers quickly grew as other like-minded women joined in cities all over the United States and Canada. Eventually the order became worldwide. In October 1886 circles of boys called Royal Guards had been formed from Sunday School classes. In 1887, men and boys sought admission and the name became the Order of the King's Daughters and Sons.[3] They were an influential group and spread their philosophy via their journal, The Silver Cross, and in a monthly column in the Ladies Home Journal.[4]

King's Daughters did not have a distinct uniform but did have a distinctive badge. The symbol chosen was the silver maltese cross of the Waldensian Christians, a 12th century breakaway group who identified one another by the silver maltese cross that each wore. In addition to their identifying cross, the watchword, "In His Name", came from the Waldensians.[5] The King's Daughter's motto represented faith, hope and altruistic service, as expressed in the lines: "Look up and not down, Look forward and not back, Look out and not in, And lend a hand."[6]

At first, "Tens" was the name used locally. This was too confining and was changed to "Circles".[7] The first circle in Canada was the Scattered Circle in the Cowichan Valley.

Bessie Maitland-Dougall arrived in the Cowichan Valley in 1886, accompanied by her husband, Frederick and by her daughter, Edith. She was acquainted with Margaret Bottome and in 1887 organized the first circle of King's Daughters in Canada. The name indicated that her many friends, scattered all over the continent, were members.[8]

The idea of a group such as the King's Daughters was popular in British Columbia. The province was expanding, the railway had arrived and with

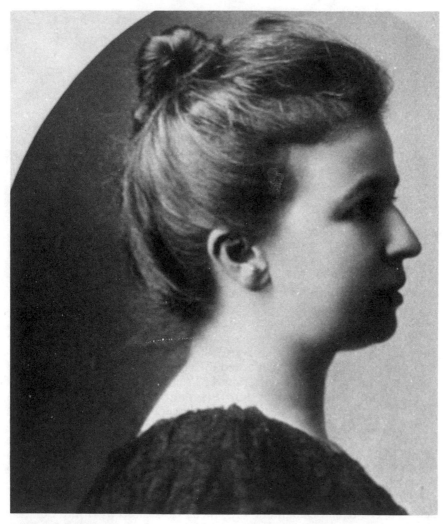

Bessie Maitland-Dougall, Founder of Scattered Circle, Kings Daughters, Cowichan, V.I.

it came businessmen and entrepreneurs with their families. It was the first secular group of women organized in the province.[9]   The first Victoria membership lists contained the names of some of the leading families. There were also circles in Vancouver, the Fraser Valley and in the Interior; each with its own project. Some examples of charitable works were aiding hospitals, work among the poor such as the provision of clothing, and the maintenance of missionaries in China. Much of the work done by these women to raise money was traditional women's work -- sewing, baking, flower shows, concerts, dances and teas.[10] Eventually, there were five circles in Cowichan: Scattered, Looking Out, Silver Cross, Happy Workers

Laying of the foundation stone of King's Daughters' Hospital, Duncan, 1910.

and Helping Hand. The latter two were from Crofton; they declined after the closure of the smelter, the people moving away.[11]

In 1896, the circles formed a provincial group. Bessie Maitland-Dougall was the first President, a tribute to the energy and prominence of Cowichan Valley women. The first provincial convention took place in Victoria on June 18, 19, and 20, 1901. There were 180 members in eight circles in British Columbia.[12] Mary Marriner noted the vigour of the Cowichan circles in her diary. The Cowichan circles raised $175.00 at their traditional sale of women's work in December for this project.[13] One member, Miss Wilson, discussed the project of a convalescent home in Duncan at the 1903 convention. At the June 1904 convention the provincial body adopted the Convalescent Home as their project. It was to be a memorial to Bessie Maitland-Dougall who had died that year. By June, 1905 they had raised $1600. The Scattered Circle undertook the bulk of the organizing work with Mrs. Macdonald and Miss Wilson acting in concert with the provincial executive of the King's Daughters. The circle opened a bank account, The King's Daughters' Provincial Convalescent Home Building Fund and donated $1000 as well as purchasing one acre of land for $100. They had every reason to believe that they would be successful in their endeavours. By 1908, there were sixteen circles and 326 members in British Columbia.[14]

Originally they planned to build a convalescent home for "tired" mothers. Later, they expanded their plans to include an emergency hospital. Controversy arose because the provincial body were supporting an institution that benefited local people. Eventually, the King's Daughters decided to continue. By March 1909, they completed plans with the architect, W.H. Wilson and announced an immediate start.[15] There was no further action until May 1910 when tenders were called for construction. At the same time, a deputation of women requested that the municipality extend King's Road (the present Jubilee Street).[16] Excavation began in September. In a grand ceremony, the Order of the Masons laid the cornerstone on

October 22, 1910. Grand Master E.B. Paul conducted the ceremony. He was rewarded with a silver trowel to commemorate this occasion. Contents of the cornerstone were a list of the names and ranks of the members of Temple Lodge 33, A.F. and A.M., a copy of the Emergency communication calling the members, a list of the officers of the Order of the King's Daughters and Sons and copies of the Victoria Daily Colonist and Cowichan Leader.[17]

To secure funds from the provincial government, The King's Daughters incorporated under the Benevolent Societies Act in 1910. In this way, if they agreed to take all classes of patients, they were entitled to a per diem grant as well as a building grant. Many small hospitals started in British Columbia at this time. The government had a policy of giving a grant for construction purposes if the community could match the sum requested. Those seeking these funds often appealed to their member of the provincial parliament (MPP) to act on their behalf when dealing with the provincial secretary. So it was W. Hayward who secured $1000 for the King's Daughters Hospital and Convalescent Home. (The name was shortened to the King's Daughters Hospital in 1916). The Cowichan Leader focussed on a fund-raising campaign starting with $180.00 in September 1910. Weekly, the paper featured the names of donors and amounts donated. By December 29, 1910 the community had raised $2100.50. In addition to the provincial government grant $2118.45 had been accumulated over the previous five years, the municipality donated $50 and Angus McKinnon donated one acre of land. Other organizations furnished rooms and the kitchen.[18]

The provincial secretary, Dr. H.E. Young, Canon Leakey and the Reverends Christmas and Holmes opened the hospital on April 4, 1911.[19] It consisted of a full basement, a main floor and a second storey that was one-half the size of the main floor.[20] Almost immediately it proved to be too small.

The Canadian Northern Railway was constructing a line to Cowichan Lake and beds were needed for the influx of male labourers, a number of whom might be expected to require hospitalization. Thus the first expan-

King's Daughters' Hospital, Duncan.

Opening ceremony King's Daughters' Hospital, 1911.

sion was a six-bed men's ward and two private rooms completed in 1912 paid for entirely by money raised by the King's Daughters and from the public. W.H. Wilson designed this as well. He planned to add an operating room, converting the existing one to a private room when there was sufficient money.[21] This was done in 1913 along with the new maternity wing. This second addition was financed by the women with a $5000 mortgage. The hospital paid the interest out of operating funds but the local circles also donated funds for this purpose and also paid the insurance.

King's Daughters supported the hospital with "women's work." They made hospital gowns, bathrobes and other linens and sold handiwork such as knitting, crocheting and baking in order to raise funds. They organized the Hospital Ball and provided tea at the Cowichan Fall Fair annually. By such means they were able to maintain their hospital.

Women ran the hospital both on the board of trustees and as the staff. The most powerful committee was the House Committee. Here, the Matron was in attendance bi-weekly. For many years, Miss Wilson chaired this committee where women had some power and control. They were involved in such diverse matters as choosing fabric for the student's uniforms, the general appearance of the interior of the institution, the purchase of food and the solicitation of donations of food, the state of the furnace, fuel consumption, the monthly patient average, spring cleaning, electricity needs, fund-raising, setting hospital fees, and the state of the equipment. Once, between board meetings, they fired the matron and hired a new one! Generally, this was a transference of women's responsibility in the home to the public sphere. Even on this committee the males were present. Dr. Stephens, and later Dr. Rutherfoord were on it because their expertise was necessary for the purchase of medical supplies. Even here, the matron who used them had to consult a male. The finance committee always was chaired by a male trustee and money matters were left to them, even though the women raised the money.

The Matron was expected to be very economical in her purchases. The board secretary dealt with insurance costs and was responsible for paying the bills although she had discretionary powers over a small amount of cash. The first three years of operation, the women conducted the correspondence. The first male manager was W.A. McAdam (later British Columbia's Agent-general in London) who worked for the King's Daughters Hospital from 1914 to 1919. After assuming his post, he handled the correspondence and dealt with the provincial government. He was replaced by E. Carr-Hilton who had been the manager of the Canadian Bank of Commerce. The secretary always attended the board meetings. The matron, in charge of the day-to-day operations, attended only when requested. These roles reflected the assumptions about the duties of men and women in the society itself. Men dealt with politics and finances; women cared, nurtured and consumed but under the guidance of men. The staff almost entirely was composed of women. The first matron was Nora Beane, a graduate of a hospital in St. Paul, Minnesota.[22] She fulfilled two duties: housekeeper and nurse. Mary Marriner worked at the Convalescent Home in 1911 as she was required. On May 30, 1911, the first probationer, Mrs. Scholfield, started work.[23] Nothing is known of her fate. Eventually, another graduate nurse and two pupil nurses, Edna Murton and Miss Rogers were added to the staff.[24] Their student uniform consisted of a lavender and white underdress topped by a white bib and apron. There was no special cap. The graduation pin was a maltese cross.

Women worked as cooks and in the laundry. Often, the garden work was

Nurses at Kings Daughters Hospital and Convalescent Home - 1914.
Front, left to right: Miss Nott, Winona Orr, Winnifred Lee.
Back, left to right: Miss Rogers, Miss New, Miss Edna Murton.
Of this group Winona Orr was a graduate nurse at that time and the others still in training. Miss Rogers and Edna Murton graduated in 1914 and Miss New in 1916.

done by the King's Daughters. Later, Chinese male labourers were employed in the kitchen and laundry; a Caucasian did the yard work. Student nurses did all the rest of the work.

It was the student nurses who did the cleaning, took care of the patients, served the meals, prepared special meals and painted the furniture. Occasionally, if the workload was heavy, housekeeping help was employed. The hours were long; twelve hours per day seven days per week. Student nurses attended lectures after shifts were completed. The matron was responsible for instructing them in the art of nursing. The local doctors lectured to them on anatomy, physiology, surgery and medicine. They also examined them at the end of the year to determine if they should advance and at the end of the three year course to determine if they should graduate. The only control that the matron had was over the choice of probationer and her dismissal, usually for poor character. This again demonstrates society's concept of the roles of men and women. The moral character of the students was the province of the matron; the intellectual aspects were the province of males.

The first two graduates of the King's Daughters' Hospital and Convalescent Home were Miss Rogers and Edna Murton in 1914.[25] Miss New graduated in March 1916 followed by Miss Bonsall[26] in 1917. This did not mean that they were the only students. Other women started the course and for various reasons did not complete the full three years. It was not uncommon for a student to take a leave of absence for reasons of health or because she was needed at home and then to later return to complete the course. Although the school of nursing was ostensibly an educational institution, in reality, student nurses were a form of cheap labor. This was the reason that the school was started in the first place.[27] Nor was this fact peculiar to Duncan's hospital. Other small hospitals had classes of students who were the main source of nursing staff, overseen by a matron or graduate nurse. It was because of inconsistent education standards and lack of professional control that the Graduate Nurses' Association of British Columbia worked for so many years for the registration of nurses.[28]

The second matron was a registered nurse, Gertrude Currie, who worked at the hospital from 1914 to 1918. Her workload was heavy. In addition to the charge of the students, she was responsible for assuring the cleanliness of the institution, purchasing foodstuffs and medical supplies, staffing the operating room as necessary, administering anesthetics and generally being about the place twenty-four hours per day, seven days per week! For this she was paid $65 per month plus room and board. Her assistant who worked night shift received $55 per month. The secretary with the less onerous tasks and responsibilities received $25 per month for part-time work.[29]

By the time she left, Miss Currie was receiving $75 per month. However, the board had to advertise the position for $85 per month in order to attract qualified candidates so they very magnanimously offered her that amount for her last month of service.[30] Miss Currie was replaced by Miss Smith (who was fired by the House Committee) and then by Miss Scott (who was hired by the House Committee). Neither were local Duncan women.

On the first board of directors, out-of-town trustees appointed by the King's Daughters were Miss Margaret Leitch, Mrs. Hasell and Mrs. Watt. Local women were Mrs. Susan Holmes, Miss Wilson, Mrs. Eleanor Macdonald, Mrs. Hamish Morten, Mrs. Florence Whittome and Mrs. Gaynor Elkington. The four males were Frederick Maitland-Dougall appointed by the King's Daughters and T.A. Wood, government agent, and Dr. H.H. Stephens, retired Royal Navy fleet surgeon, both appointed by the provincial government and A.C. Aitken appointed by the municipality of North Cowichan.[31] In 1912, the King's Daughters also appointed W.H. Elkington. Although women planned the hospital, raised much of the money required for its construction and served as trustees and provided money for its maintenance, a man was always the chairperson of the board. Frederick Maitland-Dougall served as the chairperson from 1911 until his death in 1916. Then W.H. Elkington assumed the chair. In the absence of the chairperson, one of the other male turstees presided. Only for one meeting, between 1911 and 1920 did a woman take the chair even though women outnumbered the men.

The same women served as trustees for many years. Miss Wilson remained even after the King's Daughters gave up the hospital in 1931. Mrs. Whittome, Mrs. Elkington, Mrs. Hamish Morten and Mrs. Macdonald were the others who served for the years covered by this book. Later, in 1918, Mrs. Ada Price and Mrs. J.L. Hird were added. They worked hard and faced and met challenges.

One such challenge they faced was the financial crisis in 1915. A special meeting of the House Committee recommended restraint measures to reduce expenditures. These included abolishing the post of assistant matron, not replacing a probationer who was leaving, allowing a graduate nurse to rent a room in the hospital and charging her for meals and reducing the salary of the laundry woman.[32] They also appealed to MPP Hayward to assist them in applying for convalescent soldiers to be sent to the hospital. As well, they publicized the plight of the hospital in a circular letter.[33] The provincial Kings Daughters assumed the eight percent annual mortgage interest on the $5000 mortgage.[34] Their greatest challenge was rebuilding after fire destroyed the maternity wing on March 2, 1917.

They needed the space. The patients and staff were uninjured, the former were accommodated in the sitting room, the office and the nurses' quarters. These latter were overcrowded so plans were made to erect a tent for the nurses. In addition, the new Workmen's Compensation Act required that injured workers be sent to the nearest hospital. Duncan was closer than Ladysmith or Chemainus for the workers from Cowichan Lake. It was therefore urgent to rebuild the destroyed wing.

The board decided to rebuild immediately, using the old plans. They also recommended that the King's Daughters repay $4500, the remaining mortgage owing, out of the insurance money. The insurance company paid out $6764.75 for the loss of the building and $1387.10 for the contents. Contractors tendered their bids for the building and for the plumbing and heating. The board accepted the lowest bid, that of the Island Building Company of Victoria who had constructed the wing originally. A local firm, J.L. Hird, won the contract for the plumbing and heating. Later, Island's bid increased to $5808.10 but still was retained. The contracts were signed by the provincial president and the new wing was in operation by December 1917.[35]

In the years following the First World War the King's Daughters were no longer unique. More women became elected or appointed as trustees in other B.C. hospitals. These women were an example of both the limits and the opportunities for women in British Columbia. They increased their opportunities to expand into the public sphere. However, society's perception of the roles of men and women limited their expansion and left them still controlled by the men.

The King's Daughters continued to run and to support their hospital, overseeing its expansion to sixty beds. Finally, in 1931, the financial burden became too great and the Cowichan District Hospital Association took over its management. Women's work provided insufficient economic returns for the continued independent support of the hospital.

THE PUBLIC HEALTH SERVICE
by Elizabeth Norcross

The Public Health Service came into being just at the end of Cowichan's pioneer period. As with the King's Daughters' Hospital, it was spearheaded by women. The following account has been excerpted from a history of the Margaret Moss Health Centre prepared some years ago by Florence (Mrs. Ivan) Graham.

Following the end of the First World War, Mrs. Graham wrote that a group of courageous, sincere and visionary women in the Cowichan Valley had accepted the challenge to promote a health education program in the schools. This campaign, launched by the Department of Education and sponsored by Dr. Henry Esson Young of the Department of Health, was "to instruct public school children in the laws of health and the principles of hygiene."

It was the ambition of Mrs. Margaret Moss, OBE, an honour conferred in recognition of her WWI war work, to establish such a program in the schools of the Cowichan Electoral District. In 1919, the following groups who had been active in the war effort turned their energies to the peacetime promotion of health: the Red Cross Society, both north and south Cowichan branches, the Women's Institutes of Cobble Hill, Shawnigan Lake and Duncan, the IODE chapters, and the King's Daughters co-operated and co-ordinated to form the Cowichan Electoral District Health Centre. Under the dynamic leadership of Margaret Moss, the women chosen as representatives from these organizations worked tirelessly and unceasingly to organize, administer and encourage the progress of the Health Centre. In 1920 the first Constitution was adopted, which laid the foundation for Public Health Nursing services in the Province of British Columbia.

The fact that the members of the Executive Committee formed in 1919 served continuous terms of office for years was a living testimony to their determination. Their main objective was stated as "improvement of

Health Centre, Duncan.

health, prevention of disease and the mitigation of suffering." Mrs. T. Pitt, Mrs. B.A. MacMillan and Mrs. George Owens devoted 25 years, Mrs. R. C. McGregor 20 years and Mrs. Wace and Miss Foster fifteen years of service to the Committee affairs.

In 1919 Miss Barker was employed by the Committee as the first district nurse. The foundation of the Health Centre was thus established. Funds were secured from the above-mentioned organizations. The nurse had no office, no equipment and no transportation. She depended on a bicycle and the Esquimalt and Nanaimo Railway to get from Duncan to surrounding areas.

In 1920, Miss Hall, a qualified Public Health Nurse replaced Miss Barker and the struggle for existence became critical. Only one school, Cowichan Station, had accepted the program, the demand for services was minimal and only $22.00 remained in the bank. An October 14, 1920, advertisement in the Cowichan Leader names some of the services offered: "Two nurses in residence, visits seventy-five cents, assisting doctor obstetrical five dollars, assisting minor operation two dollars." Miss Hall then resigned to become Assistant to the Director of the Victorian Order of Nurses in Calgary, and Miss Jeffares was employed by the Committee.

As the years went on, a real effort was made to extend and increase services. Funds were increased by a drive.

In 1924, offices were established in the Baron Building and two cars were purchased. Later a house was rented for the accommodation of the nurses.

Details of the expanding work of the Health Centre fall outside the time period of this book. In 1946 it became the Health Unit and the Cowichan Leader, in a tribute to the Centre said this, "The new Health Unit was a high mark to set in progressing from where the Cowichan Health Centre has left off."

A final note concluded: "In 1961 it was necessary for the Duncan Office to have a modern, useful building in which to function and again the local community responded to the need. Under the direction of the Kinsmen Club of Duncan, the required amount of money was raised locally to meet the Government's criteria to build a new Health Centre. It was most interesting that when the local Kinsmen decided upon a name for the Centre, the memory of Margarget Moss was so imprinted upon their minds that they chose to pay her final tribute in naming the building The Margaret Moss Health Centre."

THE COWICHAN WOMEN'S INSTITUTE
By Shirley Green

The idea of Women's Institutes was first brought to British Columbia in 1909 by Miss Laura Rose when she came from Ontario on her tour of Agricultural Fall Fairs, judging produce and giving lectures on dairying.

In November 1910 Miss Alice Ravenhill, a Fellow of the Royal Sanitary Institute of London, came to British Columbia and at the request of the Minister of Agriculture she organized Women's Institutes. She also wrote a series of bulletins for the use of the Women's Institutes some of which were entitled "The Place and Purpose of Family Life", "The Preservation of Food", "Labour saving devices for the Household", "Food and Diet and the Art of Right Living".

The Cowichan Women's Institute was founded in September 1912, having been organized by Mrs. Alfred Watt. It was incorporated on 18 November 1912. The names of First Officers and Charter Members will be found in Appendix II.

A Provincial Government grant of fifty cents per member was received. Over the years it was necessary to raise additional funds by putting on teas, entertainments, subletting the institute club room, alphabetical sales, home-baking stalls, dances, theatrical productions and of course each member paid an annual fee.

And so began an organization which in a quiet way was to have a considerable impact on life in the Cowichan Valley over the years. Only the less-advantaged years will be covered here for the 1920s brought a multitude of labour and time-saving devices and the rugged, early ways were soon out of mind. Household appliances of the Twenties (and even the Thirties) seem archaic now but they were "the latest thing" to the average citizen then.

The first meeting was held in September 1912 in the home of Miss Clack. The house still stands on Ingram Street in downtown Duncan though almost hidden by tall trees. Later the Masonic Hall, and then a room in the

Post Office building were used. This first meeting set the pace for the many to follow with a paper read by Miss Hadwen on "Milk", covering the production and care of milk on the farm. Succeeding meetings dealt with such diverse topics as first aid, dressmaking, gardening and cooking.

The members arranged to send displays of bottled fruit, jam, hams, bacon, poultry products and honey to the Dominion Fair to be held in Victoria.

By the latter part of 1913 plans for a lending library were made and "Book Teas" were held to fill the library shelves. Members also helped to lay out gardens at each of the district's schools.

June 1914 found the Cowichan Women's Institute hosting the Conference of Vancouver Island Women's Institutes in Duncan. Many delegates came from all over the Island and interesting discussions were heard: to name a few topics such as - modern housekeeping, babies and baby shows, domestic science, employment of women, the high cost of living, and co-operation among women's societies. An editorial in the Cowichan Leader on this occasion devoted two front-page full length columns to the work of Institute women.

With the opening of new club rooms in the Agricultural Hall the Cowichan Women's Institute was able to carry out their plan for a lending library with minimal membership fees - 50 cents for Institute members and one dollar for all others who wished to avail themselves of the books.

In August 1914 work of the Women's Institutes everywhere focussed on the war and how they could best help their husbands and sons. The Friendly Help Committee appointed at a meeting of the ladies of the district called by the Cowichan Women's Institute met with Mrs. F. L. Stephenson in the chair and with representatives of all women's societies and all churches in attendance. This committee was to find out all cases of the families of soldiers that needed "neighbouring" and to see that they were well taken care of.

Sewing and knitting were prominent among the Institute endeavours during the war. Some members also spent their time mending, sorting and packing clothes for the Belgians.

The Cowichan Women's Institute having its own club rooms, decided to buy a piano on the instalment plan so that the rooms might be available for sub-letting in the evenings.

At the Institute meeting in May 1915 it was noted that the Red Cross work was of necessity occupying much of the memberships' time and a committee was formed to tackle this job. The minutes at this time list an impressive quantity of hospital supplies sent through the Vancouver Branch of the Red Cross.

In 1916 Annual Meeting the minutes make the first reference to Mrs. Blackwood-Wileman, president. Of the many active members of the organization, she was one of the most active. The Cowichan Leader's tribute to her appears at the end of this essay.

Through the war years members were very busy. There were the Red Cross Committee and the Friendly Help Committee as well as regular meetings at which they heard addresses or discussed matters of particular interest to women. They were looking into jam-making and canning as a

Mr. W.H. Hayward, M.P. Mrs. Hayward & Violet Hayward. 5 Feb./05.

possible industry, basket-making as a handicraft. With all these interests the president was able to report at the beginning of 1917 that membership had increased from the initial 30 to 147.

The library and interest in it had grown to the point that it was decided to set up an independent library committee for 1917 to work in co-operation with the Institute; consequently five members of the Institute worked together with five non-members.

Also in 1917 some 45 members of the Institute took part in a presentation of the Gilbert and Sullivan Comic Opera "Trial by Jury" a production which was a huge success in every way with the proceeds divided between the Blue Cross and Red Cross funds. In July of that year the Cowichan

Women's Institute records carry this note. "Mrs. Hayward reported that owing to a change about to be made in the Mainland and Island Red Cross Societies, we have decided to call ourselves Cowichan Women's Institute War Workers as we still wish to remain an independent body and hope to carry on our good work to help the men at the front who are sacrificing so much for us."

The Women's Institute succeeded in maintaining all activities. In September 1917 they were looking into the matter of school consolidation which was brought about two years later.

In November of that year they passed a resolution calling on the Government to take steps to obtain indentured Oriental labour for the period of war "on the lines in which it is now provided in France and other parts." Related to this theme, in April of the next year they endorsed a resolution from the Women's Institute at Kalamalka to petition the Government to have all interned aliens put to work to earn their own food.

The library committee could report that the library had about 100 members, but there was room for more. Later in the year the Cliffs School was closed and a large number of its books were donated to the library.

Back on the national issues: In June 1918 National Registration was to be attempted. The Cowichan Women's Institute room was placed at the disposal of the National Registration Registrar on June 22, and members of the Institute and the IODE volunteered their services for this work.

Among the great variety of speakers and topics heard at 1918 meetings were: Mr. C.H. Hopkins on poultry; Mrs. George Henderson on the Canadian School system; Mr. Hopkins again speaking on "Insects, our friends or foes"; Miss Edith Ravenhill demonstrating a steam pressure cooker; Mr. Stevenson on bulbs and their care; Miss Helen Stewart, librarian from Victoria who spoke on (1) conservation of food, (2) life in France, (3) library work; Mrs. Burchett on music in the schools.

It was a very full program for 1918 especially considering the fact that all meetings were cancelled from September to the end of the year because of a national flu epidemic. The grand Victory Ball planned for January 30, 1919 had to be postponed to Easter Monday for the same reason.

In the meantime, traditional concerns of the Women's Institute were kept in mind. Health of school children was up for discussion at one meeting. The embarrassing state of the school library was the subject of another report as it appeared that only 50 books still were in good condition. By contrast, the adult library had added 155 new books to its stock in the preceding year with 15 more on order.

Mindful of the responsibility bestowed upon women with the obtaining of the vote, the Cowichan Women's Institute members arranged a monthly round table conference on civic and provincial laws.

In April, following months of discussion, it was decided to get a district nurse from the Victorian Order of Nurses. This placed another obligation on the organization to raise funds to pay the nurse. On the general subject of health it was resolved to ask the Mayor and Council to have notices posted requesting people not to expectorate on the sidewalks.

The Cowichan Women's Institute Library had by this time become the Cowichan Public Library which was hailed as progress.

1915. Early Buick, possibly 1912 model. Mr. R. Blackwood-Wileman, Mrs. Blackwood-Wileman and ?

At its June meeting president, Mrs. Blackwood-Wileman, reported on some of the most important subjects in which the Institute had been interested - the consolidation of schools, the district nurse, teaching of humane subjects in the schools, and the Blue Cross surplus funds.

Other unrelated matters came up for discussion during the summer of 1919 such as assisting with an entertainment to raise funds for boy scout uniforms. Also, they requested City Council to take steps to ensure that horses were not left standing indefinitely on city streets in hot weather.

Obtaining a district nurse was found to give rise to unexpected problems. However, by December of 1919 a district nurse was in residence in Duncan and "available to all those desirous of nursing care who live between Westholme and Hillbank."

Sadly, Mrs. Blackwood-Wileman who had worked so hard in this and other causes, died at this time. The Cowichan Leader paid tribute to her as follows:

"Mrs. Adelaide Blackwood-Wileman, 1852-1919: Her activities in this District are written large. More than anyone else she was directly responsible for the consolidation of the schools in Duncan and North Cowichan. This was but one phase of her work in connection with the Cowichan Women's Institute of which she has been president for the past four years, the Library, the District Nurse, the inauguration of the Blue Cross Society, the Cowichan Chapter IODE and the Children's Aid Society are but a few of the works in which she took a leading part. She has passed literally 'in harness' pointing to her fellow women to revive the old domestic crafts of spinning and weaving and to carry on the projects she succeeded in instituting after much opposition.

Mrs. Blackwood-Wileman was gifted with exceptional powers of organization and her influence extended far beyond Cowichan. She became a member of the Advisory Board of the Women's Institute in 1917 and succeeded Miss Alice Ravenhill in the chairmanship. On several occasions, as on her last trip, she was selected by the Government to represent the Province in Women's Institute gatherings.

Cowichan can ill spare one whose influence has been so marked on all that tends to improve country life. She set an example during the war. She faced the problems of peace undaunted. She leaves a splendid record of service and inspiration to those who are here and those who will come after."

This tribute to Mrs. Blackwood-Wileman could also have applied to many of the members of the Cowichan Women's Institute of the period from 1912 to 1920. Not only those whose names appeared most consistently in the meeting minutes and in newspaper reports, but to those whose names appeared only in membership lists. They are the ones who provided the initiative energy and generosity to carry out plans successfully. Their team work has prevailed through the years and is still much alive in the present day Institutes of Cowichan, Somenos, Koksilah, Lake Cowichan and their neighbours, Cobble Hill and Shawnigan Lake.

Rosalie Winifred Ashburnham (nee Barnard)
(Mrs. Lawrence Ashburnham)
and
Doreen Ashburnham-Ruffner
by Doreen Ashburnham-Ruffner, daughter

The name of Ashburnham goes back to 1913 at Cowichan Lake. A cousin of my mother's who had previously immigrated to Vancouver, British Columbia, sold us some five hundred acres of lake front property, sight unseen. We set sail from England for Canada with promises of green pastures, peach orchards and a three-bedroom house with barns and outbuildings. Our party included my father and mother, Lawrence and Winifred Ashburnham, and Mrs. Farrer, a long-time friend of the family. Mother's maid, Grace, came too. She married Fred Reed of Maple Bay. My nanny and myself were to follow in May of 1914.

The family arrived by horse stage at Lake Cowichan in December of 1913 and were taken up to the lake property by boat. They prepared to move into a small furnished house until they could build the large one (fifteen rooms in all), which the families had planned to use as a shooting lodge. They were going to have sportsmen from England who would come yearly for the shooting season. The small, furnished house turned out to contain a rusty iron stove, one kitchen table, three rickety chairs and a couple of old bed springs. The family had to return to the Lakeside Hotel and there they remained over the New Year, my mother terrified of "celebrating loggers" shooting off revolvers to see in the New Year.

Finally adequate furniture was obtained and there the family lived until the new house was completed. All material for it had to be hauled up the lake by scow.

Neighbours were few and far between at the lake. Gordon Archibald was our nearest neighbour. He had a small bay on his property which made an excellent harbour. We used his landing stage until we built ours. My first real impression of Cowichan Lake was being helped off the boat at Archibald's landing. Being pitch dark, we did not realize until too late that he had only that day moved the landing. So instead of walking off onto the path, we plunged headlong into a thicket of wild roses. I can remember saying to my father, "If this is Canada, I want to go home to England!"

Mrs. Farrer's children, Marcia and Tony and their nurse arrived the first week in August, just beating the start of the First World War. The war, of course, spoiled all plans of a shooting lodge but we lived there happily for many years.

It was a paradise for children. We had horses, boats and wonderful fishing and swimming. When we were older we had shooting. Blue grouse, willow grouse, pigeons and ducks abounded. We were overrun by deer. Mr. Archibald became our tutor and Mother coped with our French. While we lived in the country we were never allowed to lower our manner of living. We "changed" to formal dress for dinner every night and learned all the social graces.

As children we raised countless rabbits which no one could bear to eat when they were served to us at the table. We loved pig-killing time and used to take the intestines, clean them out, inflate them and--much to our parents' horror--float around in the lake, using them as life belts.

Winters we either went to California or Victoria. It was dreary at the lake, and in those days there was a lot of snow.

I remember my mother trying to bake a cake. Her first effort was so terrible that it was refused by people and animals; even the pigs turned it down!

We had geese that were the bane of Mrs. Farrer's life. Every time she would go into the downstairs kitchen to watch the enormous slabs of gingerbread she would make for us, and bend over to test the progress, Gertie, our grey goose would rush up and peck her sharply on her nether portions!

I do not think either my mother or Mrs. Farrer had ever even seen the inside of a kitchen. Boiling water was an adventure. However, for many years we had two Chinese servants, plus my nurses. We also had hired men to help keep up the property, so no one suffered hardships.

In those days we were self-supporting. We had our own milk, cream, butter and cheese. We slaughtered our beef, lamb and pork. We grew all of our own vegetables and had a root cellar. Small fruit abounded, both wild and cultured. Our cupboards were full of every type of preserve, chutney, pickle and all varieties of canned fruits. We made our own wines and beer. We shot deer for meat in addition to the farm animals. The lake had a lot of trout and we had chickens, turkeys and guinea hens. We salted down beef, cured hams, preserved eggs in isinglass and really shopped only for staples.

We entertained frequently and had guests from all walks of life. I have pictures of Prince Arthur of Connaught and Lord Pembroke pretending to throw Tony into the lake. Lord and Lady Byng spent time with us when he was Governor General of Canada, as did many other notables and all of our dear friends. There was a combination "general store" and post office at the foot of the lake. The train only ran once every two weeks to points up-island. There was one other store and a Chinese laundry, also a boat landing for people to come and purchase their supplies. People were few and far between and logging was just starting.

I remember an incident at one such camp in the Upper or big lake as we called it. Two loggers returned to the big float house on which the crew lived while logging that particular area and having spent the weekend celebrating, they got into a knife fight. They went outside and only one returned. The police went around to all the houses warning parents to keep their children in as there was an escaped murderer at large. We were all agog and rumors ran rampant. Sadly, six weeks later, while dipping up water off the float, the Chinese cook pulled up the man's body with the bucket. He apparently had fallen in and drowned.

I had a little red canoe which, a day before the body was recovered, had gotten loose and floated across the lake. The freight boat recognized it as mine and took it in tow and tied it up at the loggers' float house. The logging boat was instructed to take the body to the foot of the lake for dispatch to Victoria for burial. The boat captain decided that my canoe would be fine for that so the soggy, decaying remains were thrown into it. Upon reaching the foot of the lake the canoe was tied up at the landing stage to await the next move. At that moment, I arrived with my father to pick up our weekly groceries and mail, and on spying my red treasure, took off across the float and took one flying leap into it. What a catastrophe! There was one sodden screaming child with the decomposed remains!

It was the scene of Tony Farrer's and my cougar fight which received so much publicity in August 1916, and finally concluded by my becoming a member of the Victoria Cross-George Cross Association as recipient of the Royal Albert medal for heroism awarded by H.M. King George V. This was the first known attack by a cougar which sprang out of the forest, attacking Tony who was badly mauled and scratched about his head and arms. I resolutely stayed with him, finally driving the animal away into woods where it was later shot by Henry March. I am still flown to England every two years for a reunion and have notable visits with the Royal family either at Buckingham Palace or Windsor Castle.

My family remained until the house burnt to the ground in 1929. We lost everything as we had no insurance. It was a wooden house, and being located that far from civilization with no fire protection, the insurance rates would have been excessive.

In the early thirties we built a huge boat-house, complete with four bedrooms, large living-room and bathroom. We spent many happy summers there before selling it to the Rounds family and moving to California after a few years.

My father died in Santa Cruz in 1943. My mother died in Redondo Beach in 1968. I now live in south central California with my daughter and granddaughter, and look back with pleasure on days that one will never see again.

The site of our house which burnt was dedicated by the government as a public park in memory of my father. On my visits to Canada I frequently go there and sit by the water and dream of those early days starting some sixty-seven years ago.

Gwyneth Ashby (nee Stephenson)
(Mrs. Lancelot Ashby)
1894-
by her daughter Rowena D. Fuller

My maternal grandfather, Frederick L. Stephenson, born in Stratford-on-Avon, England, had an adventurous turn of mind. While attending Dublin University, he decided to seek a new life in Canada. He arrived in Victoria in 1886 where he duly met and married my grandmother, Emily.

My mother, christened Gwyneth, was born in Port Simpson, British Columbia, on June 22, 1894.

Later her parents lived in Ladysmith, moving to Cowichan (by train) when her father was appointed Rector of St. Peter's Church at Quamichan and St. Andrew's Church at Cowichan Station in May of 1914.

Gwyneth lived with her parents at St. Peter's Rectory, in Quamichan. The Rectory is still standing although much altered and the wide verandas are gone.

Only cold water was available in the bathroom and kitchen of the Rectory when the family first took up residence. A basin and tin bathtub were in the bathroom and the facilities consisted of an outhouse at the end of the path.

On one occasion Gwyneth rode her horse, Babe, to Mains' butcher shop in Duncan to pick up the family's order, then, on a dare, crossed the street and rode through the back entrance of the Cowichan Merchants, through the store and out the front door.

On September 1, 1914 she entered training as a nurse at the King's Daughters' Hospital where the Matron was Miss Gertrude Currie.

My mother will be 92 years old this year.

Grace G. Baiss (nee Ellis)
(Mrs. Geoffrey Baiss)
1885-1984
by her daughter Diana J. (Jose) Hewlitt

My mother, Grace G. Baiss, was born in Hungarton, Leicester, England, the seventh daughter of the Reverend John Ellis and Anne Ellis. At the age of nineteen she left her large family of sisters to marry my father in 1907. Geoffrey G. Baiss had travelled to South Africa and the Argentine before

Baiss Farm on Richards Trail.

deciding to farm in the Duncan area. The choice was due to a relative's previous arrival.

Mother knew nothing of farming as she was a city child. She had a small graveyard of pies that had failed (she could not cook), and what do you do with a failed pie? Bury it! That is, of course, after the chickens had refused to risk breaking their beaks, not to mention what it might do to their digestive systems.

Our mother told us of the pigs that got intoxicated after eating fermented apples. They escaped, but we never did hear the end of that story.

When our parents went to socials, we three children rode in the back of the buggy where we were obliged to sleep during the festivities.

Oh yes, indeed, there was a pump where we could draw water from the well, and a wood stove where she learned her cooking skills.

Home for my mother was first on Richards Trail, followed by Herd Road and Eagle Heights. Three children were born to this marriage--Jocelyn (Joy), Dick, and Diana (Jose).

Grace Baiss opened the Black Cat Tearoom in 1924, helped on the farm, and cooked for the help. This busy life ended in 1984, almost reaching a century.

Grace Baiss and Dorothea Baker.

Native lady doing the Baiss laundry as Grace Baiss looks on. c.1907.

Grace Baiss and baby, and the new Premier Washer. c.1918.

Opening of Cowichan Agricultural Hall in 1888.
In doorway: F.H. Price, T.A. Wood & W.H. Elkington.
Standing centre: Theodore Davie, Q.C. & C.E.B. Davie, Q.C.
Seated lower step: James Norcross

Dorothea Gilderdale Baker (nee Ellis)
(Mrs. Hugh C. Baker)
1881-1974
by her daughter Dorothea M. Savory

My mother had a very hard life here in Duncan. She married Hugh C. Baker, a fourth generation Canadian, in 1910, the same year that she came to North America. They lived in Tonnawanda in the United States, then in Eastern Canada and in Phoenix, Arizona, where my father died on Christmas day.

Left a widow with three small children and very little money, my mother came to Duncan in 1919 because her sister, Mrs. Baiss, was living here.

I remember that my mother did the washing outside the back door in summer with a hand-worked machine and a scrub board. We children helped put the clothes through the wringer. There was electric light in the house; one naked bulb hung in the middle of the room into which you had to grope your way to find the string and pull on the light. We had no electric gadgets at all. A wind-up gramophone was our greatest pleasure.

A small shack had been built over a little creek with a trap door opening to the creek. Here a large earthen crock was kept into which was put the butter (home churned by all of us taking turns), the milk, and meat - when we had some - which was not often. Our favourite hiding place was to open this trap door, crawl in and hide under the floor, especially if there were extra chores to be done.

The only heating in the house was the fireplace in the sitting-room and a large wood-burning stove in the kitchen. It was a constant problem, bringing wood in and getting it dry. Often the oven was full of kindling drying, making a pleasant smell of cedar steaming. The oven was used sometimes to warm our feet in the cold weather, resulting in horrible chillblains.

The kitchen was the main living room of the house, everything went on there. While my mother coped with cooking meals, preserving fruit and vegetables or making jam, we children sat around the kitchen table doing our homework or reading. There were two clothes racks on pulleys overhead and the ironing was done with flat irons heated on the stove. The stove also heated the water so this was a central point in our lives. No one wanted to leave the kitchen because the rest of the house was so bitterly cold. My mother had the cold task of lighting the fire in the morning and of starting the morning porridge and setting the bread.

It was a constant struggle for my mother to make ends meet. Her sisters in England helped with finances as much as they could and one brother of my father came and helped on the farm for a while. Life as the daughter of the Reverend John Ellis and Mrs. Annie Ellis in a small vicarage in Leicester had not prepared my mother for this kind of life. I remember the Indians coming around and selling mother a salmon for twenty-five cents and some old clothes. My mother grew sweet peas and gladioli for the Crosland Brothers Seed Farm and worked in her sister's tea room in Duncan to help make money. No family allowance or pensions existed in those days.

We had chickens, a cow and two horses. My brothers milked the cow and I was supposed to look after the chickens. My mother had told me not to learn to milk, for then the boys would stay playing ball at school and not come home to milk. To get groceries, mother or one of us had to entice the horse from the field, hitch her up to the buggy and go down to Duncan to what is now Bucky's Sport Shop for general supplies. How scared we all were when the horse reared when one of the first cars drove by us! Mother managed to keep a tight rein.

We had a happy childhood with plenty of fresh fruit and vegetables, eggs and homemade butter. Mother made jam and preserved fruit. Vegetables were salted down in a large crock and the apples stored in a small cellar. To get to the cellar we had to go out of the house to an outside door, something no one wanted to do in the winter.

Mother only made one trip back to England when her father died.

She died in 1974 and I now live in the home where we grew up.

Harriet Woodhall Bell
1886-1970
by her niece Helen G. Maltby

My aunt, Harriet Woodhall Bell, arrived in Duncan with her parents in October of 1910. She lived on First Street.

She first worked for Mr. Prevost who had a stationery store where Powel's Men's Wear used to be located (a brick building next to Bank of Commerce). She subsequently worked for the Post Office and after that became a Government Telephone Operator for the Gulf Islands in an office above the Post Office in the old Post Office building. This was during the early 1920s (or earlier) to 1931 or 1932.

She was a well known organist for various organizations. She played the organ at the Presbyterian Church for many years and for the Christian Science Church in the 1960's.

For many years she was associated with the McHaffie-Beevor-Potts Medical Clinic.

Auntie also sang at church and at various musical concerts. She played the piano in a small group which provided music for community dances. She loved to play cards, especially canasta and bridge.

She had many, many friends in the community and she always loved to visit our home, bringing us treats galore! She was very good at entertaining us when we were children and was very patient, indeed.

Aunt Harriet died in 1970.

Katie Bell (nee Smith)
(Mrs. Ralph Bell)
1895-1962
by her sister-in-law Gwen Smith

Katie was 16 years old when she came to the Cowichan district. She attended the high school in Duncan. She usually walked to school down the railway track from Herd Road and sometimes took the train home in the afternoon. The fare was then ten cents from Duncan to Somenos Station.

She started to train as a nurse at King's Daughters Hospital but ill health forced her to give it up. Later she graduated from the hospital in Vernon and returned to Duncan where she nursed at the King's Daughters Hospital until her marriage in the early 1920s. She then moved to Kamloops.

Mary Theresa Brown (nee O'Connor)
(Mrs. Oscar C. Brown)
1884-1950
by her daughter Kathleen Getz

In 1907 Mother left County Kerry, Ireland, to join relatives in Canada and a sister living in Cowichan. Two years later she married Oscar Charles Brown, a native son and a well-known builder in the area. Their first home was on the corner in Duncan where the Williams and Davie Law Office now is located. After selling their property at that location to make way for the British Columbia Telephone building, they built their new home on the corner of Trunk Road and McKinstry Road, where it still is standing. I remember mother telling us that there were very few homes in the area and that all around were fields of wild flowers in the spring.

My mother was a life-long member of St. Edward's Catholic Church and in those days worked very hard to raise money to maintain the church as their members were so few. When the Altar Society was formed in Duncan in 1910 Mother was elected secretary-treasurer, the only office needed at that time.

She was a member of the Irish Society which had a fairly large membership. They were quite an active group here during the 1930s, and, of course, their main event of the year was the St. Patrick's Day dinner, as always well attended by the public.

My mother's main interest, however, was always her home and family. This was more than a full-time job with seven children--five boys and two girls, Herman, Bernard, Agnes, Wilfred, Hubert, Gerald and Kathleen. In spite of a very busy life with a large family, she always had time to welcome their many friends.

Violet M. Carr-Hilton (nee Walter)
(Mrs. E.W. Carr-Hilton)
1874-1953
by her daughter Pat Lines

My mother came from London, England, in 1895 to join and marry my father. He was then in Tacoma, working for the Bank of British North America. In 1911 Mr. and Mrs. Carr-Hilton came to Cowichan where Mr.

E.W. Carr-Hilton house situated where Cowichan Lodge now stands, built c.1911.

Carr-Hilton opened the Duncan branch of the Bank of Commerce. Mr. Carr-Hilton, English by birth, started the cricket club here in what is now McAdam Park, in 1913. For a time cricket was very important in Cowichan. The famous Don Bradman came with the Australian team and played Cowichan here. Other notables played cricket here, including Ronald Colman and Nigel Bruce of Hollywood. Violet Carr-Hilton was a charter member of the IODE in Cowichan, and also a member of the Women's Institute, possibly a charter member. When her daughter, Patricia, opened a dance studio in Duncan, Mrs. Carr-Hilton played the piano for her students.

Lillian Clack
1873-1963
Compiled by the Researchers

"My first memory of her was when I was about five years old," Ned Miller said. "My mother called me in to the front room to meet a tall and very pretty young lady with long, golden hair who was proposing to start a kindergarten in Duncan."

Miss Clack, to whom Ned (E.F.) Miller referred, was a very special person in Duncan's life, from the time of her arrival from England about 1910 to her precipitate departure during the Second World War.

273

It is only a slight exaggeration to say that there is no long-time resident of Duncan over the age of 70 who is not anxious to contribute a fond memory of Miss Clack. "I was one of her first kindergarten pupils," "I took piano lessons from her," "I studied water-colour painting under her."

The first kindergarten classes were held in premises over the butcher shop which later became Mains', standing where H.W. Dickie's office is now. Then the classes were moved to the upstairs of the Norcross Building at the corner of Front (now Canada Avenue) and Kenneth Streets. The next move was to a house that stood across the street from the United Church on the northwest corner of Ingram and Jubilee. This was while Miss Clack's house was being built on the opposite corner. In that house she lived for as long as she remained in Duncan.

Ned's story continued: "I think it was then that she began teaching music, and most of the young people of the town took lessons on piano from her. She was a very accomplished musician and was in constant demand to accompany visiting singers from Victoria and other cultural centres. She also taught art at that time, painting, drawing, et cetera. Her pictures were in all local shows. Her speciality was dogwood, but she painted many other subjects."

Another correspondent has contributed: "She was a wonderful teacher. Her pupils found everything very interesting and made good progress, with never any discipline problems." (Besides kindergarten, she taught pupils in the early elementary grades.)

"Among her particular friends," continued this lady, "she seemed to have the most in common with the Misses Wilson of The Cliffs. They also had a school and shared her love of flowers and gardening."

Lillian Clack was one of the younger members of a family of twelve. She was born in London and her father taught art in Kensington. He was well-to-do as he owned a house on the Isle of Wight to which he invited such people as H.G. Wells, George Bernard Shaw and others in that circle.

What brought Miss Clack to Duncan? It is something of a mystery that will probably never be solved. Ned Miller, who believed himself to be the only visitor she ever admitted in her last years, says, "She apparently left England on her own and cut herself off from her family. When she was in her final illness in a nursing home, I wrote to a brother in Manitoba and received a rather curt reply to the effect that she had not kept in touch with them and they felt no responsibility for her. However, when she died, a relative appeared. I wanted to buy one of her pictures, but it was no go. I couldn't even get a picture I had given her years before."

It was a sad end to a career that had been spent taking an active part in and contributing to Duncan's cultural life.

Just as the reason for her coming to Duncan is a mystery, so is the reason for her departure. One story is that her nerves were shattered by the late evening noise from a bowling alley which had been built next door. Another is that malicious gossip affected her. She walked out abruptly with just a suitcase and found a tiny house in North Vancouver where she lived as a recluse and spent hours playing Chopin on the piano by herself.

"Some time in the 1940s," Ned Miller wrote me, "I met her on the street and after that visited her often. Eventually she was taken ill during a very cold spell and the oil for her stove was used up. Neighbours finally entered the house and found her unconscious. She was taken to a nursing home where she lived for some time, but eventually died there. The only Duncan people at her funeral were Eva and I and Girlie (Evelyn) Grassie who was teaching in Vancouver. I couldn't contact anyone else."

It was an unhappy end for one whose memory is cherished by so many.

Louise Bertram Clement (nee Thomson-Currie)
(Mrs. William Alexander Clement)
1870-1966
by her daughter Elizabeth L. Clement

Louise Thomson was born in Orillia, Ontario, the daughter of Frank and Dorothy Thomson. Her father inherited an estate called Lenthill in Scotland near Melrose. This was entailed property which therefore could be inherited only by succession, and to claim it he had to take the name of Currie, thus becoming Frank Thomson-Currie.

In 1898, my mother, Louise Thomson-Currie, went to Britain with a chaperone and several other young ladies on the occasion of Queen Victoria's Jubilee. She kept a diary which is very interesting. As no Canadian flag could be found in London, she bought a white silk flag with a Union Jack on the upper left corner and appliqued three maple leaves and a beaver made of olive green sateen. Waving, cheering and clapping they saw Sir Wilfred Laurier go by. He looked up, seeing the young ladies and their flag.

With her husband, William Alexander Clement, whom she had married on October 26, 1904, she arrived in the Cowichan Valley during the summer of 1914.

My father was a civil engineer but in 1913-1914 there was no engineering going on in Vancouver, necessitating a move. Travelling by boat to Victoria and by the Equimalt and Nanaimo Railway to Duncan, they settled on the north-east corner of Bell-McKinnon and Herd Roads. Here the family was to take up chicken ranching. Life on a chicken farm in Somenos in those days was quite an undertaking but I never once heard my mother complain. The original Herd Road house burned down many years ago.

There were two children, Stuart Alexander and Elizabeth Louise (the writer).

The Alfred and Charlie Crane families were our neighbours. The ladies came to call when we first arrived. The conversation got around to preparing chickens and cooking them with these women remarking on how difficult it was. My mother was asked how she did it and replied, "Just split the chicken open at the back end and put your hand in and pull everything out." "Oh!" they said, "we tried to do it with two spoons!"

At all times my mother got up early and made breakfast. We always had porridge, oatmeal or wheat, sometimes bacon and always toast made over wood coals at the front hole in the stove. We had a wire toaster the same as people use now to broil hamburger. We children had milk to drink while the adults had coffee, which was boiled for three minutes in an enamel coffee pot. Mother had a rolled up brown paper plug that she put in the spout of the coffee pot to keep in the aroma.

After breakfast, beds were made and floors mopped with an O'Cedar mop. The mop was treated with O'Cedar oil and had a nice odor. Dusting was done frequently. On Saturdays it was my job to wash over the kitchen floor. If I had to be asked to do it there was no reward, but if I did it without being asked, my Dad gave me ten cents.

Mother made all of our bread, cakes, cookies and buns while teaching me to do likewise. She was very proud of her Scotch shortbread which she had learnt from an old Scottish woman. In turn she taught me and much later her grandson. She preserved enough jam, pickles, fruits and vegetables to last the winter. For several years, she bought half a pig and cured bacon and hams.

In the spring and summers, it was her responsibility to care for the young chickens once they were out of the incubator and into the brooder houses. These houses had to be kept at a certain temperature or the chickens would feel cold and start crowding together, suffocating the ones on the bottom of the pile.

Clothes, bedding, tablecloths and towels all had to be washed by hand with water heated in a copper boiler on the stove. If very soiled, a scrubboard was used. Then we used a plunger-like upturned funnel with a long wooden handle that was used to work up and down in the washing to force water and soap through the clothes. Later, Dad bought a wooden washing machine that worked by hand. In winter this was done in the kitchen and in summer on the back porch. We had a long line with a pulley in the kitchen. There was a wooden clothes rack that could be let down by a cord, filled with articles, and then pulled up again to the ceiling. It must have been about six feet long.

In autumn, the young hens were moved from one hen house to the regular laying hen house after dark. Everyone helped to carry them (two or three in each hand), and what a squawking time it was! Mother helped gather eggs, clean hen houses and feed the chickens. I always helped by turning eggs being incubated. This was done twice every day.

The well was quite near the house so all the water we used was pumped and carried in pails. We had a large bathtub but no piped-in water. Mother made all my clothes, I suspect she made her own, too. We used oil lamps which had to be trimmed and the chimneys polished daily. When mantle lamps came, the lighting was improved as they gave off a more intense light.

The vegetable garden was really my dad's, but Mother always helped. She loved flowers and had pink peonies, a lovely pink rose called "La France," and snapdragons. At the front she had several broom bushes; the ones that are yellow and red. Right at the gate she had a pale pink flowering currant.

At least a couple of times every summer Mother and Birdie Estridge would plan a picnic to Maple Bay. We took our horse and wagon, making a day of it. Once we travelled to Cowichan Bay to the Regatta which was a wonderful experience. There were Indian canoe races, sailing races--and for me the best of all--highland dancing. Some summer evenings, Mother,

Birdie, Stuart and I took the wagon and went fishing for trout at the "long bridge" at the north end of Somenos Lake. We also took picnics to the river flats at Sahtlam and Skutz Falls.

We got our milk from the Smiths (father of Wilfred and Morris) and then from the Estridges; both farms had trouble with their cows getting sick and dropping their calves. I realize now that they were infected with brucellosis. We were very lucky not to get undulant fever as the milk was unpasteurized. Both farmers had to destroy their cows, plough their fields and grow crops for several years before getting more cows.

We had a telephone which was the last telephone on the line so messages were telephoned to us or people came in the night to telephone the doctor. When Armistice was signed I know we got a call at about 11:00 p.m. to tell us the war was over. I was in bed asleep and the ringing of the telephone woke me up.

Louise Anna Estridge
(Mrs. John J. Estridge)
1856-1931
by a family friend, Elizabeth Clement

John and Louise Estridge came from England and first settled near North Battleford, Saskatchewan. They had 11 children, the eldest boy staying in England. There were nine boys and two girls, Jack, still in England, Cecil, Charlie, August (Gus), Hubert, Bill, Hugh, Katherine (Birdie) and Madge. The youngest son married a girl from Crofton, Mary Oullette. He was killed and she married Clare Johns of Chemainus and bore two daughters.

John and Louise lived on Herd Road and were there when we came in 1914. Mrs. Louise Anna Estridge was a kind and good neighbour. Mr. John Estridge was a typical Victorian English husband. Beets could not be used in the summer when they are tender as beets were winter vegetables. They dealt at the Cowichan Merchants, and if that store could not supply what Mother or Birdie wanted, they would have to wait for it and would not go to any other store to seek it. The Cowichan Merchants was strictly where they dealt. Peanut butter appeared so Birdie bought some but father would have none of it, "His grandfather never had it, his father never had it, so why should they?" They lived on a farm and Birdie had never eaten corn on the cob until she had it in our house; to her father that was cattle food! Birdie was a good friend to Mother and they corresponded for years after each had left Somenos.

Mrs. Estridge was a wee, tiny woman and all the boys were six feet tall or more. She also raised turkeys for many years. She made wonderful Devonshire cream.

Mrs. Estridge told the story of their trip to North Battleford. They arrived at the lakehead by boat and then had to find some means of travel to their destination. There was quite a large group of settlers. When the men came back from seeking wagons, horses or oxen, the woman camped next to Mrs. Estridge asked her husband which he had bought and when he said oxen she said, "Oh, I am so glad because now we will be able to have milk."

Every covered wagon had a brazier or fire pail hanging at the back. One day as they stopped for lunch Mrs. Estridge took the fire pail and set it down on the gravel beyond the wagons to boil a kettle. The next thing she knew a herd of cattle had come along and she had to grab up the brazier and run. It was still hot so she put it down on the prairie and immediately the grass caught fire. It took the men all afternoon to stamp out the grass fire as it raced across the dry prairie.

Birdie tried to teach me to crochet with little success but she did manage to teach my brother and me to dance the two-step, three-step and the waltz.

Mrs. Estridge died in 1931 and Birdie died in Vancouver in 1983 or 1984.

Jane Evans (nee Plaskett)
1889-1976
by her son Stanley T. Evans

Mrs. Jane Evans was a cousin of the Plaskett family who settled in Duncan around 1905. One of them, Mrs. Clara (Plaskett) Peile returned to England in 1911 where her son Harrison was born. She returned to Duncan in the summer of 1912 and brought her cousin Jane Plaskett with her as her companion and to look after the baby.

They travelled on the Empress of Ireland just two months after the Titanic sank. It did not ease their minds when the S.S. Empress of Ireland also ran into trouble during the eleven day crossing when it had a boiler room explosion. (This liner sank the next year on the St. Lawrence with a heavy loss of life.) Clara and Jane had another upset when the train from Halifax had a fire break out on it when they were near Winnipeg. They finally arrived in Duncan.

Jane Plaskett had planned on returning to England but these disasters changed her mind so she never returned. She continued to live with her cousin Clara and family while she worked as a waitress in Sutton's Tea Room on Station Street. Some of the Duncan businessmen used to give this shy English girl a very bad time with their teasing.

Jane met and married James Evans of Koksilah in November 1912 and they moved on the McLay Willowbrook Ranch, then owned by his mother, Margaret McLay Evans. In June 1914 their first son, Stanley, was born.

At the start of the First World War Clara Peile's husband, Harry, joined his regiment in England leaving his ailing wife and son in Duncan. When Clara Peile passed away in November, 1914 her baby son was left in the care of Jane Evans. She took care of him until his father returned in 1919.

While living at Willowbrook a second son, Norman, was born to Jane in April, 1917. In 1920 the Evans' moved to a new home at Koksilah next to the old Koksilah school. Their third son Gordon was born in December 1922. Jane worked alongside her husband doing her share in clearing the land, driving the horses at haying time and cultivating their vegetable garden. She was an excellent knitter and during the Second World War knitted many pair of socks for the troops overseas. She was also a charter member of the Koksilah Women's Institute.

Jane was widowed in 1959 and continued to live at her home tending to her flower garden until her health started to fail. Latterly, she lived at the homes of her sons until she passed away February 26, 1976 at the age of 87.

Florence Fawcett (nee Eden)
(Mrs. Rowland C. Fawcett)
1877-1962
by her daughter Barbara L. Fawcett

Mother, with her family of three brothers and two sisters, lived in an eighteen-room house near the centre of Oxford, England. Mother very badly wanted to be a school teacher, and although quite well enough off to send her to Cheltenham College to study, her father refused because he wanted the three girls to stay at home and to look after him.

Mother started a Ragged School in the poor part of Oxford, gathering all the small children of Oxford to meet in a large room which she rented. She would go around to the bakeries and buy day-old buns for a good tea for them. They enjoyed a hymn sing, a simple Bible lesson and a short prayer. She also conducted a "Girls Club" and taught them how to sew and knit.

My Uncle Frank had come to Victoria, and by her letters he could feel how unsettled she was, so he invited her out to attend his wedding. It was after that that she came to Duncan.

On her trip across the Prairies, it was snowing and blowing and she thought to herself, "After this wedding I am returning to England as soon as possible." When she reached Victoria the wild roses and broom were in blossom and she changed her mind. This was in May of 1913.

Mother had already booked her return trip on the Empress of Ireland which sank in the St. Lawrence estuary. The telegram which she sent to her brother, George, was delivered to the wrong destination. You can imagine how worried her family was, thinking she had been on the Empress of Ireland!

We lived in an apartment above the Esquimalt and Nanaimo Railway station, now a heritage building. My father was station agent here.

How Mother did the washing for the six of us in winter I do not know. I remember we had a hand wringer and one clothes rack operated by two pulleys. In the summer she carried her load of washing down the railway track beyond Trunk Road and hung it up on clothes lines down there. Mother told me that by the time she had hung the last garments up, the first were dry; it was so hot.

When we were babies, the roads in town were gravel and the sidewalks wooden. The only other sidewalk in Duncan stretched from the Duncan Garage corner to the corner of McKinstry and Trunk Roads. Many a time Mother pushed our pram along this route. One day, when Evelyn was a baby, Rowland suddenly darted into the road into the path of a car and called out exultantly, "I made him stop, didn't I, Mama!" No harm happened to him, but Mother told the driver of the car to give him a sound spanking to teach him a lesson.

Three daughters and one son were born when we lived in the apartment above the E & N station. In October of 1922 her husband was taken ill and taken to the King's Daughters' Hospital. The children were sent to Victoria to relatives and Mr. and Mrs. David Ford (postmaster), offered her a home with them.

After her husband's death on January 4, 1923, she had a house built on Holmes Street which still stands. As the Canadian Pacific Railway refused her a pension, and a person had to be absolutely destitute to get government aid, she took in a few boarders to provide for herself and family. She realized it would take considerable money to provide for and educate four children, so in 1924, with the backing of Mr. Ken Duncan, she borrowed $5,000 and built a large house on Relingferg Road (later Coronation Avenue) to accommodate ten paying guests as well as herself and her family.

It was hard work every day of the week for many years but all four children completed high school and went on to various professions. I would like to pay tribute to my mother who gave so much of herself for all four of us. She was indeed a pioneer.

Edith Davidson Fleetwood (nee Batchelor)
(Mrs. George H. Fleetwood)
1882-1794
by her son W.J.H. (Jack) Fleetwood

My mother, Edith Davidson Fleetwood, was educated at the Montrose Academy and at a finishing school in Montrose, Scotland, where she was born in 1882. From a family of fourteen children, seven boys and seven girls, she trained at the Royal Sick Children's Hospital in Aberdeen, then emigrated to California in 1907. She practised nursing there until 1910 when she came to Kelowna, British Columbia where she met my father, George H. Fleetwood. She nursed in Kelowna and in Vancouver before marrying in 1913.

When she told people she was moving to the Cowichan district, she was warned, in hushed whispers, that, "the district was peopled with a very dissolute, fast set, with sport as their God."

Mother refused to move to Cowichan Station until my father had running water in the house.

Periodically she was called on to use her medical experience, mainly in midwifery, during her life at Cowichan Station where she was an active member of St. Andrew's Anglican Church W.A., although born a Presbyterian.

She died in 1974 in her ninety-second year and is buried in St. Andrew's Churchyard, Cowichan Station. She was red-haired, a very strong and very determined woman.

Miss Dorothy Geoghegan
1896-
from interviews by the Researchers

Dorothy Geoghegan was born in 1896 in Devonport, England, of an Irish Royal Navy doctor and an English mother who had been born in Ottawa. The family emigrated to Canada in 1912. They chose to settle in Cowichan because an old friend, Dr. Stephens, was already there. Dr.

Miss Norah Denny and Miss Dorothy Geoghegan at an early Cowichan Girl Guide Camp.

Geoghegan had built a home on Westcott Road in Somenos prior to the arrival of Mrs. Geoghegan and the two children.

Dorothy finished high school in Duncan, one of only four students in her class. She took the first two years at the college in Victoria, at that time an affiliate of McGill University. The last two years were in Vancouver at the University of British Columbia which was housed in army cabins on Twelfth Avenue. A graduate in 1917, she returned to Cowichan to teach with a Miss Young who conducted classes from her home on Bell-McKinnon Road. Among her students she numbered: Annie, Betty and Ivy Arthur, Hamish Mutter, Anthony Burgess, Peter Edwards, Madeleine Grieves, Cathy Townsend and others.

In the holidays she sought outdoor employment and worked at the apple orchard of Dr. Rutherfoord and anywhere else to augment her meagre earnings. She recalled the careful wrapping in tissue paper of the apples packed in boxes.

In 1920 she was sent back to England by her parents to stay with friends. She planned to stay there indefinitely but her mother became ill so she returned to Canada within the year.

Prior to going to England she started the first Girl Guide company in Cowichan. She enquired everywhere to find someone capable of taking her place while she was away. So this is how she came to know Miss Denny who was delighted to carry on the work.

On Dorothy's return the two continued on the Guide work together and also decided to start a private school for day pupils. Miss Denny had worked on the farm of Harry Holmes who suggested they rent his late parents' home which was vacant at the time. They gathered sixteen pupils including Jack Davie, Esme Mutter and sister, and founded Queen Margaret's School in April of 1921. Soon it was apparent that larger quarters were needed. With financial assistance from England, they built the original school at the corner of Government Street and Gibbins Road. Miss Denny and Miss Geoghegan helped prepare the land, even felling trees.

Miss Geoghegan is well remembered by former pupils and Guides for her lovely singing voice. She taught them many songs and was also an excellent teacher of Latin. She is still teaching today in her home.

On a final note, Miss Geoghegan was the first female church warden at St. Mary's Church, Somenos.

Louisa Green (nee Spencer)
(Mrs. Frank Green)
1873-1965
by her son Trevor Green

Louisa Green was born in 1873, in St. Athan, Glamorganshire, Wales. Her parents, Michael and Fanny Spencer, owned a small farm there, but later they lived for some years at Monkton Manor Farm in the small village of Stogursey.

After the death of her father, the family moved to Taunton and the children, a son and seven daughters, attended various schools to further their education. Louie, as she was known, enrolled in a boarding school in Bradford, Yorkshire.

In those far-off days, following graduation, there were few openings or positions that a young girl might consider without risking "social suicide." One might become a successful governess or nurse or stenographer, but to work in a shop or as a waitress indeed would be a backward step. Louie was anxious to be independent rather than to follow the sheltered and uneventful existence of her family in Taunton and the odd restrictions of the 1890s. (For instance, she was harshly criticized by her mother and elder sisters for having acquired a bicycle!)

She therefore became a governess to the young children of several prosperous families and this involved delightful interludes in the Scottish Highlands, visits to London, and memorable holidays on the south and west coasts of England. She had studied music at school and became an accomplished pianist, another qualification for the young governess.

The most memorable interlude occurred when she accepted the post of English-speaking governess to a wealthy Russian family who were living in Moscow. This was a great adventure and a rare experience for any young woman. In those days to travel through Europe by train, unchaperoned, was inviting danger, or so her family were convinced. Her employer was affiliated with the firm of Faberge (Court Jewellers to Tsar Nicholas II), and his lifestyle was indeed a most gracious one with a fine town-house, many servants and a comfortable abode in the country in which to spend the summer months.

After having lived for almost two years in Moscow and having mastered the rudiments of the difficult Russian language, it was with regret that, due to the failing health of her mother, Louie returned to the family home in Taunton.

Prior to these incidents, cousins from Victoria had been travelling from Canada to England and establishing acquaintance with members of the Spencer tribe. These were the sons of David Spencer, uncle to Louie, who years before had founded the David Spencer Limited stores in Victoria, Nanaimo and on the mainland. Friendships had developed and the Victoria family issued warm invitations and offers of hospitality to those who might consider a visit to Canada. After the death of her mother, the sale of the family home and another term as governess to a notable family in Shropshire, Louie felt the urge to travel again, this time to Canada and more particularly to Victoria, where there was promise of a post of governess to the two small children of one Captain Neroutsos who was in the service of the Canadian Pacific Railway.

Thus, in 1906, she left from Liverpool for Montreal, travelling on the S.S. Virginia. Among the passengers on board she met an Irishman, Walter Sinton, travelling likewise to Victoria, British Columbia, who spoke in glowing terms of the free and challenging life in the new outpost.

Upon arrival in the city, Louie found a warm welcome awaiting her with the Spencer cousins, then resident in what is now the Victoria Art Gallery on Moss Street. They were most kind and warm-hearted and she found much of interest and delight in the "new world," especially the freedom from hide-bound restrictions, and the opportunity to be an individual.

The position as governess to the Neroutsos children continued for perhaps a year until they had outgrown the need for such guidance, after which Louie decided to train as a stenographer or secretary. This involved mastering shorthand, and also using a dictaphone, a recent innovation in those distant days. Eventually employment in offices in Tacoma and Vancouver followed and, latterly, a return to Victoria where she became secretary to Justin Gilbert, a court reporter.

During the first year in Victoria, through Walter Sinton with whom she had travelled by train to Victoria, she met his cousins, a family named Green who were also from Ireland. They consisted of elderly parents, three sons and five daughters. The eldest of the sons, Frank Green, was at this time living at Cowichan Lake where his two brothers had built the first Riverside Inn. Eventually he and Louie Spencer came to meet in Victoria and she found his accounts of the pioneer life in the backwoods of Vancouver Island fascinating and challenging. In due course, accompanied by one of her cousins as chaperone, she made her first visit to what was destined to be her future home. The journey was made by train to Duncan, then by horse stage to the Lake. Needless to say, the magnificent forest of virgin timber, the tranquil lake and the beautiful river more than exceeded the highest expectations of the emigree from England.

Both Louie Spencer and Frank Green shared the longing for independence, freedom and the challenge of the pioneer way of life, the benefits of which were not to be found in the city. They were married in 1909 at St. Peter's Church in Quamichan, their sole attendants being the Henry March family who had arrived at Cowichan Lake before the turn of the century.

Frank Green drove his horse stage to Duncan, twice weekly, the twenty-one mile trip taking four hours each way to convey passengers and mail and small freight to either destination; this routine included an overnight stop in Duncan.

This was a totally different way of life for the young wife raised in the sheltered atmosphere of an English background. The skills of cooking were completely new to her, the daily chores in the small log cabin had to be dealt with, and in due course, the caring and upbringing of her two small boys became another facet of her busy life. She faced these challenges with faith and with courage. Longing for the homeland was seldom considered.

There were few other women in the area then. Frank's brother and sister-in-law lived nearby and a Colonel and Mrs. Haggard occupied a summer home downstream, but the pioneer Henry March family, Louie's closest friends, lived eight miles away beyond Honeymoon Bay so that contacts were infrequent.

As the early years passed by, it was evident that the pioneer life at Greendale, on the river, delightful as it was in many ways, could never be a prosperous one. With the future of her two sons to consider, Louie Green envisioned a plan of operating a sort of summer camp or guest house on the property. Proximity to the river and its excellent fishing areas, the wonderful lake, the abundance of game for the sports-minded and the peaceful atmosphere and surroundings all suggested that this venture should prove a success.

Thus in 1917, Louie Green began catering to her first visitors and the tattered Guest Book, dated 1918, contains a most interesting roster of names.

From then on her life became more and more involved. Several guest cottages were built and tents were acquired for summer overflow. There were countless meals to prepare, further housekeeping routines to follow, until by mid-October the last fisherman had departed and a hiatus of several months ensued until, by early March or mid-March, the season would commence again.

The passing years saw gradual improvements at Greendale. A telephone was installed and a bathroom with an adequate supply of hot and cold water became a necessity.

From the early 1920s, as the business prospered, a cook was engaged to serve from mid-March until mid-September, by which time the Victoria families with their many children had returned to the city and Louie could cope, single-handed, until the season closed in October.

A brief visit to England, in the winter of 1927, convinced Louie Green that without doubt, Vancouver Island had truly become home to her. It seemed as if the English country life had become more than ever restricted and insular. The countryside, needless to say, was no less beautiful and enchanting, but now, with husband and sons at Greendale and many close friends, she was happy to return from the homeland to await a busy spring season in 1928.

In 1947, Frank Green died at the age of eighty-six, and for some years thereafter occasional visitors appeared at Greendale, usually during the fishing season. By way of diversion, Louie resumed her teaching of the piano, set aside since her early career as governess, and looked forward to the weekly visits of her young pupils. This may well have been one of her contributions to the village scene, although in the early 1920s she had filled a position on the local school board. She continued to live on at Greendale until 1963 when she moved to Cherry Point Lodge, a rest home near Mill Bay, where she passed away in January, 1965, at the age of 92.

Fanny Catherine Greig (nee Jiggle)
(Mrs. James Greig)
-1927
by her daughter Ethel M. Wilson

My parents, James and Cathy Greig, their sons, Edward James, aged eighteen, Herbert John, aged fifteen, and their daughters, Doris Margaret, aged nine and Ethel Maude, aged six, came to Duncan in May in 1911.

As there was a boom on in Duncan (and elsewhere) at that time, it was at first impossible to obtain decent housing. For a short time, the family lived in a house right in town. It turned out to have bed bugs! It was also inconvenient. In a short time, owing to extremely sad circumstances, a new house on Nagle Street came on the market. The owners had two tiny boys who became very ill with dysentery, then the most prevalent disease killing many babies and young children. Mr. and Mrs. White lost one son on a Monday, buried him on a Tuesday, only to lose the next son on Wednesday and bury him on Thursday. It was no wonder the parents quickly sold their home and went back to England.

My mother had to work hard. She had a wood burning kitchen range with a reservoir. Water (cold only) came from the tap at the kitchen sink. The drain boards were wooden. There was no bathroom, the country toilet being in a section of the woodshed. Ablutions were performed at the kitchen sink and in the "hip bath." There was no way of cleaning the house except with a long-handled broom and a brush and shovel. The washing machine was one that had to be constantly turned by hand, and there was much canning and jam-making to be done.

There was a wire-sided "safe" in the pantry (off the kitchen), and milk, delivered daily, usually kept for a day. There was no ice to be obtained. Bread was brought to the door daily. Everything arrived in a horse-drawn cart, even the fresh meat. There were shops downtown, a bakery, butcher shop and other small stores and the large Cowichan Merchants (now Eaton's).

As there was no ice obtainable, butter was kept in a hole in the ground under the house in the summer. As it was often so hot the evening dinner was cooked on an open fire outside. One evening I remember the dog running off with the roast of meat!

My mother was very kind to some brides who arrived from England in 1911. She helped them with their babies, even being present when one poor women had a terrible and difficult birth on the kitchen table.

The recreation at that time was simple though probably adequate. There was much entertaining in the homes, teas, dinners and musical evenings. The card game "Five Hundred" was popular. There were also many church activities.

The hard time was during the First World War. Both sons, of course, enlisted, one being wounded, but both returned safely. The two girls attended the nearby consolidated elementary school and later the secondary one.

My mother made do with little. She was handy with her needle and our English relatives sometimes sent clothing and material to go with it. Sometimes a dressmaker, Miss Frazer, came in for a day.

Much of the family life was centered around St. John's Anglican Church where the whole family was encouraged to sing in the choir and to attend and later teach in the Sunday School. Lonely bachelors, such as Mr. Carlton Stone, were brought home after the service for lunch. One day a theological student was there, a Mr. Buck, whom my mother inadvertently called Mr. Doe!

I rememember a surprise party for Mother's birthday one year. Neighbours came with lovely carnations (a dozen pink, large beauties), delicious food and music. Three ladies from not far away sang solos. When I arrived home from school the party was in full swing.

When my mother died in another house in 1927, the milkman said, "I have never seen so many women in tears as I did this morning. Mrs. Greig

has gone to her reward."
She was much beloved by her former neighbours.

Laura Sophia Margaret Hansen (nee Sorenson)
(Mrs. John Eric Hansen)
1886-1943
by her daughter Eva Beech

Mrs. Hansen, my mother, came from Asinglse, Isle of Sjalland, Denmark and was born there in 1886. Her parents came from the same area, the town of Viby. As a young woman she worked in the cookhouse department of a large dairy farm about fifteen miles from Copenhagen. She met John Eric Hansen there as he worked on the same farm outside with the stock. They married in 1904.

Her husband's oldest sister, Mary Thugerson, from Somenos sent for them to come to this beautiful valley of Cowichan. There was a small Danish settlement there including Sjyrup, Thugerson, and later Petersen and Hansen, and at Westholme, Sonderguard and Quist. Three girls and twin boys were born in Denmark, the twins passed on at three months before they emigrated to British Columbia in about June of 1912. I was told that the ship from Liverpool was seven days late arriving in Halifax, ordinarily a fourteen-day sail, as they had to watch for icebergs; the Titanic had sunk in April.

Mrs. Hansen and her forty-day-old baby, Eva, were both very ill when they arrived at Halifax, so they stayed there for two weeks before taking the train to Vancouver. The family arrived on Bell-McKinnon Road early in July and stayed with the Thugersons until a small house was built next door. Later there were "add-ons," but first a large barn, many chicken houses and rabbit hutches were built.

My parent sold milk, cream and eggs to Duncan's Creamery and later all kinds of vegetables, especially Spanish onions. There was a variety of fruits too, strawberries, raspberries, currants, plus poultry and rabbits sent to the market. The money from this was used for staples such as flour, coffee, tea, salt, pepper, et cetera, and sewing material. Mother made all clothes for herself and the girls. Everything else that we needed came from the farm.

Mother had four more daughters, seven in all. Things were rough during the war years, especially with the influenza. At one time everyone was in bed with the flu except two, Mary and Eva, who had to do the housework and the nursing. Outside help was hired for the care of the stock.

Our parents joined the church at Somenos where the Mountain View Cemetery is now. The church was taken away in the 1940s, I believe. We got the mail across the street at Mr. Hystead's post office and store, and we girls went to the Herd Road school. Buses transported children to Duncan's first two-storey stone elementary school on Nagle Street, beginning January 2, 1920.

Cooking was done on a large iron stove which had a reservoir for hot water. At first water was drawn from a well in the backyard but later a pump was installed on the back porch which was a great deal more convenient. There were many acres of land to the farm and the Island Highway now runs through the bottom land. In 1916 and 1919 the snow was up over the fence posts.

It was about three miles to Duncan's Station, and we drove there in a small buggy with a box in the back, like a surrey but without a fringe. It was about 1918 when we got our first car, a Ford pick-up.

The farm was sold in the early 1920s and the whole family went back to Denmark to visit for one and a half years, returning to Cowichan in 1923 to a fair-sized farm at Vimy. Mother did the same things there, but had no dairy to manage. She lived there for the next 20 years until she passed away in 1943, leaving her husband and seven daughters.

Carlota Elisa Hassell (nee Robertson)
(Mrs. Frederick P. Hassell)
1883-1970
by her daughter-in-law Eleanor Hassell

Carlota Elisa Robertson was born in Scotston, St. Cyrus, Scotland in 1883. She was one of four daughters of James and Helen Robertson.

The family moved to the United States and "Charlie" went to the Annie Wright School in Tacoma, Washington. Meanwhile her father bought a house on Lakes Road looking on Quamichan Lake.

She joined the South Cowichan Tennis Club and played with Edie Share and was one of the earliest members.

Charlie married Fred Hassell in 1910 and they built a house on Quamichan Lake. They had nineteen and a half acres of beautiful lake front property and Fred cleared a lot of it and started a farm.

Fred joined up when war broke out and went overseas in 1915. Charlie and her very young son, Alister, followed him in 1916 and remained in England until the war was over.

They used to go to dances in Duncan by horse and buggy. It was during one of these dances in 1919 that they were told their house was on fire. They tore home to find everything gone and only the chimneys standing.

They put up a tent in their garden and proceeded to build again around the remaining chimneys. The house is still standing on Indian Road near the Lake.

Charlie had a terrific sense of humour and took tragedy with a stout heart.

Charlie's father was a great whist player and she and he played together a great deal. From that came Charlie's own passion for bridge which she enjoyed until her death in 1970.

288

Kathleen A. Kennington (nee Morgan)
(Mrs. Allan Kennington)
1874-1950
by her daughter Kathleen A. Wilkinson

The Kenningtons arrived in the Valley in 1907. Their eldest daughter, Sylvia (Inky), was just 4 years old. The second daughter, Kathleen (John), was born in 1908 in the Inverarity House, Somenos. They came out either to join, or at the same time as, the Stepneys, Hogans, Robinsons - all coming from Pincher Creek, Alberta.

Not long ago, an item in the Cowichan Leader from the diary of one of the Miss Marriners stated, "Mrs. Kennington's and Mrs. Hassell's tea at the (South Cowichan Lawn Tennis) Club today poured with rain and nobody came!" This was early August 1908. Tea at this club was a very social event on Saturday afternoons, with a damask tablecloth, silver teapots and cake trays, plates of dainty cucumber sandwiches, small scones and scrumptious cakes. Rain or shine, the attending hostesses had to be there in case someone arrived, even if tennis wasn't played. Much of this is hearsay to me, but the practice remained until I was married 21 years later and may still do! However on this day, when "nobody came," Mummy would have had to go out and catch 'Johnny,' our very temperamental sorrel pony, hitch him to the democrat (which was a sort of passenger wagon with a seat in front and space for bales of hay at the back), load up her cakes, polished silver, wood and starched cloth (the cloth pressed by flat irons on a wood stove!). Then came the drive from Somenos to pick up Mrs. Hassell at Quamichan, who would bring her teapot, cloth and cakes - all of which would mean long hours of cooking and polishing. Another four miles brought them to Cowichan Courts via Tzouhalem road. The climax to this really was that I arrived three weeks later! How Mummy managed, I can't imagine. I'm sure she stayed well behind the high table and long tablecloth.

We had a floating camp (boat house) on Cowichan Bay just east of the wharf, anchored with four concrete blocks about 200 yards offshore. Here I played happily at the age of five or six in my rowboat, paddling and rowing about "catching fish." I fell in one day when no one was about! My father believed that children and puppies automatically swam if they fell in. I did, though old Chief George from the Indian Reserve came to help me out.

It was quite a usual occurrence to see the Kenningtons sailing down the bay, having worn out our anchor rope. Capt. Lane in the 'Sokum' would come and tow us back again. These were trying times for Mummy. Water was carried in pails from a creek and put in a boat. Imagine washing and ironing for two children, using buckets of water. Mummy couldn't swim and wasn't really very fond of the water but always seemed gay and cheerful because the rest of us loved it so much.

They used to play polo on the Experimental Farm grounds at Koksilah, a beautiful sight. Once, Sylvia, aged four, seeing her father on 'Johnny' with rider and horse careening down the field after the ball, rushed out to greet him. Mummy caught her just in time! My mother was a superb rider herself and looked lovely in her riding habit. She rode side saddle. I still remember her riding when I was six or seven, just before the 1914 war.

I remember the day when Sylvia and I saw Mummy and Daddy off to drive to Victoria in our new car, a grey Dart, to go the Government House Ball, the paraphernalia they took! This, too, was before the first war. They stopped half way, staying at the Shawnigan Lake Hotel. I think it was a C.P.R. Hotel at the station, also near the narrow, precipitous Malahat Drive that descended to Victoria.

There may be discrepancies in these memories, some are from diaries, old letters to family in England and 'tales my mother told me!'

Gertrude A. McLay (nee Van Norman)
(Mrs. Robert McLay, Jr.)
1888-1982
by her nephew Stanley L. Evans

Gertrude Van Norman was born in Bobcaygeon, Ontario in 1888. In 1905 she came to Cowichan with her parents, her father making the move because his employer, a lumber company, was moving to the area. The family first lived in a house in Duncan near the present Duncan City Hall but Gertrude moved to Victoria where she worked in a clothing store.

In 1911 she married Robert McLay and ran a tearoom and confectionery on Craig Street. Their home was on Koksilah Road and the first house at Eagle Heights, south of the Cowichan River. Robert operated a mill at Cobble Hill and built a store in 1912 that became the Cowichan Merchants and is now the T. Eaton Company store.

Robert drove a 1912 McLaughlin car and Gertrude a Studebaker. Later she would relate how her wrist was broken when the car "coughed" while she was cranking it.

She cleared land, burning out stumps, and cut her own firewood with a crosscut saw. For a time she lived at Cowichan where she enjoyed fishing.

After the death of her husband from multiple sclerosis, she moved to a small house on Polkey Road. Still active in her later years she climbed on the roof to put out shingle fires while in her late seventies and eighties, but her house was eventually burned down.

The McLays had no children. Gertrude passed away on June 30, 1982 at the age of 94.

Maud Menzies (nee Foster)
(Mrs. James Menzies)
1884-1968
compiled by the Researchers

Depression times in Britain before the First World War caused Maud Foster's parents and her two brothers, E.(Ted) W. and George A. Foster to emigrate to Canada and the Cowichan Valley in 1913, and all remained here.

Maud had employment as a nanny at a home in Crofton for a time and later worked as a clerk in the Mercantile Ladies' Wear. She was a gifted pianist, a natural player, and often played the piano at the movie house for the silent movies.

Following her marriage to James Menzies in 1915, son of John and Shusann Menzies, they moved into their own home on the land pre-empted by John Menzies. Later the land was divided and they farmed fifty acres of their own.

Maud had five sons, and like many women of the times she had few conveniences when beginning her life on the farm where she cared for her family and took her share of farm chores. She made and sold butter, also milk, eggs and potatoes. She also hosted Sunday School picnics on the farm.

Widowed in 1935 and with all of her sons then living in North Vancouver, she also moved there.

She died in 1968 in her 84th year.

Elizabeth Morley
(Mrs. Walter Morley)
by her grand-nephew Ronald G. Morley

My great-aunt, Elizabeth Morley, came to Cowichan in 1903. She and her husband, Walter Morley, operated the Post Office and a store at Tzouhalem, across the road from St. Ann's Mission Church property, from 1903 to 1921 when he died.

Elizabeth Morley was born in Ireland and died at Tzouhalem but I am not able to give dates or her maiden name.

During the years she was at Tzouhalem she gave medical aid to the Indian people and also to the Convent School.

Tzouhalem Post Office. St. Ann's Church, Priest's Home c. 1912.

Margaret Moss
(Mrs. Claude Moss)
-1937
compiled by the Researchers

There is a building in Duncan which bears the name of a woman in a well-deserved tribute to her exceptional community service. It is the Margaret Moss Health Centre.

Mrs. Moss was born in Scotland and died there, but spent many of the intervening years abroad. For a period of time immediately following the Boer War she lived in South Africa where she was in charge of educational services. It appears that she and her husband then came to Canada and made their home at Cowichan Station.

Most of the information that we have concerning her is obtained from a retrospective article published in the Cowichan Leader on February 2, 1961 on the occasion of the opening of the Health Centre building.

During the First World War she returned to England with her husband, Colonel Claude Moss. Margaret Moss did war work and eventually was made superintendent over 1,200 women and girls working in an airplane factory. In its issue of April 11, 1918, the Leader proudly announced that the first Canadian Wren was a resident of this district, this being Margaret Moss. She rose to vice-admiral in the Service and received an OBE in recognition of her work.

Cowichan Station was home, however, and the Mosses returned here where Mrs. Moss immediately got busy promoting the establishment of a public health nursing service for the district. The major secular women's organizations of the area were drawn into this cause under her leadership. A society, with a constitution drawn up by Colonel Moss was formed and Mrs. Moss was its first president, serving in that capacity for a total of fifteen years in two separate terms.

In addition to her work on the Health Centre Committee, Mrs. Moss served two years on the Cowichan Station School Board.

When Colonel Moss died, his widow returned to Scotland, her own death occurring shortly afterwards in 1937. The Cowichan Leader in the course of lauding the work of the Cowichan Health Centre in 1946, said, "The late Mrs. Claude Moss, who founded the organization, is revered in memory as a lovable woman of unusual ability and talents."

Phyllis Nairne Neel (nee Kingston)
(Mrs. Edmond William Neel)
1884-1959
by her daughter M. Nairne Casgrain

After all these years my memories are a bit faded, but a few incidents do stand out. There was the winter of 1916, the year of the big snow, when my older brother and I spent most of our days sliding down the roof of the farmhouse into huge piles of snow which reached almost to the edges of the roof. This was great fun for a six-year-old and a nine-year-old! I seem to remember my father telling me that there was sixteen feet of snow that winter and I can recall his struggles to cut a path down to the barns to care for the livestock.

Another incident I do remember vividly is the birth of twins on Christmas Eve. They were not expected until February so their unexpected arrival caused somewhat of a panic situation in the household. I remember my older brother, a younger sister and myself being herded upstairs in charge of the maid while the cook and, presumably, my father took care of the emergency downstairs. By the time the hired man had hitched up the horse and buggy and had gone to fetch the doctor and the latter had put in an appearance, the babies had arrived and apparently my mother was sitting up in bed knitting!

My brother was sent to a boarding school on Salt Spring Island at an early age, but I went to a local day school and walked two and a half miles to get there and two and a half miles back.

The house was said to be built in 1905. My Father did not build it as he came out here in 1907 and Mother followed the following year with the new baby. As far as I remember, it was very comfortable, having a furnace, indoor plumbing with a separate toilet and bathroom and--for those days-- a very up-to-date kitchen. Most of the houses in the Cowichan Station area at that time were extremely comfortable and I doubt if anybody cooked on the hearth or had to draw their water from a well. In many ways the homes were more comfortable then than they are today as they all had proper dining rooms, with one, if not two, spare rooms for overnight or longer

Deep Dene on Cowichan Harbour, May 1905. Home of Mr. & Mrs. Stanley Dighton.

time visits; for the most part the kitchens were very spacious.

My mother's sister, Joan, came to Canada a year or two after mother's arrival. She arrived and married, settling at Coombs. I can remember her family arriving by sleigh, to spend Christmas with us, having made the trip in two days.

I think the big event of the day on the farm was getting the milk down to the station to meet the train every day. In those days Cowichan Station was quite a little community with a hotel, two grocery stores, two Chinese laundries and several other little stores. There was also a community hall and a post office.

In the summer Mother and four children were bundled into a buggy and taken to Cowichan Bay where we used to spend a month at a boarding-house known as Deep Dene. It was a very popular spot, particularly with people from the Vancouver area.

The one big treat during the winter was a trip to Victoria by train, to see the annual Christmas pantomime. I think the train ride took around three hours and from what Mother told me, I gather she spent the entire time in the washroom with one or other of the children who were all given to train sickness; something we all grew out of, thank goodness.

Mother was an accomplished pianist and did a great deal of accompanying at local concerts. I recall being very impressed that when she was playing at the local theatre a sheet of music slipped off the piano and strayed down onto the floor. Mother did not bat an eye but kept right on with the music.

Mother was in her 75th year when she died in 1959.

Lilyan Gladys Pollock (nee Bell)
(Mrs. James D. Pollock)
1896-1969
by her daughter Helen G. Maltby

Our mother, Lilyan Gladys Bell (Pollock), arrived in Duncan with her parents on a dark, rainy night in October, 1910. There were no street lights or sidewalks and they had a muddy walk to the house on First Street from the E & N Station. It was a depressing arrival, but the next morning the sun came out and the view of Mt. Prevost from the back porch was so beautiful that Mum knew she never wanted to return to town life in the North of England.

For some years she helped her mother with housework but was not allowed to do much cooking--she might waste food! So it was not until she married in 1917 that she actually started to cook. She and James D. Pollock were married in St. Andrew's Presbyterian Church by the Rev. A.F. Munro and went to live at Hillcrest Lumber Company which was just getting started in Sahtlam.

Her first house had a well near the kitchen with a pump in the kitchen. Coal oil lamps provided light and, of course, there was an outhouse. She had two children, Jean and Robert. Then she and her little family moved to their house on Godden Road (now Beech Avenue) here they lived for over two years while Dad opened up the Hillcrest town yard at the corner of Canada Avenue and First Street. Stewart and Mary were born in the Godden Road house. In 1924 the family moved back to Sahtlam.

Mum's second house at old Hillcrest was larger but still had a pump in the kitchen to draw water from a nearby well. The living room had a wood heater and the kitchen had a wood cookstove with a reservoir on one side for heating water. A wonderful supply of hot water was available from the dry kiln which had a barrel beside it into which near-boiling water constantly poured. Everyone carried it home in buckets. This house had an added-on bathroom which had no heat. However, there was a wonderful large wooden tub lined with metal--quite unique! When it was cool, the children were bathed in a tub in the kitchen. This house was quite close to the mill's wastewood burner. The roof of the house was made of iron, but in 1928 sparks got into a low stump which was partly under the house and at approximatey 7:00 p.m. on a May evening fire broke out under the house. Help came quickly with big fire hoses with Lem Traer, Hillcrest Woods Superintendent, who also lived at Hillcrest, in charge. The fire soon was extinguished but there was a great deal of water damage.

Bill and Helen had been born in this house and so there were six children. Neighbours kindly took us in until a new house was built.

Our new house was built by Oscar Brown and his crew who finished it in two weeks. It was a quarter of a mile from the mill and so we no longer worried about sparks from the burner. The inside was all finished with cedar V-joint. There was a large kitchen with a wood-stove and ceiling drying racks for the washing. In the pantry there was a sink with hot and cold running water, and a cooler vented to the outside. There was a large living room with a wood heater (always taken out in summer) and three bedrooms for parents, boys and girls. The bathroom had a proper bath and basin but for several years had no toilet. Best of all, this house had AC power. Our previous house latterly had lights, but now we were able to have an electric washing machine to replace the hand-operated washer. We also had an ironer on which Mom became very proficient at ironing all the boys' shirts. Larry and Dick were born while we lived here.

In 1936 Dad became ill and died, leaving Mum with eight children from 18 years of age to two years. We left Hillcrest and went to live in the house on Beech Avenue. Mum was a wonderfully kind, patient mother--one of the most truly unselfish people you could ever find. She never attended school; her parents wanted her help at home so they got a doctor's certificate stating that her eyes were too bad for her to attend school. Her father taught her at home and she was better educated than many people who go through school today. Her handwriting was beautiful and her spelling was accurate. She wrote lovely letters. However, she always felt the lack of schooling and encouraged her children to work well at school.

She loved music and took violin lessons from Mr. W.A. Willet who conducted the Cowichan Amateur Orchestra. She played in the second violin section in the early 1920s, while our father was in the first violins. When the Victoria Symphony started coming to Cowichan she was a faithful listener at the concerts. Like her mother, she was most hospitable and had frequent visitors. She especially enjoyed having the children in the neighbourhood come to call.

During the war she knitted and sewed as a member of a group of women providing clothing and bedding for refugees. Over the years all five of her sons were Boy Scouts and after the war she worked for the Quamichan Troop. For her efforts, she was awarded a "Thanks" badge.

She devoted her life to her family and to helping others. She was a spiritual woman who loved and guided us through the most difficult times, we were indeed fortunate in having such a wonderful mother.

She died in 1969.

Bessie Harriet Rudkin (nee Whitelaw)
(Mrs. A.J. Rudkin)
1854-1930
by her daughter Irma Burrows

My mother was born in St. John's Wood, London, in 1854 of English parents by the name of Whitelaw. She told us that as a schoolboy her father made Queen Victoria's envelopes for pocket money. I have the scissors he used.

In 1912 my parents with five daughters and a maid came to settle in the Cowichan Valley. I believe they chose Cowichan because their daughter, Dorothy, had come out the previous year to marry Trevor Hicks. I was only nine years old at the time but I believe that my parents were encouraged and assisted in making this move by the British Women's Emigration Society.

The family made arrangements to travel by the Allan Line ship Grampion, and while the furniture was being packed up the family was scattered to various relatives. As the sailing date drew near, there was anxiety about getting all of us collected at the railway station because there were railway strikes on at that time.

When we disembarked at Saint John the escort lady made arrangements for us to take the train to Montreal. Continuing westward in the colonist car of another train, a wheel of our coach caught fire and put the heating system out of order. When it was restored it seemed impossible to regulate the heat and the seats were almost too hot to sit on.

There was a small stove in our colonist car on which we cooked all our meals. There were sackcloth curtains, and grey blankets were supplied either by the railway or the Emigration Society. Crossing the prairies we saw some buffalo which was exciting for us, but we were glad to be met by Dorothy in Vancouver as no one was feeling very well at the time. The family stayed in Vancouver a few days while our parents and sister Muriel went to Duncan to make arrangements for a place to live. When they arrived in Cowichan, Mother was found to be ill with double pneumonia. Dr. Dykes attended her and Mrs. Hadwen nursed her through it.

For our first six weeks in Cowichan we lived in a rented house, poorly furnished, while we waited for the arrival of our furniture and could move

Bessie Harriet Rudkin, nee Whitelaw, 1854-1930. Mrs. A Rudkin, c.1917.

into our own home. Father (Arthur John Rudkin) bought a property on Quamichan Lake which had a fairly new house only seven or eight years old, and a young orchard of Cox's Golden Pippin apples. This house had a perfectly good furnace but Father, perhaps because he was not used to central heating, never put it into use. The house was heated by three fireplaces which Mother kept going through the cold weather, Father being occupied outdoors. To accommodate us, Father added two bedrooms to the second floor of the house and made other alterations. In summer when the well ran dry we hauled water from the lake in barrels which was then pumped into the cistern in the house.

There were twelve and a half tons of our furniture in twelve packing cases and there was some doubt in Victoria if they could be loaded on the Esquimalt and Nanaimo Railway. However, that was accomplished. A piano was shipped in the one-and a half-ton packing case. On arrival at Duncan, the cases were delivered one at a time by Frank Kingston on his wagon.

Mother's first postcards home to family and friends in England had one message, "Am living in the middle of a forest. In front of us is a lake with mountains beyond, and we are surrounded by Indians." I think that when Mother got over her first homesickness, she was quite happy in her new home.

The whole family made a trip back to England one year, and in 1930 Mother returned by herself and died in England that year.

My mother's children were: Kathleen Marion (Booth), Edith, who died young, Dorothy (Hicks), Muriel (Wilkinson), Phyllis Joy (Bateman), Lois (Booth), Arthur (who died in infancy), and Bessie Irma (Burrows).

Annie Smith (nee Speakman)
(Mrs. James Smith)
1867-1940
by her daughter-in-law Gwen Smith

Annie Smith's pioneering days were not in this district but in Alberta where she came in 1891 from Manchester, England. She travelled west on one of the first trains on the railways which at that time was completed only as far as Red Deer, Alberta, riding in a caboose on a work train. She taught school until her marriage to James Smith in 1894.

The family came to Cowichan in 1911 for reasons of her health and lived on a farm on Herd Road.

She was a member of the Methodist Church (later the United Church), and was a life member of the Women's Missionary Society of which she was a devoted member.

Annie lived on the Herd Road farm until shortly before her death in 1940 at the King's Daughters' Hospital, Duncan, and was interred at Mountain View Cemetery, Somenos.

Mona Solly (nee Primrose Wells)
(Mrs. Leonard Fordham Solly)
1892-1982
by her daughters Ruth P. Holman
and
M. Grace Solly

Mother was a young girl, about 16 years old, when she left England with her parents, Dr. and Mrs. A. Primrose Wells, to live in Creston, British Columbia for the benefit of her father's health.

After a time in England during the First World War, to contribute to the war work needed there, they came back to Victoria and to Cowichan in 1920. They lived on Norcross Road where the house, much altered, still is standing.

Mother, together with her sister, was employed at Crosland Brothers Seed Company on Green Road. The company was run by Sam and Ralph

Crosland who had come from England and grew sweet peas for seed. The brothers were well known and respected businessmen in this area.

Our mother and her sister helped to pick and sort the seeds for packaging and distribution.

Mother met our father, Leonard Fordham Solly. He had bought land and farmed on the Bell-McKinnon Road, later known as Solly's Farm. They were married in Victoria in 1921.

Mother particularly enjoyed her flower garden and preparing displays, which she entered at the annual shows at the old Agricultural Hall.

Phyllis M.B. Springett (nee Wallich)
(Mrs. Eric C. Springett)
1897-1985
by her nephew Bernard Wallich

Phyllis Springett was born in 1897 in Cheltenham, England, the daughter of Collings and Mary Leonora Wallich. She came with her parents and only brother, Maurice, to Cowichan in 1911.

Phyllis Springett, nee Wallich, 1897-1985.

Phyllis was a keen horsewoman and in the early days ran a riding school in Duncan. For many years she trained horses and rode in the Vancouver Island shows.

In 1926 Phyllis married Eric C. Springett who had arrived in Victoria from England in 1920. He was a British Columbia Land Surveyor and had attended Guelph Agricultural College where he studied animal genetics. Following their marriage they operated the Hiawatha Dairy Farm at Quamichan where Eric built a magnificent log home for his new bride. The buildings still stand and the farm can be recognized by the distinctive white stucco barn and silos. Phyllis had her riding school here.

In 1937 they sold this and bought property on the original Corfield farm land at the head of Cowichan Bay. There they built another home which for nearly forty years was a landmark visible from Cowichan Bay and the Old Island Highway.

During the war years, 1940 to 1944, while her husband was Overseas with the Canadian Army, Phyllis was a Placement Officer for the Emergency Farm Labour Service and was also active in the Aircraft Identification Service for the Royal Canadian Air Force. The threat of Japanese air attacks was very real in those days. Following the war she worked many years for the Floral Art Shop in Duncan and with Mrs. Daphne Mutter for a short while operating a craft supply shop in Duncan called the Hobby Horse. She served on the Duncan Hospital Auxiliary.

In 1972 the Springetts sold the Cowichan Bay property and built another home at Cherry Point. Here Phyllis took up painting quite seriously and was active in organizing classes and displays for district artists.

Following the death of her husband in 1983, Phyllis moved to Penticton to live near her nephew and his wife, Bernard and Anna Wallich. She passed away in 1985.

Anna Marie Swanson (nee Borg)
(Mrs. Carl Albin Swanson)
1886-1964
by her daughter Ethel M. Davis

When my mother, Anna Maria Borg, left her home town of Goteborg, Sweden, in 1906 to "see America" she was about twenty years old. Travelling by boat to New York, then by train across Canada, she came to North Vancouver where she was married the next year to my father, Carl Albin Swanson. She had worked in hotels at times before her marriage.

Because of employment being available in logging, they came to Cowichan in 1913 and to life on a house boat (floathouse) at Cowichan Lake. It was very primitive! One had to walk to shore to the outdoor toilet. Our house boat was towed around the lake to wherever our father was working.

My mother always had flower boxes on the house boat, as well as a garden ashore. She had chickens, ducks which laid their eggs in the lake, and a cow. She made most of our clothes.

We had coal oil lamps and later gas lamps. There was a wood stove in the kitchen and a heater in the living room.

There were three girls in the family by that time, Edith, Ethel and Annie (Bonnie). My younger sister, Bonnie, fell into the lake twice and my mother jumped in fully clothed to rescue her. We went to a one-room school where the teacher sometimes was not much older than the students. Students had to board in Duncan or Victoria to go to high school.

The women were all very friendly and had their tea parties, card games and dances. When our parents went to a dance, they took us. There were no babysitters in those days. When we were very young we slept on the coats in the cloakroom; then, as we got a little older, we sat on the benches and watched our parents and their friends.

My parents never got back to Sweden to visit their families. There was no spare money in those days. It must have been a very hard life for my mother with three little girls and no relatives from her home to help her, but she was always cheerful and no one ever went away without flowers, vegetables, eggs or cream.

Sarah Elizabeth Thorpe (nee Clements)
(Mrs. Alfred D. Thorpe)
by her son Alec Thorpe

My parents, Sarah E. Clements and Alfred D. Thorpe, were married in England and lived for a time at Portslade, England, before leaving by boat for Canada. They travelled across the continent by train, arriving in Duncan in November of 1911.

They came to Cowichan because my father had a son, Roland, living here and Father also had a job in Duncan.

They lived in Duncan from November of 1911 until September of 1914 when they moved to Sooke and lived there for two years, followed by two years in Victoria and then back to Duncan in 1918. In September of 1918 they moved to Nanaimo but returned to Duncan in 1930. They are both buried in St. Mary's Anglican Cemetery, at Somenos.

My mother, Sarah Thorpe, was a member of the Women's Association of St. John's Church (Anglican), and did lovely needlework for the church. Her three children were named Doris, Clement and Alec.

Louisa Tombs (nee Rice)
(Mrs. Thomas E. Tombs)
1870-1935
by her daughter May Cleough

Louisa Tombs was born in Worcester, England in 1870, marrying Thomas E. Tombs in 1897. Their four children, Bert, Stanley, Roland and May, were born in England.

The family emigrated from England to Duncan in 1913, Louisa preparing many parcels of food supplies in advance for the family's use on the ship and on the train across Canada. The family came to Duncan because that was where relatives, the Pitt family, lived.

In November of 1916 Bert was killed overseas and Thomas, who was managing the Quamichan Hotel, died the following month. Louisa and the children moved into the hotel which she managed until 1919, with the help of Don Pitt.

She then moved to a house on Festubert Street which is still occupied by her daughter, May. Louisa died in 1935.

Alice Georgina Townsend (nee Adams)
(Mrs. Frank T. Townsend)
1864-1940
by her granddaughter Sally A. Smith

Soon after arriving in Duncan in 1908, Alice and Frank Townsend with Adrian, aged six years, and Kathleen, aged four years, settled in a house on the corner of Jubilee and Kenneth Streets where a barber shop is located today. The house was later moved to Tyee Street and is still occupied.

As a young girl in England, Alice took an apprenticeship as a milliner with the firm of William Whiteley, Westborne Grove, London and upon completion of her apprenticeship worked for a number of years with this firm.

Soon after arriving in the Cowichan Valley she opened her first millinery shop on Station Street, approximately where the White Hart Tea Shoppe is located today.

With her training and artistic talent she was soon called upon to design

Station Street, Duncan, in 1909. Photo from Sally Smith.

and sew the beautiful hats that were worn during that era. Many customers came from Victoria to have a hat especially designed or remodelled to match their outfits.

Her shop also specialized in fabrics, materials, laces, trims and fine women's wear.

The following are some of the women who were employed in the millinery shop: Mrs. Harris, Pearl Symons, Bessie Armour and Jean Van Norman. Some years later this shop was relocated on Station Street, where the I.D.A. Pharmacy is located today.

Mary Leonora Wallich (nee Wallich)
(Mrs. Collings Wallich)
1867-1938
by her grandson Bernard C. Wallich

Mary Leonora was born in Norfolk, England, the daughter of the Reverend L.C. Wallich and Fanny (nee Wilkinson).

Mary Lenora Wallich, c.1890. Mrs. Collings Wallich, 1864-1938.

Mary married her first cousin, Collings Wallich in 1890. He was a tea planter in Darjeeling, India. Their first child, Maurice, was born in 1896 in India. Their daughter, Phyllis (Springett), was born in 1897 in England. Around 1907 or 1908, Mary and Collings retired to their farm in Gloucester, England.

A long-time friend, Colonel Tom Moss, who had settled in Cowichan, persuaded them to leave England for Canada. They arrived in Cowichan in 1911. They built a home named Cotswald on a hill overlooking the Cowichan Bay Road, then the Island Highway. The road, which ran past their home to Cowichan Bay, was called Wallich Road, now Hillbank Road.

Being the wife of an India Tea Planter and "gentleman" farmer, Mary was accustomed to a fairly high quality of life, attended to by household servants and all that went with it. Though her new life in Canada presented many challenges, she soon became well known for her great talent in art and music. She also was tireless in her efforts to help the sick, the needy and recent immigrants in the community. She was organist for many years at St. Andrew's Church, Cowichan Station. Her beautiful water colour paintings of Cowichan scenery and plant life are treasured today in many private collections throughout the district. The Old Stone Church was one of her favourite subjects. She also wrote short stories and poems, published in the local and Victoria papers. She was a lifelong member of the Imperial Order of the Daughters of the Empire.

In later years, Mary contracted diabetes, eventually losing her eyesight. She always longed to return to her Norfolk home but accepted the privations of a pioneer wife without complaint.

Mary died at the age of 71 years in 1938. She lies beside her husband in St. Peter's Churchyard, Quamichan.

Margaret Ray Springett (nee Hill), 1862-1927, wife of Louis C. Springett, who came to Vancouver Island in 1902 with their seven children: Tom, George, Percy, Mai Lawrence, Irene Sprot, Lorna Davidge and Josephine Chater. The first Springett home was at the intersection of Norcross and Westcott Roads and later they moved to Maple Bay. Margaret assisted by her daughters operated the Bay of Maples Tea Rooms. In June 11, 1914 issue of the Cowichan Leader she ran the following advertisement.

> *"Bay of Maples Teahouse and Restaurant*
> *Large verandah looks over the sea.*
> *Always cool and shady.*
> *Fresh strawberries and cream.*
> *Meal tickets, 10 for $3.65.*
> *Rooms to let, Sites for campers.*
> *Launch and rowboats for hire*
> *Fishing.*
> *Contact M.R. Springett."*

Louis Springett was an artist with great painting skills and many of his landscapes, wild bird and dogwood pictures are still in evidence around Vancouver Island.

(This information excerpted from "The Springetts of Maple Bay" by their great-grandson Dennis Minaker, with his kind permission.)

Eleanor Fry, Henry Fry, Daniel Mainguy, Bessie Mainguy, Harold Mainguy at the Mainguy home, Chemainus River, Westholme.

Eleanor Fry, nee Edgson, Mary Edgson. Keturah Edgson, nee Hutchins. Seated: Fannie S. Blythe nee Edgson.

Fanny Sophie Blythe, nee Edgson, 1874-1965.

The Family of David & Margaret Evans.

l. to r.: William, Bessie, Margie, John, Father, Mary Ann, Mother, Robert, Esther, Robina, James, George & Harry.

Taken in 1906.

G. Estridge.   J. Young.   Norcross   Norman.   H. Cook   Blackstock.   D. Stephenson.
Redfern   T. Corfield.   Lt. A. Lane.   Capt McGuire. (Q.M).   Young   Le Croix.
                                                C. Thorpe.

July 1915. Cowichan Boys in the 52nd C.E.F. at Vernon Camp.

Duncans School — April, 1910 (later known as Zenith School).

Front row, l. to r.: Magnus Henderson, ?, ?, Marshall Smith, Stylie Hamilton, ?, ?, Albert Dirom, ?, ?, Gordon Weismiller.

Back row, l. to r.: Flora McKinnon, Grace Murton, Olive Ford, Robina Evans, Linnie Fear, Winnie Murton, Olive Henderson, Blanche Truesdale, Stan Weismiller, June Ventriss, Wilfred Christmas, Lydia Campbell, George Evans, Nona Smith, Stanley Henderson, Teacher, Albert Dickinson, Corfield, Green.

Old Somenos School Class of 1912
Cor. Norcross Rd. & Somenos Rd.

Back row: Jim Kier, Maude Auchinachie, Margie Evans, Sybil Henslow, Teacher Thomas Levy, Madge Estridge, Eva Auchinachie, Florence Davie, Ted Marsh.

Second row: Alan Kenning, Sid Kier, Reg Estridge, Cecil Henslow, Hec Marsh.

Front row: Mac Marsh, Alec Bell, Kathie Kenning, Marion Kenning, Elsie Auchinachie, Abie Kenning, Stan Auchinachie, Bill Auchinachie.

From Arthur Lane's album.

Local theatrical company outside Agricultural Hall, Duncan. 31 Jan.1906.

*Back row: George Cheeke, Miss Miles, Ronald Wilson, Louis Springett and
Arthur Lane.*

Front row: Mrs. R. Bazett, Mrs. S. Dighton, Stanley Dighton, Mrs. Cheeke.

*29 July 1911. Deep Dene party leaving "Sokum" after a picnic.
"Au Bon Revoir et Bon Voyage."*

22 June 1911 — Festivities for the Coronation of George V (Wilcuma).

Cowichan Bay Regatta July 1910.

Cowichan Bay Regatta 1914.

Early view of Cowichan Bay Waterfront south of wharf with Buena Vista Hotel. c.1910.

"City of Nanaimo" off wharf Cowichan Bay Regatta. July 2, 1906.

3-horse team and mower at Chisholm Farm. C.1916.

314

Chisholm farm — feeding the chickens.

Haying at Bradshaw farm. c.1916.

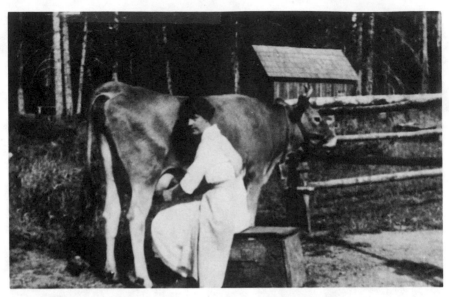

Nancy Bradshaw 1883-1957.
Nancy Bradshaw arrived in Cowichan in 1907. She was typical of many of the farm women of the time who so ably and willingly pitched in with the chores such as the milking, haying, looking after the poultry, gardening, etc.

And threshing accomplished at Kingston farm.

316

Rural mail delivery in 1915 near Quamichan Lake in a 1912 Ford.

Agate Sutton's Tea Room. C.1910.

1910 photograph of Margaret (Alexander) Sutton's home in Duncan where her daughter Agate Maud (Sutton) Smithson opened a tea room about this time.

Wedding of Billie MacAdam and Inez Duncan.

Left to right — under verandah roof:
Mr. & Mrs. Carruthers, Miss Wilson, ?, Mr. Stillwell, Margaret Duncan, Reg Gooding, Rev. Christmas, Bella Holmes, ?, Miss Clack, ?, Mr. Paterson, ?, Ronald Wilson, ?, ?, Mrs. Smithson, Willie Paterson, tree, ?.

Bride and groom: Billie MacAdam & Inez Duncan.

Left diagonally top to bottom:
Mr. Clague, Mrs. Clague, Lionel Stevenson, Mona McDonald, Mrs. W. Paterson, Phyllis Holmes, Sonny Allen, Mrs. K.F. Duncan, Stewart Paterson, Jean Paterson.

To right of bride and along further:
Mrs. W.C. Duncan, Mr. W.C. Duncan, Mrs. Lomas, Mrs. Mackay, Kate Robertson, Annie Paterson, Chrissie Paterson, Alma McDonald, Kenneth Duncan.

Babe in arms — Jean Duncan.

Alderlea Methodist Church Choir. 1915.

Kathleen & Bobbie Whittome riding in a sleigh. 18 Jan./1905.

320

Cliffs School — Tweedledum & Tweedledee and others from a performance of "Alice in Wonderland" — Elizabeth Sherman & Mary Waldon.

Skating party. Quamichan Lake.

"Mother Reading"
Mrs. J.W. Dickinson, wife of Alderlea Methodist Minister 1910.

South Cowichan Lawn Tennis Club.
Long skirts did not prevent one enjoying the game in 1912.

Madeleine Kingston riding side saddle. c. 1906.

Watching the Hayward Cup Final in 1912. Kingston vs. Ryall.

Alice Malbon.

Harriet Ruby Symons Thorpe outside Thorpe's Furniture at Craig and Station Streets. 1914.

Medal presented to Ruby Symons for excellence in High School Entrance Examinations in 1902.

"Good Luck Wreath" made from hair of many members of the Evans Family wrapped on fine wire frame. Cowichan Valley Museum.

Edwin & Mary Ellen Guns, c.1896.

Methodist W.M.S. meeting in the Whidden's garden, 1918.

Appendix I

List of Pioneer Women of Cowichan in the 1860s
(The list which follows was compiled by John N. Evans about 1930. He was not himself a resident of Cowichan in the 1860s and our research has shown that a few of the women he names did not arrive in the Valley until the 1870s. These names have been marked with an asterisk. - The Editors)

Mrs. Neil Bell
Mrs. David Alexander
* Mrs. David Alexander, Jr.
Mrs. Fry
* Mrs. Fry, Jr.
Miss Elizabeth Blackmore
Mrs. Thomas Skinner
Mrs. Bremener
Miss Mary Skinner
Miss Emily Skinner
* Mrs. Ambrose Skinner
* Mrs. Tait
Mrs. Beaumont
* Mrs. (Rev.) David Holmes
Mrs. (Rev.) Reece
Mrs. John Hales
Mrs. Mathew Bottrill

Mrs. Randall
Mrs. Archibald Dodd
Mrs. Williams
Mrs. Archibald Kier
Mrs. James Kier
Mrs. Hale
Mrs. Bednall
Mrs. William Manly
Mrs. John Morley
Mrs. Sinclair
Mrs. Allard
Mrs. Milton Edgson
Mrs. Shaw
Mrs. Pat Brenan
* Mrs. William Drinkwater
Mrs. Leask

Appendix II

First Officers and Charter Members of the Cowichan Women's Institute: 18 November, 1912

President Mrs. J.M. Hayward

Vice-President Mrs. H. Morten

Secretary Miss S. Hadwen

Charter Members:

J.M. Hayward
Aileen Steward
S.L. Flintoff
D. Morten
M.S. Hanson
A.E. Holmes
H.A. Alexander
C.M. Morton
M.A. Inverarity
A. Ligertwood
Katie Bowden
M.E. Wilson
M. Dwyer
M.E. Duncan

M.B. Somerville
C.M. Jackson
E.A. Groves
F.M. Jackson
Sybil Hadwen
A.M. Green
C.E. Hassell
E.C. Leather
L. Walbraham Taylor
C. Patterson
M. Chambers
G. Elkington
A. Duncan

Appendix III

The Pioneer Researchers group is indebted to the following for their assistance in providing photos and information for this book.

Photo credits:

C. Bradshaw, B.F. Burrows, J. Duncan, K. Derby, I. Desrosiers, E. Dobell, G.E. Elkington, P. Feeney, H. Frost, D. Field, M. Filion, S. Garriock, A. Green, E. Green, M. Haslam, E. Holm, J. Hunter, L.M. Jaynes, N. Johnston, E. Kier, C. Leger, P. Lines, D. MacAdams, M. McKay, H. McNichol, J. Marsh, W. Mayea, B. Mellor, E. Norcross, H. Mutter, G. Prevost, F. Price, D. Roberts, D. Ryan, D. Savory, E. Sherwood, S. Smith, S. Stewart, M. Stone, D. Turner, D. Vaux, B. Wallich, G. Weld, J. White, D. Wilkinson, D. Minaker.

Also: B.C. Provincial Archives, Cowichan Valley Historical Museum, J. Dickinson Album, A. Lane Album, B.C. Maritime Museum.

The King's Daughters and Their Hospital Bibliography

I PRIMARY SOURCES

(i) Government Records

B.C. Provincial Secretary, GR1549, Public ARchives of British Columbia.

(ii) Other Records

Minutes, International Order of King's Daughters and Sons of British Columbia, Volume I and II, Provincial Archives of British Columbia.

Minutes, King's Daughters Hospital, Volume I, Provincial Archives of British Columbia.

(iii) Newspapers

Cowichan *Leader*
Victoria *Daily Colonist*
Victoria *Daily Times*

(iv) Private Papers

Mary Marriner Diary

II SECONDARY SOURCES

Elliott, Gordon, ed. *Memories of the Chemainus Valley: A History of the People.* Chemainus, B.C.: Chemainus Valley Historical Society, 1978.

Gugle, Sara F. *History of the International Order The King's Daughters and Sons 1886 - 1930.* Columbus, Ohio: International Order of the King's Daughters and Sons, Incorporated, n.d.

Finlay, J.L. and D.N. Sprague. *The Structure of Canadian History.* Scarborough: Prentice - Hall of Canada, Ltd., 1979.

Latham, Barbara and Cathy Kess, eds. *In Her Right: Selected Essays on Women's History in B.C.* Victoria: Camosun College, 1980.

Latham, Barbara and Roberta Pazdro, eds. *Not Just Pin Money: Selected Essays on the History of Women's Work in British Columbia.* Victoria: Camosun College, 1984.

Norcross, E. Blanche. *The Warm Land: A History of Cowichan.* Duncan, B.C.: Island Books, 1959; revised 1975.

Whittaker, Jo Ann. "Dogs and Seals are trained. Nurses are educated. Aren't They?: Nursing Education in Canada, 1874 to 1930." B.A. Honours Dissertation, University of Victoria, 1984.

"The Search for Legitimacy: Nurses Registration in British Columbia 1913 - 1935." Unpublished paper, University of Victoria, 1984.

Footnotes

to Essay "The King's Daughters and Their Hospital"

[1] Sara F. Gugle, *History of the International Order The King's Daughters and Sons 1886 - 1930* (Columbus Ohio: International Order of the King's Daughters and Sons, Incorporated, n.d.), pp.24-25.

[2] *Ibid.,* passim, p.22. They were members of the Episcopalian, Methodist and Presbyterian Churches in New York City.

[3] *Ibid..* However, there was little evidence of their active participation in the Cowichan Valley other than as support for their wives.

[4] *Ibid..* p. 30.

[5] *Ibid.* p. 24.

[6] *Ibid.* p. 23

[7] *Ibid..*

[8] *Ibid..* p. 408

[9] Victoria *Daily Times* (VDT), June 15, 1908, p. 16.

[10] Victoria *Daily Colonist* (VDC), September 4, 1902, p. 5.

[11] *Ibid..* June 22, 1904.

[12] *Ibid.* June 19, 1901. p. 2

[13] Mary Marriner Diary, October 31, 1902; July 31, 1903.

[14] VDC June 13, 1908, p. 20.

[15] *Ibid..* March 16, 1909, p. 9.

[16] Cowichan *Leader* (CL), May 12, 1910, p. 4.

[17] *Ibid.* October 27, 1910, p. 1.

[18] *Ibid.* January 26, 1911, p. 1.

[19] *Ibid.* April 6, 1911, p.1

[20] *Ibid.* September 22, 1910.

[21] British Columbia Provincial Archives (PABC), GR 1549 Provincial Secretary, Box 1, File 11.

[22] *CL*, March 30, 1911, p. 1.

[23] Mary Marriner Diary, May 30, 1911.

[24] CL, August 27, 1914, p. 6.

[25] *Ibid.*

[26] *Minutes*, King's Daughters' Hospital, February 16, 1916; April 18, 1917.

[27] PABC, GR 1549, Box 1, File 11.

[28] Jo Ann Whittaker, "The Search for Legitimacy: Nurses' Registration in British Columbia 1913 - 1935," (Unpublished paper, University of Victoria, 1984).

[29] PABC, GR 1549, Box 2, File 11.

[30] KDH *Minutes*, August 14, 1918.

[31] CL, October 27, 1910, p. 4.

[32] KDH *Minutes*, July 25, 1915.

[33] *Ibid.* August 18, 1915.

[34] CL, March 5, 1914, p. 7.

[35] KDH *Minutes*, passim.

Chapter Notes — Section I

The Researchers experienced some difficulties following the death of Miss Norcross, and were unable to locate or replace her Chapter Notes to Section I.

Chapter Notes — Section II

[1] E. Blanche Norcross, *The Warm Land* (Vancouver, Island Books, 1975), p. 22.

[2] Ibid., p. 23.

[3] Ibid,. p. 23, 24.

[4] Ibid., p. 23.

[5] Frank A. Peake, *The Anglican Church in British Columbia*, (Vancouver, Mitchell Press, 1959), p. 31.

[6] Williams' British Columbia Directory 1882-1883. (Victoria), p. 140.

[7] Papers of first Cowichan Historical Society (Miss Wilson), (Provincial Archives).

[8] G.W. Owens (compiler), *Heritage of One Hundred Years:* Duncan United Church 1869-1969, p. 14.

[9] Norcross, *The Warm Land.* p. 21.

[10] Papers of First Cowichan Historical Society (Provincial Archives).

[11] Norcross, *The Warm Land.*

[12] Don Morton, *A Goodly Heritage.* (The Corporation of the District of North Cowichan), p. 3.

[13] David R. Williams, *One Hundred Years at St. Peter's.* (Duncan, B.C.), p. 16.

[14] Norcross, *The Warm Land.*

[15] W.H. Olsen, *Water Over the Wheel* (Chemainus Valley Historical Society, 1963, First Ed.)., p.76, 80.

[16] Williams' *British Columbia Directory*, 1882-1883, p. 143, 144.

[17] Ibid., p. 136.

Chapter Notes — Section III

[1] E. Blanche Norcross, *The Warm Land* (Vancouver, Island Books, 1975), p. 47, 48.

[2] Minutes of St. Peter's Guild, in private hands.

[3] G.W. Owens, *Heritage of One Hundred Years* (Duncan United Church 1869-1969) p. 22.

4. Ibid., p 17.

[5] B.C. Gazette. Dr. Rowbotham is described in the Gazette as a Justice of the Peace, Deputy Surgeon General, retired, of Quamichan. Served the Cowichan District as coroner from Febtury 18, 1887 to January 11, 1888.

[6] Hand-down history.

[7] Norcross, *The Warm Land*, p. 53.

[8] Hand-down history.

[9] David R. Williams, *One Hundred Years at St. Peter's* (Duncan), p. 37.

[10] Norcross, *The Warm Land*, p. 48, 49.

[11] Cowichan Leader (Duncan, B.C.), 14 November 1912.

[12] Mary Marriner Diary, 14 September 1896. (In private hands).

[13] Papers of first Cowichan Historical Society. (Miss Wilson. Provincial Archives).

[14] Norcross, *The Warm Land*, p. 50.

[15] John F.T. Saywell, *Kaatza* (Sidney, B.C. 1967), p. 38 and ff.

[16] Ibid., p. 3.

[17] Norcross, *The Warm Land*, p. 51.

[18] Hand-down history.

[19] Provincial Archives.

Chapter Notes — Section IV

[1] Elwood White and David Wilkie, *Shays on the Switchbacks* (Victoria, B.C. 1968), p. 1.

[2] Fairfax Prevost, Correspondence with his mother, in private hands.

[3] Vincent Moore, Angelo Branca, *"Gladiator of the Courts."* (Vancouver, Douglas and McIntrye, 1981), p. 7, 8, 9, 217. Teresa (Mrs. Filippo) Branca gave birth to her third child, Angelo, when her husband was running the store on Mount Sicker. They left for the mainland as soon as the infant was old enough to travel.

[4] E. Blanche Norcross, *The Warm Land.* (Vancouver, Island Books, 1975), p. 58.

[5] Elwood White and David Wilkie, Shays on the Switchbacks, p. 6.

[6] E. Blanche Norcross, *The Warm Land*, p. 61.

[7] The Enterprise, (Duncan, B.C.), February 24, 1900.

[8] The Cowichan Leader, advertisements and announcements, 1910-1915.

[9] Mary Marriner's diaries, in private hands.

[10] Frances Hogan, St. Edward's Altar Society 1910-1944: Catholic Women's League of Canada St. Edward's Council 1944-1960. (Duncan, B.C., Cowichan Leader).

[11] The Cowichan Leader, announcement, March 12, 1910.

[12] Ibid., news, 1912.

[13] E. Blanche Norcross, *The Warm Land*, p. 65.

[14] The Cowichan Leader, June 26, 1913.

Miss Norcross' notes regarding references 15 to 22 are not available.

[23] Ibid., March 25, 1930, p. 3.

[24] Ibid., February 13, 1917, p. 4.

[25] Ibid., February 20, 1919, p. 5.

[26] Ibid., March 6, 1919, p. 3.

[27] Ibid., March 20, 1919, p. 1.

[28] Ibid., September 14, 1916.

[29] Ibid., March 22, 1917.

[30] Ibid., February 22, 1917.

[31] The Cowichan Leader, February 14, 1914.

[32] Ibid., April 12, 1917, p. 5.

[33] Ibid., May 29, 1919, p. 1.

[34] Ibid., February 20, 1919, p. 1.

[35] Ibid., October 16, 1919, p. 1.

[36] Ibid., January 4, 1917, p. 2.

[37] Minutes of Cowichan Women's Institute.

Sources Consulted

Published Works

Brown, Ashley G. (ed.) *British Columbia: Its History, People, Commerce, Industries and Resources*. Sells Ltd., London 1912.

Dougan, R.I. Cowichan My Valley. Duncan, B.C. 1973. (2nd ed.)

Dunae, Patrick A. Gentlemen Emigrants. Douglas & McIntyre, Vancouver, B.C. 1981.

Gregson, Harry. A History of Victoria, J.J. Douglas Ltd., Vancouver, B.C. 1970.

Gustafson, Lillian (compiler), Elliott, Gordon (ed.) Memories of the Chemainus Valley: A History of People. Chemainus Valley Historical Society. 1978.

Lugrin, N. de Betrand. Pioner Women of British Columbia. Women's Canadian Club of Victoria, B.C. 1928.

Macfie, Matthew. Vancouver Island and British Columbia: Their History, Resources and Prospects. Longman, Green. 1865.

Moore, Vincent, Angelo Branca "Gladiator of the Courts." Douglas & McIntyre, Vancouver, B.C. 1981.

Morton, Don. A Goodly Heritage.The Corporation of the District of North Cowichan.

Norcross, Elizabeth Blanche. *The Warm Land*: A History of Cowichan. Island Books, Duncan, B.C. 1975 (2nd ed.).

Olsen, W.H. *Water Over the Wheel*. Chemainus Valley Historical Society. 1963 (1st ed.).

Ormsby, Margaret. *British Columbia: A History. The Macmillans in Canada.* 1958.

Owens, G.W. (compiler). Heritage of One Hundred Years: Duncan United Church 1869-1969.

Peake, Frank A. *The Anglican Church in British Columbia.* Mitchell Press. Vancouver, B.C. 1959.

Rattray, Alexander. *Vancouver Island and British Columbia.* Smith Elderk & Co. 1862.

Saywell, John F.T. Kaatza. The Chronicles of Cowichan Lake. Cowichan Lake District Centennial Committee. 1967.

Williams, David R. One Hundred Years at St. Peter's. Duncan, B.C.

Williams' *British Columbia Directory* 1882-1883. Victoria, B.C.

Manuscripts, Newspapers, Diaries and Papers

The Daily (British Colonist). Victoria, B.C.

Cowichan Leader. Duncan, B.C.

Cowichan Historical Society papers, 1928-1935. Provincial Archives.

Guide to British Columbia 1987-78. N.D. N.P.

Hogan, Frances. St. Edward's Altar Society 1910-1944: Catholic Women's League of Canada St. Edward's Council. 1944-1960. Duncan, B.C.

Diaries of Edward Marriner. Provincial Archives.

Diaries of Mary Marriner. In private hands.

Journal of Bishop George Hills. British Columbia Diocesan Archives.

Minutes of North Cowichan Municipal Council.

Minutes of City of Duncan Municipal Council.

Tax rolls. Municipality of North Cowichan.

Minutes of the Cowichan Women's Institute.

Index

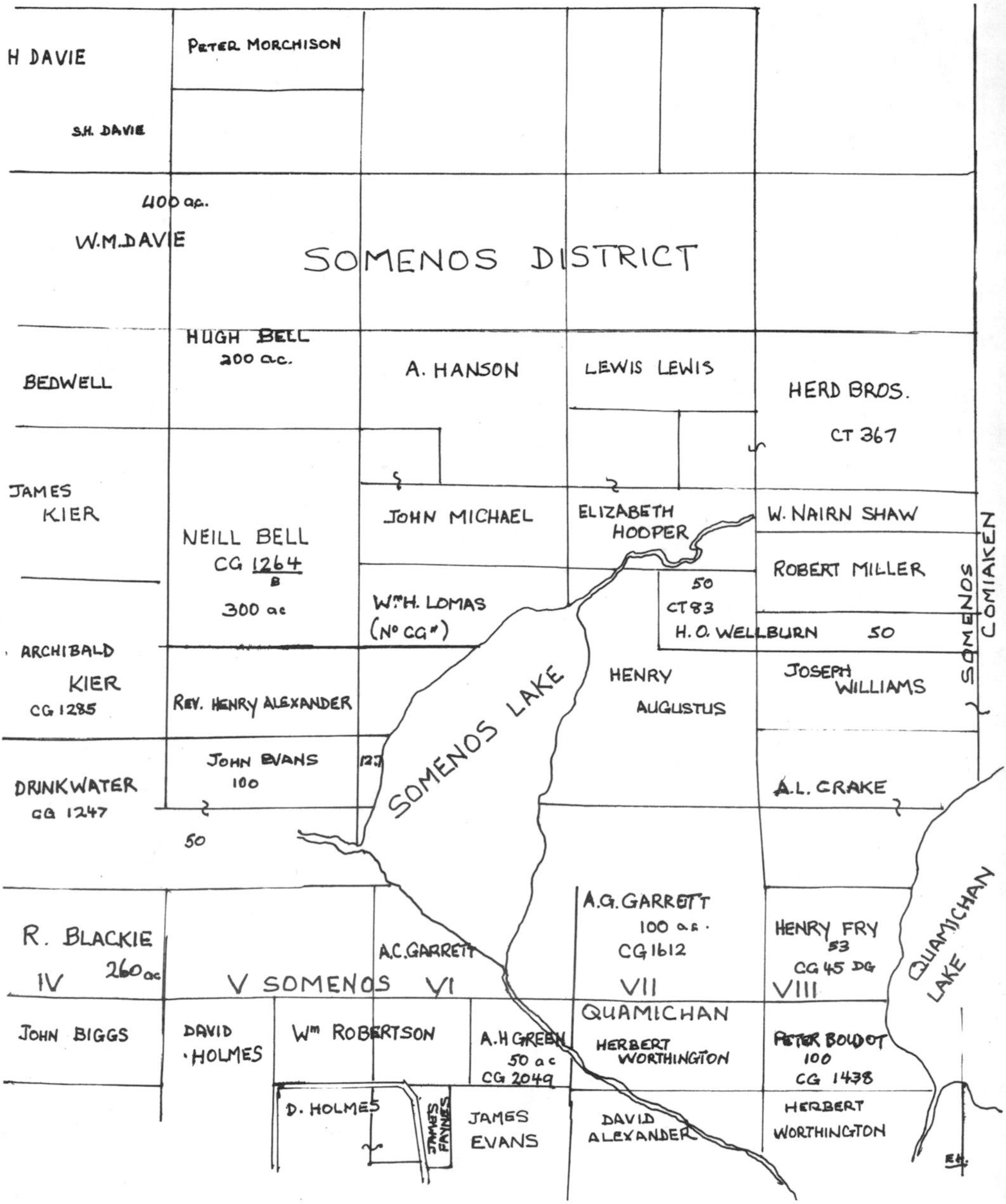

SOMENOS DISTRICT

H DAVIE

PETER MORCHISON

S.H. DAVIE

400 ac.
W.M. DAVIE

HUGH BELL
200 ac.

BEDWELL

A. HANSON

LEWIS LEWIS

HERD BROS.

CT 367

JAMES KIER

NEILL BELL
CG 1264
B

300 ac

JOHN MICHAEL

ELIZABETH HOOPER

W. NAIRN SHAW

ROBERT MILLER

50
CT 83

H. O. WELLBURN   50

Wᵐ H. LOMAS
(No CG #)

ARCHIBALD KIER
CG 1285

REV. HENRY ALEXANDER

HENRY AUGUSTUS

JOSEPH WILLIAMS

SOMENOS LAKE

DRINKWATER
CG 1247

JOHN EVANS
100

127

50

A.L. CRAKE

COMIAKEN

SOMENOS

A.G. GARRETT
100 ac.
CG 1612

HENRY FRY
53
CG 45 DG

QUAMICHAN LAKE

R. BLACKIE

IV   260 ac

A.C. GARRETT

V SOMENOS   VI

VII

VIII

JOHN BIGGS

DAVID HOLMES

Wᵐ ROBERTSON

A.H GREEN
50 ac
CG 2049

QUAMICHAN
HERBERT WORTHINGTON

PETER BOUDOT
100
CG 1438

D. HOLMES

JAMES FAYNES

JAMES EVANS

DAVID ALEXANDER

HERBERT WORTHINGTON

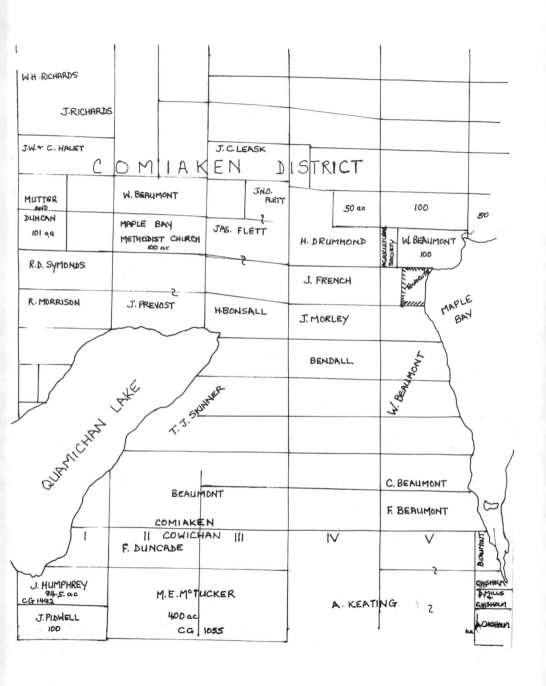

COMIAKEN DISTRICT

W.H. RICHARDS

J. RICHARDS

J.W. & C. HALET

J.C. LEASK

MUTTER AND DUNCAN 101 9.9

W. BEAUMONT

J.N.O. FLETT

50 ac

100

50

MAPLE BAY METHODIST CHURCH 100 ac

JAS. FLETT

H. DRUMMOND

AGRICULTURAL SOCIETY

W. BEAUMONT 100

R.D. SYMONDS

J. FRENCH

BEAUMONT

R. MORRISON

J. PREVOST

H. BONSALL

J. MORLEY

MAPLE BAY

BENDALL

W. BEAUMONT

QUAMICHAN LAKE

T.J. SKINNER

C. BEAUMONT

F. BEAUMONT

BEAUMONT

COMIAKEN

I

II   COWICHAN   III
F. DUNCADE

IV

V

BEAUMONT

J. HUMPHREY 84.5. ac CG 1432

M.E. McTUCKER

A. KEATING

CHISHOLM & MILLS & CHISHOLM

J. PIDWELL 100

400 ac CG 1055

A. CHISHOLM

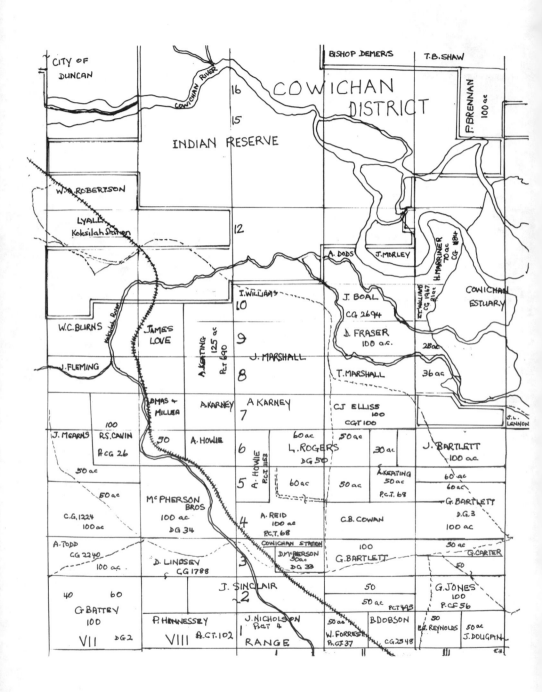

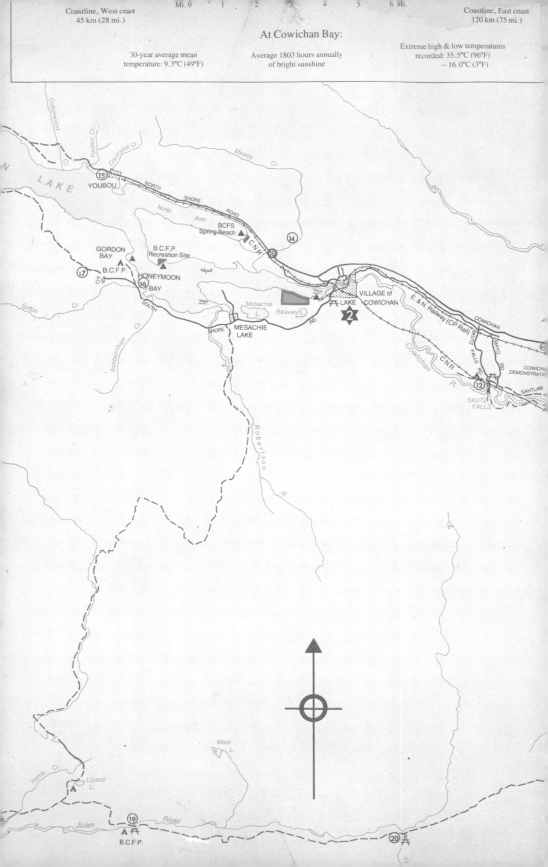

At Cowichan Bay:

Coastline, West coast 45 km (28 mi.)		Coastline, East coast 120 km (75 mi.)

Mi. 0   1   2   3   4   5   6 Mi.

30-year average mean temperature: 9.3°C (49°F)

Average 1803 hours annually of bright sunshine

Extreme high & low temperatures recorded: 35.5°C (96°F) − 16.0°C (3°F)

Cottonwood Cr.

Youbou Cr.

Coonskin Cr.

Meade Cr.

LAKE

(15) YOUBOU

NORTH SHORE ROAD

North Arm

BCFS Spring Beach

(14)

C.N.R.

(13)

GORDON BAY
B.C.F.P.

B.C.F.P. Recreation Site

HONEYMOON BAY

(17)

(16)

SOUTH SHORE ROAD

Sutton Cr.

Ashburnham Cr.

Mesachie L.

Beaver L.

MESACHIE LAKE

ROBERTSON RD.

Cowichan LAKE

VILLAGE of COWICHAN

(2)

E & N Railway (CP Rail)

COWICHAN

SKUTZ FALLS RD.

MAYO RD.

C.N.R.

Cowichan R.

COWICHAN DEMONSTRATI

(12)

SAHTLAM

SKUTZ FALLS

Robertson R.

Maid L.

Harris Cr.

Lizard L.

(19) B.C.F.P.

Juan River

(20)